WITHDRAWN
SMU LIBRARIES

D1211886

Tudor Men
and
Institutions

TUDOR MEN AND INSTITUTIONS

Studies in English Law and Government

Edited by Arthur J. Slavin

Louisiana State University Press
BATON ROUGE

We dedicate this book to
Walter Cecil Richardson.

"To truth its state is dedicate."
Shelley, *Prometheus Unbound*

ISBN 0–8071–0227–X
Library of Congress Catalog Card Number 72–79337
Copyright © 1972 by Louisiana State University Press
All rights reserved
Manufactured in the United States of America
Printed by LithoComp, Inc., Smyrna, Georgia
Designed by Dwight Agner

∠219559

iNTRODUCTiON

These essays, published here for the first time, share two characteristics. However wide their range of subject matter, each
throws some light on the nature of Tudor rituals of rule. And
each does so by dealing with some governor or institution of
government or problem of law related to that aggrandizement
of power we associate with the Tudor dynasty.

It is no longer evident to us, as it was to James A. Froude,
that we must look exclusively to Henry VIII's reign in order
to understand the actions on which the later constitution rested.[1]
Medievalists have never tired of showing us how the Tudor
accomplishments rested on the adaptation of old uses to new
purposes.[2] And rightly so. Whether we accept the notion of
G. R. Elton that there was a Tudor revolution in government,

[1]. James A. Froude, *History of England, from the Fall of Wolsey to the Defeat of the Spanish Armada* (12 vols.; London, v.d.), IV, 236–43.

[2]. See A. R. Myers, *The Household of Edward IV* (Manchester, 1959), 48–49; B. P. Wolfe, *The Crown Lands* (London, 1970), 67–75; and P. Williams and G. L. Harriss, "A Revolution in Tudor History?" *Past and Present* No. 25 (July, 1963), 3–58.

FONDREN LIBRARY
Southern Methodist University
DALLAS, TEXAS 75222

or reject it outright, is now no longer as keen a question as it once was.[3] For Professor Elton has himself spent the best part of the last fifteen years fruitfully modifying his own views. Other scholars too numerous to catalogue have shown how deeply laid are the fifteenth-century roots of Tudor practices.

On that foresworn roll none stands higher than Walter C. Richardson. Every essay in this collection touches some problem familiar in his work. More than most, his prize-winning book on Tudor chamber administration stressed the basically medieval methods of Henrician government.[4] In outlining the scope of that work, Professor Richardson insisted that we must understand the relations of power and efficiency to wealth. He also insisted that our understanding of those things would depend in some measure on our study of careers below the first rank men of Wolsey's stature and Cromwell's significance. His work has shown the truth of this by the establishment of the importance of John Heron, Reginald Bray, Walter Mildmay, and numerous other lawyers and administrators known earlier merely by reputations inherited from sometimes malign chroniclers.

His books have illustrated the possibility of making demonstration do the work once left to authority. Not that such studies were unprecedented in American scholarship or in the great tradition of English administrative history done by the British. On these shores the late F. C. Dietz pioneered studies of Tudor revenue and its administration.[5] And in England G. R. Elton, Harry Bell, and Joel Hurstfield followed in the footsteps left by T. F. Tout, whose work on administration

3. See the debate in *Past and Present*, Nos. 25–32, the focal point of which is Elton's *The Tudor Revolution in Government* (Cambridge, 1953).

4. Walter C. Richardson, *Tudor Chamber Administration, 1485–1547* (Baton Rouge, 1952), awarded the Herbert Baxter Adams Prize of the American Historical Association, given for the best work in European history by an American scholar, once in two years.

5. F. C. Dietz, *English Government Finance, 1485–1558* (Urbana, 1920), and the various other studies in the University of Illinois Studies in the Social Sciences, Vol. III, No. 2 and Vol. VIII, No. 2.

unfortunately left off in the fourteenth century.[6] Yet Professor Richardson did rescue from obscurity certain men and institutions.[7]

His special merit lies in his repeated demonstration of the roles played by "the countless . . . politically inconspicuous administrators" who raised armies, collected taxes and land revenues, governed courts, and in general made the government work to the degree that it did.[8] He also pointed out how poorly stocked the literature was in studies of some quite conspicuous politicians who were important administrators. One need only mention his hope that there might soon be solid studies of Sir Thomas Audley, Sir Ralph Sadler, Sir Richard Rich, Sir Thomas Wriothesley, Sir Walter Mildmay, Sir William Paget, and Sir William Petre.[9] His reason for so doing he made clear: "Institutional history, however accurate in detail, becomes meaningless when separated from the dominant personalities of the period who gave it life and color."[10]

The table of contents of this book affords a reminder of Professor Richardson's achievement. For it brings together the first scholarly expositions of some themes vital to the history of administration and also elaborates on men and institutions either dimly known or known chiefly heretofore in his own works. This book also treats at length problems in our understanding of the education of lawyers and the rule of law, which is especially fitting in the light of the work on lawyers and the Inns of Court which Professor Richardson will soon send

6. Professor Elton's contribution ranges over many articles, a couple of monographs, his volume on the Tudor constitution, and the essays in his *Star Chamber Stories.* See H. E. Bell, *An Introduction to the History and Records of the Court of Wards and Liveries* (Cambridge, 1953); and Joel Hurstfield, *The Queen's Wards* (London, 1958).

7. Walter C. Richardson, *Stephen Vaughan: Financial Agent of Henry VIII* (Baton Rouge, 1953); *Mary Tudor: The White Queen* (London and Seattle, 1970); *History of the Court of Augmentations* (Baton Rouge, 1961). *The Royal Commission Report of 1552,* a careful examination of some Edwardian reform efforts, will soon be published in the *Archives of British Culture* series.

8. Richardson, *Tudor Chamber,* Introduction, *passim.*

9. Richardson, *History,* 66–67.   10. Richardson, *Tudor Chamber,* viii.

to press. Law and reform were the twin concerns of his very early work on the Court of the Commonwealth.[11]

Since these essays have also in common this relationship to Professor Richardson's life's work, my colleagues and I thought it appropriate to dedicate the volume to him. We hope to do him honor in the measure that we continue the labor of illuminating the conditions of Tudor governance and of the men, institutions, and law of which it was composed.

Arthur J. Slavin

11. Richardson, "The Court of the Commonweal," *Papers of the Michigan Academy of Science, Arts and Letters*, XIX (1933), 476–95. The manuscript of *The Inns of Court and the Renaissance* is complete and in final revision.

CONTENTS

Introduction   v
Arthur J. Slavin

I   **Sir Thomas Audley: A Soul as Black as Marble?**   3
Stanford E. Lehmberg

II **The Fall of Edward, Duke of Buckingham**   32
Mortimer Levine

III **Lord Chancellor Wriothesley and Reform of
Augmentations: New Light on an Old Court**   49
Arthur J. Slavin

IV **The Hundred Years War and Edward
IV's 1475 Campaign in France**   70
J. R. Lander

V   **Notes on the Early Tudor Exchequer of Pleas**   101
DeLloyd J. Guth

VI **The Exchequer of Chester in the
Last Years of Elizabeth I**   123
W. J. Jones

VII The Essex Puritan Movement and the
     "Bawdy" Courts, 1577–1594   171
     Jay P. Anglin

VIII The Enforcement of Royal Proclamations under
     the Provisions of the Statute of
     Proclamations, 1539–1547   205
     R. W. Heinze

IX   The Matriculation Revolution and
     Education at the Inns of Court
     in Renaissance England   232
     Louis A. Knafla

X   The Rule of Law in Sixteenth-Century England   265
     G. R. Elton

Tudor Men
and
Institutions

Stanford E. Lehmberg

SiR ThOMAS AUDLEY: A SOUL AS bLACK AS MARbLE?

Recent scholarship has been kind to some of the chief ministers of Henry VIII. Thomas Cromwell, long considered an unscrupulous Machiavellian, has been transformed by G. R. Elton into an administrative genius holding moderate political views based on his training at the common law and in Parliament.[1] Richard Rich, for centuries hated for his probable perjury against Sir Thomas More and esteemed (in More's words) "very light of tongue, a great dicer, and of no commendable fame," [2] emerges from Walter Richardson's sympathetic reassessment as a model servant of the state, endowed with unusual resilience and tact.[3] Thomas Wolsey, regarded by even

1. G. R. Elton, *The Tudor Revolution in Government* (Cambridge, 1953); "The Political Creed of Thomas Cromwell," *Transactions of the Royal Historical Society*, 5th ser., VI (1956), 69–92.

2. William Roper, *The Life of Sir Thomas More, Knight,* in Roper and Harpsfield, *Lives of Saint Thomas More,* ed. E. E. Reynolds (London, 1963), 43.

3. Walter C. Richardson, *History of the Court of Augmentations, 1536–1554* (Baton Rouge, 1961), 61–67; *Tudor Chamber Administration, 1485–1547* (Baton Rouge, 1952), 316–18.

his admiring biographer A. F. Pollard as being ambitious and bellicose, has been pictured by J. J. Scarisbrick as an advocate of European pacification, never motivated by dreams of the papacy.[4]

Other less fortunate officers have not yet been treated to the adequate studies which, as Professor Richardson once commented, "would add immeasurably to the administrative history of the period." [5] One such figure is Thomas Audley, successively speaker of the Commons and lord chancellor, ennobled by Henry VIII as Baron Audley of Walden. It will be our purpose here to reexamine his career and reconsider the traditional judgment of it.

That verdict has been essentially negative. A few writers, it is true, have praised Audley: the Restoration biographer David Lloyd held that

His Soul ennobled his Body, and his Body graced his Soul: The one quick, solid, apprehensive and judicious; the other tall and majestick: *King Henry loved a Man;* and here was one whose Austerity was allayed by Debonairness, whose Gravity was sweetened with Pleasantness; whose Knowledge was as large as his Authority, whose Wit was equal to his Wisdom; whose Memory was strong, and Judgment solid.... He understood *business* well, and *men* better; and knew King Henry's temper better than himself.[6]

But the majority opinion has been severely critical. Edward Foss, in his biographical dictionary of English jurists, wrote that Audley undoubtedly equalled, "if he did not exceed, all his contemporaries in servility":

His interpretations of the law on the various criminal trials at which he presided are a disgrace not only to him, but to every member of the bench associated with him, while both branches of the legislature are equally chargeable with the ignominy of passing the acts he introduced, periling every man's life by the new treasons they invented,

---

4. A. F. Pollard, *Wolsey* (London, 1929); J. J. Scarisbrick, *Henry VIII* (Berkeley and Los Angeles, 1968).

5. Richardson, *Augmentations*, 67n.

6. David Lloyd, *State Worthies, Or, The States-Men and Favourites of England Since the Reformation* (London, 1670), 72–73 (1st ed.; 1665).

and every man's conscience by the contradictory oaths they imposed. . . . The consciousness that the odious laws he had introduced might be turned against himself, and that his fate depended on the momentary whim of an inexorable tyrant, may most probably have brought on, only five years afterwards, that illness which terminated in his death.[7]

Foss judged on legal grounds and found Audley wanting. A more general writer, that delightful antiquary Thomas Fuller, admitted Audley to his gallery of *Worthies* but charged him with greed. "In the feast of Abbey lands, king Henry the Eighth carved unto him the first cut (and that, I assure you, was a dainty morsel), viz. the priory of the Trinity in Aldgate ward London, dissolved 1531, which, as a van-courier, foreran other abbeys by two years, and foretold their dissolution. . . . He had afterwards a large partage in the Abbey lands in several counties." He was buried at Saffron Walden with a "lamentable epitaph," most likely of his own composition; his magnificent tomb is made of a marble "not blacker than the soul, nor harder than the heart, of him whose bones were laid beneath it."[8]

These judgments raise a number of questions. How did Audley achieve his spectacular rise? What exactly were his responsibilities and accomplishments in Parliament, the courts, and the Council? How deep was his learning? How much wealth did he amass, and by what means? Was he guilty of corruption, partiality, or avarice? Evidence exists to answer most of these queries, and historians—if they are not to lay themselves open to criticism like Foss's—ought to examine it carefully before delivering their verdict.

We should begin with a brief survey of Audley's career. Although little documentation concerning his early life survives, a contemporary record lists his birthplace as Earl's Colne, a

---

7. Edward Foss, *Biographia Juridica: A Biographical Dictionary of the Judges of England* (London, 1870), 27–28. Part of this passage is quoted in a footnote to Audley's biography in G. E. C[okayne], *The Complete Peerage* (new ed.; 13 vols.; London, 1910–49), I, 349.

8. Thomas Fuller, *The History of the Worthies of England* (3 vols.; London, 1840), I, 507–508; William Addison, *Audley End* (London, 1953), 12.

village near Colchester in Essex, and reliable sources agree on the year 1488.[9] The occupation of his father, probably named Geoffrey, is not known, but there is no evidence to support the conjecture that he held the status of gentleman.[10] More likely he was a yeoman farmer. In some manner young Thomas gained an elementary education, perhaps (like Wolsey) through the Church: there was a priory at Colne. He almost certainly attended Cambridge, probably as a member of Buckingham College, a Benedictine foundation open to the laity.[11] At some date, possibly immediately after leaving Cambridge, Thomas also studied law at the Inner Temple.[12]

We next find him back in Colchester, where he was admitted as a burgess in 1514 and appointed town clerk soon after.[13] Presumably he began the practice of law. By 1520 he was prominent enough to be named a justice of the peace for Essex—he held the office for the rest of his life—and a member of the commission of gaol delivery for Colchester Castle.[14] In 1523 he was first sent to Parliament as a burgess for Colchester. Henry VIII seems to have had an unusual, and unexplained, interest in the election, but there is no reason to believe that he dictated the choice of members.[15]

Although we know nothing about Audley's activities in this Parliament, we may well suppose that he attracted notice. Certainly he began, soon after, to accumulate offices which would not come the way of an ordinary borough member. This was

9. W. Gurney Benham (ed.), *The Oath Book or Red Parchment Book of Colchester* (Colchester, 1907), 147; Philip Morant, *The History and Antiquities of the County of Essex* (2 vols.; London, 1768), I, 138. The date is confirmed by (and perhaps derived from) Audley's epitaph, which states that he was fifty-six when he died in 1544.

10. In, *e.g.*, J. A. Manning, *Lives of the Speakers of the House of Commons* (London, 1851), 172.

11. J. B. Mullinger, *The University of Cambridge from the Royal Injunctions of 1535 to the Accession of Charles the First* (Cambridge, 1884), 64–65.

12. He was later, in 1526, autumn reader at the Inner Temple.

13. Benham, *The Oath Book*, 147.

14. *Letters and Papers of Henry VIII* (21 vols.; London, 1862–1932), III, i, 1081, hereinafter cited as *L.P.*; references are to document number rather than page number.

15. W. Gurney Benham (ed.), *The Red Paper Book of Colchester* (Colchester, 1902), 26; cf. S. E. Lehmberg, *The Reformation Parliament, 1529–1536* (Cambridge, 1970), 12.

the Parliament in which Wolsey experienced such difficulty extracting a subsidy from the Commons, and it may be that Audley was one of the few to support the request.[16] At any rate Audley was named a commissioner to collect the subsidy in his home county, and he may have become a protégé of Wolsey's, even a member of his household.[17] In 1525 he was named to Princess Mary's council; in 1526 he was appointed attorney of the Duchy of Lancaster; in 1527 he received the honorific title groom of the chamber.[18]

Like Thomas Cromwell, Audley benefited from Wolsey's fall rather than being dragged down by it. Indeed Audley's initial position seemed considerably more promising than Cromwell's. He was easily elected to the Reformation Parliament in 1529, now as a knight of the shire for Essex, while Cromwell had to scramble for a borough seat. And he was immediately chosen speaker of the Commons.[19] He clearly favored the king, whose justice and mercy he praised in his disabling oration; he was himself eulogized by More, the chancellor, who reported Henry VIII's conviction that Audley was wise, able, and discreet.[20]

In 1532, after the Submission of the Clergy, More resigned the great seal, and Audley again profited. Doubtless because he had managed the Commons well for the king, Audley was appointed lord keeper and asked to preside over the Lords.[21] In 1533 he became lord chancellor.[22] By this time he was one of the leading councillors: he was the chief official remaining in London when the king and Cromwell visited Calais in 1532,[23]

16. Lehmberg, *The Reformation Parliament*, 1–2.

17. *L.P.*, III, ii, 3504, 3585; IV, ii, 1331.

18. *Dictionary of National Biography;* Robert Somerville, *History of the Duchy of Lancaster* (London, 1953), I, 407.

19. Lehmberg, *The Reformation Parliament*, 27, 80.

20. Edward Hall, *Hall's Chronicle* (London, 1809), 765.

21. *L.P.*, V, 1069, 1075 (a very full account of the delivery of the great seal to Audley), 1295 (on the making of a new seal), 1499 (9).

22. *Ibid.*, VI, 73.

23. *Ibid.*, V, 1421, 1430, 1475–76, 1517. In 1536 the council sometimes met at Audley's house: *Ibid.*, XI, 219, 285.

and he was very active in preparing drafts of proclamations and parliamentary legislation.[24] During the summer of 1533 he found the press of governmental business so great that he could not leave London, despite a serious illness which may have been precipitated by overwork.[25] In 1534 he helped negotiate a treaty with the Scots.[26] He opened the Parliament of 1536 with a long oration on the king's unhappy marriages and the problem of the succession.[27] He was hated by the rebels in the Pilgrimage of Grace, during which he was placed in charge of preserving order in Essex and was again for a time the principal councillor in London.[28] He presided at the trials of More, the Carthusians, Anne Boleyn and her associates, the Marquis of Exeter, Lord Montague, Sir Geoffrey Pole, Sir Edward Neville, Sir Nicholas Carew, Lord Dacre, Thomas Culpepper, Francis Dereham, and several of Catherine Howard's relatives.[29] (All but Pole and the Howards were executed.) In 1537 he took part in the christening of Prince Edward and the funeral of Queen Jane which followed all too soon on its heels.[30] A year later he buried his own wife, daughter of the Suffolk squire Sir Thomas Barnardiston, and was reported to be taking "great thought" about his future.[31] Within three months he had married Elizabeth, the daughter of Thomas Grey, Marquis of Dorset. Audley wrote Cromwell that the king had commanded the new marriage, though he had no cause to regret it. It was certainly a token of his new social status.[32]

24. Lehmberg, *The Reformation Parliament*, 135n., 204, 206, 210, 225, and MSS cited there; *L.P.*, VIII, 147. Audley's role was primarily that of a legal expert: see especially *L.P.*, XI, 382 (3).

25. *L.P.*, VI, 842, 927, 976, 982, 1049, 1063.

26. *Ibid.*, VII, 647, 1032.

27. *Journals of the House of Lords* (London, [1888]), I, 84; J. A. Froude, *History of England from the Fall of Wolsey to the Defeat of the Spanish Armada* (2nd ed.; London, 1858), II, 509–11.

28. *L.P.*, XI, 599, 714, 788, 860; XII, i, 6, 201, 853.

29. *Ibid.*, VIII, 609, 666, 974, 996; X, 876, 848, 908; XIII, ii, 979, 986, 1182 (1); XIV, 290, 931; XVI, 1395, 1470.

30. *Ibid.*, XII, ii, 911, 1060. Subsequently Audley gave Edward a piece of plate each New Year's: *ibid.*, XIII, i, 5; XIV, 5; XV, 1.

31. *Complete Peerage; L.P.*, XIII, i, 170.

32. *L.P.*, XIV, ii, 775 (the MS is Cleopatra E. VI, fol. 193, B.M.).

An even more obvious sign appeared in November, 1538, when Audley was ennobled with the title Baron Audley of Walden.[33] For several years he had been accumulating lands—we will return to that subject when we come to consider his wealth—and he had climaxed his campaign of acquisitions in Essex with the grant of the monastic site at Walden in March, 1538.[34] In 1540 he was installed as a knight of the Garter.[35]

Lord Audley continued to be involved in Henry's matrimonial projects. He helped make the marriage treaty between the king and Anne of Cleves; he attended Henry at her reception in England; he was sent to tell Anne of the king's "alteration of countenance," and rendered depositions during the annulment proceedings.[36] When Cromwell fell from favor Audley did nothing to help him (apparently only Cranmer and Fitzwilliam dared to speak out), and he assumed some new responsibilities, though no new offices.[37] He was deeply involved in Catherine Howard's debacle: he advised Cranmer to write out the charges against her, and he was sent for in haste when Henry learned of them.[38] In his speech opening the Parliament of 1542 he inveighed against Catherine, "aggravating and exaggerating her misdeeds" according to Eustace Chapuys.[39] Perhaps fearing the approach of death and eager to carry out some philanthropic scheme, he refounded and endowed Buckingham College, Cambridge, changing its name to Magdalen.[40] In May, 1543, he witnessed the signing of a treaty between Henry VIII and Charles V.[41] He is last recorded as attending

33. *Ibid.*, XIII, ii, 933.   34. *Ibid.*, XIII, i, 1115 (23).
35. *Ibid.*, XV, 560.
36. *Ibid.*, XIV, ii, 286, 572; XV, 14, 18, 845, 850, 860, 908.
37. *Ibid.*, XV, 804. The relationship between Audley and Cromwell is considered more fully below.
38. *Ibid.*, XVI, 1328, 1331, 1333–34, 1366.
39. *Ibid.*, XVII, App. B. Cf. *Journals of the House of Lords*, I, 164; Froude, IV, 135–37.
40. *L.P.*, XVII, 283 (9). Audley's will ordered his executors to draft statutes for the college; these provided that his heirs and successors—the owners of Audley End—should continue to name the masters of the college, an unusual arrangement which remained in effect until 1925. Cf. Mullinger, *The University of Cambridge*, 69–70; Addison, *Audey End*, 216.
41. *L.P.*, XVIII, i, 603.

a Council meeting in July. His will is dated April 19, 1544. On April 21 he resigned the great seal.[42] Nine days later he was dead.

Thus the bare bones: now the scrutiny. One must comment first that Audley's was clearly an amazing career, even by Tudor standards. The only Henrician figures carried higher by the revolving wheel of fortune—Wolsey and Cromwell—were dashed to death and disgrace; Audley, somehow arresting its descent, died peacefully, in high honor, able to bequeath enormous wealth to his heirs.

It is not easy to plumb the secrets of Audley's success. His rise to prominence is particularly difficult to explain. According to one tradition he served so ably as steward to the duke of Suffolk that he came to the king's attention.[43] If so this must have been while he was in his early twenties. Another possibility is that he was briefly a captain at Calais: a Thomas Audley is so recorded in 1515, although it may not have been the future chancellor.[44] (Confusingly enough, Audley's own brother and two of his nephews were also named Thomas.) But both theories seem improbable. It is much more likely that Audley's efficiency and ambition were first apparent to the residents of Colchester, who were so well pleased with their bright young clerk that they sent him to represent them in Parliament.

We have already speculated on Audley's part in the Parliament of 1523. The session obviously marked a turning point in his career, a progress from the local to the national scene. No doubt Audley now concentrated on making himself useful to persons in positions of authority. Able administrators were badly needed, and Wolsey (among others) must have been glad of Audley's help. Perhaps during this period, too, it became apparent that Audley had no personal conviction or conscience

---

42. *Ibid.*, XIX, i, 459. The will was proved in the Prerogative Court of Canterbury and is now in the PRO, PRO II. 31. f. 783.

43. *Dictionary of National Biography;* William Howard-Flanders, "Thomas, Lord Audley of Walden, 1488–1544," *Transactions of the Essex Archaeological Society* (new ser.; X, 1909), 290.

44. *L.P.*, Addenda, II, ii, 1513.

which would interfere with his service to the crown, and that he knew how to turn the fall of his superiors to his own gain. We must couple with this some pure luck, which opened the chancellor's position at just the time when Audley was ready for it. (How common is the sight of able men passed over merely because the jobs they could handle are not vacant!)

During the decade of the 1530's Audley and Cromwell worked closely with each other, and their relationship is of special interest. They must have been thrown together in the Parliament of 1523, and later in Wolsey's service. Cromwell can hardly have been responsible for Audley's appointment as speaker in 1529—if anything, it is more likely that Audley aided Cromwell in achieving office—but Cromwell surely helped Henry select Audley as More's successor, and thereafter the two must have seen each other, when they were both in London, nearly every day. When they were not, they wrote often and at length. During Cromwell's visit to Calais in 1532, for example, Audley sent him eight letters in four weeks.[45] On the whole the secretary and the chancellor got on well; in 1539 Audley said that he would be hurt if Cromwell did not spend a night with him at Walden, and there are other signs of personal friendship.[46] But the relationship was sometimes strained, perhaps because it was uncomfortably obvious that Cromwell was the master and Audley the servant. As Chapuys wrote in the biography of Cromwell he sent Cardinal Granvelle, "the Chancellor is only his tool." And it is just possible that the jealousy was reciprocated: Cromwell may have envied the prestige that attached to the chancellor's office. At least we have Chapuys' word that although Cromwell had "so far refused to take the great seal himself, people say he will be persuaded to catch at it before long."[47]

In 1535 and 1536, particularly, disputes over jurisdiction

45. *Ibid.*, V, 1408, 1430, 1437, 1450, 1463, 1476, 1514,-1518.
46. *Ibid.*, XIV, ii, 154. A number of letters express confidence that Audley will show favor to the writer at Cromwell's request: cf. *e.g. ibid.*, VI, 1441; VII, 594, 647.
47. A full text of this dispatch (*L.P.*, IX, 862) is printed in William Thomas, *The Pilgrim*, ed. J. A. Froude (London, 1861), 107–108.

and patronage arose and criticisms were exchanged. The earliest affair concerned the appointment of an undersheriff for Middlesex. Audley had begun by writing the sheriffs of London, who duly appointed his nominee; when Cromwell attempted to fill the post he was told that all they had was at the king's disposal but that they could not revoke their promise to the Lord chancellor. Finally Audley was forced to write Cromwell, reminding him that a similar conflict had arisen the year before, when Cromwell had promised not to interfere again. Audley complained that he had few opportunities to advance his servants, while Cromwell had many; he begged that his appointment be allowed to stand. But the matter was not settled so easily. Cromwell was adamant, and Audley wrote once more that he was "right well content ye take your pleasure in it [an obvious and obsequious lie], praying you to consider that it is given me, and that of good congruence and reason ye cannot take it from me." [48]

At this point another issue increased the friction. Audley had nominated Dr. John Vaughan to a vacant benefice in the diocese of St. Asaph, but since Bishop Standish had just died, Vaughan could not be instituted, *sede vacante,* without the consent of Cromwell as vicegerent in spirituals. [49] Once again Cromwell wished to make the appointment himself and called Audley thankless. The chancellor had to write denying "eny ingratitude" and insisting abjectly that he set more by his "lovynge frend [Cromwell] then eny will or riches in the world." Although the benefice belonged to his office, he would gladly have granted it in accordance with the wishes of the king or Cromwell. A lengthy defense followed:

I was a poor honest man before it plesid the Kynges mageste to call me to myn office, and more better accepted then for my poor degree then I am now with all myn estate. And yet I have servyd his Grace truly and his peple indifferently. I medyll with as few thynges as ever did chauncelor, I am not so chargeable to the peple as chauncelors have ben, I thynke never chauncelor lesse sett by. And yet

---

48. *L.P.,* IX, 273, 432, 370, 450.   49. *Ibid.,* 511.

I am right wel content with the litell medelynges that I have, mer-
velynge mooche why I shuld have eny occasions of onkyndnes mynys-
trid to me, prayinge you if ye thynke eny onkyndnes in me or know
eny fawt by me, tell it betwixt you and me and ye shal fynde me
conformable, what so ever ye do. . . . I covyte rather to liff an honest
liff honestly then to liff in an honorabill estate with reproche. And
thus fynally it may like you to understand that I wil alweys conforme
my self to all thynges that the Kynges highnes shal comaund me,
and be oon of your poor frendes if ye wil so take me, and if ye
refuse me I wil not striffe, but take paciens in al adversytez, nothyng
elles desiryng but honestie without offence to my master or reproche
to my frende.[50]

It seems impossible to follow the matters up conclusively.
Probably Audley wanted the undersheriff's post for Robert
Dyne, one of his "poor servants"; a year later Dyne was still
being identified only as a servant of the chancellor's.[51] The
records of the Welsh bishoprics for this period are seriously
defective and include no reference to Vaughan.[52] But Dr.
Vaughan, who was busily visiting monasteries in Wales, himself
admitted that all benefices of which the bishop was patron were
now in Cromwell's gift.[53] The chances are that Cromwell prevailed in both cases: a mutilated letter to him, apologizing for
"remiss behavious and negligence" and seeking restoration of
the "good times before showed," may well be from Audley.[54]
It is conceivable that Chapuys was right and that Cromwell
pressed the issue of patronage with the hope of discrediting
Audley and becoming chancellor himself. The next year there
was no such dispute; Audley wrote in September, 1536, that
Cromwell's desire concerning the undersheriff of Middlesex
had been accomplished.[55]

Fifteen thirty-six did bring a lesser squabble. By his own
account Audley was driven into a "foolish choler" and "con-

50. Cottonian MS Titus B. I, fol. 365, B.M. (*L.P.*, IX, 528).

51. *L.P.*, IX, 450; XI, 1385. Dyne had probably come from Essex with Audley;
there was a John Dyne at Walden (*ibid.*, XIII, ii, 307).

52. Cf. John Le Neve, *Fasti Ecclesiae Anglicanae, 1300–1541*, XI: *The Welsh Dioceses*,
ed. B. Jones (London, 1965), v–vi.

53. *L.P.*, IX, 511.   54. *Ibid.*, 863 (November 21, 1535).

55. *Ibid.*, XI, 465.

ceived unkindness" when he saw a warrant made out to Christopher Hales which would have infringed the privileges granted Audley by the king. Audley hoped Cromwell would not meddle in a matter from which he could draw no profit, and he reminded Cromwell that he had not interfered with spiritual persons when Cromwell was master of the rolls. If necessary, Audley concluded, they could join in milking the Church. A month later he added that he had "never yet compounded for no religious house, wherein I have found myself a little grieved." [56] There are also signs that the activities of Audley's servant Bothe, deputy clerk of the peace in Staffordshire, ruffled Cromwell's temper.[57] But in the main Audley and Cromwell worked in tandem effectively. Each evidently realized that he needed the other. Moreover, there *was* enough profitable business for both of them.[58] Audley's failure to stand by Cromwell during the difficult days of 1540 need not be interpreted as proof of animosity: Cromwell's fall, rather, opened new avenues of preferment which an opportunist like Audley could scarcely have been expected to ignore. In fact Audley did not advance himself significantly after Cromwell's execution. He might have been regarded as being next in line for the position of chief advisor, but he lacked Cromwell's genius and may already have been showing his age. Besides, the king resolved to manage more of his affairs personally, and to divide responsibility for the rest between a number of councillors.

So much for office; now for wealth. Perhaps the most striking aspect of Audley's career was his ability to acquire land. Three factors seem to account for his success: luck, which threw vast monastic estates on the market; inside information, which enabled Audley to know what was going when; and persistence, which he exercised in repeated letters begging Cromwell to further his suits.

What Audley wanted, naturally enough, was a house in London and a landed estate in Essex. Since he inherited nothing

56. *Ibid.*, 296, 465.   57. *Ibid.*, 158.
58. *Ibid.*, 296.

of consequence, he had to beg for both. As lord keeper he had been given the use of Norwich Place, described by Chapuys as the best house in Westminster, but he was not satisfied and desired a great London residence of his own.[59] Early in 1533 he discovered just the thing and wrote Cromwell that he would like the "poor house" lately belonging to the priory of the Holy Trinity in Aldgate, commonly called Christ Church. Although he was in debt—he had had to purchase plate and other requisites of office—he believed he could bear the charges if the king would pay him the £100 due for his work as speaker in the previous session of Parliament and lend him £600 on good security.[60]

Audley did not receive the priory immediately. Sometime later he wrote Cromwell another long letter, "scribbled this morning in my bed," accompanying the grant of Christ Church which he had drafted for (as he hoped) the king to sign. There was further pitiable talk of poverty; never had chancellor so little to live on. Audley's own lands, he claimed, were not worth so much as £40 a year, and he had recently been forced to sell a house, probably in Hoxton, to pay his most pressing debts.[61] (The chances are that the dwelling was not grand enough for a chancellor and that Audley was glad to be rid of it.) He was informed that the old houses at Christ Church were worth no more than £120—he could have made more than that, he insisted, practicing law rather than serving the king!—and would cost above £600 to repair; he had therefore included some profitable lands in his draft grant, "so that the one might help the other." If he received this boon he would buy Cromwell a couple of geldings, order daily prayers for the king and queen to be offered in the old priory church,

59. *Ibid.*, VI, 180. A letter of October 1532 is dated from Norwich Place: *ibid.*, V, 1450. Chapuys added that the king had given Audley an annuity of more than a thousand ducats out of the revenues of Westminster Abbey, but he may have been mistaken. Audley held some former Abbey property, but only as trustee for the king: *ibid.*, V, 627 (23).

60. *Ibid.*, VI, 2, printed in full in *State Papers of Henry VIII* (London, 1830), I, 388–89.

61. Cf. *L.P.*, V, 1721, a letter of 1532 dated from "Hoxon."

and never ask anything further. Surely he should be given the means to sustain his position in society: "if a Chancellor of England, when he dieth, have not 200 marks of land, it is to be noted, when a merchant and one of the law will not be so satisfied." [62]

Finally Audley was successful, no doubt after a good deal more badgering. Grants of March, April, and June, 1534, gave him the property he desired. [63] Though the buildings may indeed have been in bad repair (Audley said that no one could live there in the winter until a "house of office" was restored) they must have been much more valuable than he made out. [64] Stow had childhood memories of the prior's keeping "a most bountiful house," and the priory, founded by Henry I's Queen Matilda, included a great church with a steeple and a "ring of nine bells well tuned." Despite his promise of prayers Audley offered to give this building to the parishioners of St. Katherine's, the adjoining parish church, but "having doubts in their heads of after-claps" they refused the donation. Stow continues:

Then was the priory church and steeple proffered to whomsoever would take it down, and carry it from the ground, but no man would undertake the offer; whereupon Sir Thomas Audley was fain to be at more changes than could be made of the stones, timber, lead, iron, etc. For the workmen, with great labour, beginning at the top, loosed stone from stone, and threw them down, whereby the most part of them were broken, and few remained whole; and those were sold very cheap, for all the buildings then made about the city were of brick and timber. [65]

62. *Ibid.*, VI, 927 (not dated; placed in *L.P.* at July, 1533). Audley would have seen Cromwell personally but was "very ill at ease" and had taken a glister.

63. *Ibid.*, VII, 419 (28), 587 (10), 962 (26). The land Audley wished for revenue was probably the manor of Braughing, Herts., formerly held by Nicholas Hancock, the last prior of Christ Church. This was granted to Audley in December, when the earlier grants were confirmed: *ibid.*, 1601 (35). Audley's title was further ratified by a private act of Parliament in 1536 (Lehmberg, *The Reformation Parliament*, 243).

64. The annual value of the priory's possessions in London was given as £355 13s. 6d., but it is not certain that Audley obtained all the property and pensions involved. *L.P.*, XII, ii, 777, where misdated; probably of 1532.

65. John Stow, *Survey of London* (London, 1956), 127–29. After Audley's death the property passed to his son-in-law, the 4th duke of Norfolk, and was called Duke's Place.

None of the old edifices was good enough for Audley, who built afresh on the site of the church. In later years he sold a number of tenements and shops within the precincts of Christ Church, including the Saracen's Head, an inn which was bought by a yeoman of the guard.[66] It was at his "grete mansion howse . . . yn the saide parishe" that Audley died.[67]

The estates in Essex were more scattered and were acquired over a longer period of time. We know that Audley owned property in Colchester as early as 1527, and in 1531 he was granted another parcel of land there, with adjacent pasture and a watermill.[68] This was relatively insignificant, but in 1536 the chancellor made a considerable coup: Henry gave him St. Botolph's Priory in Colchester, together with three manors in Essex, four advowsons, and twelve specified annual pensions, worth £134 3s. 4d. a year, and an annuity of £300.[69] Later in the same year Audley consolidated his holdings by exchanging property with the Abbey of St. John's, Colchester,[70] and he was granted the manors of Terling and Leighs, which had been surrendered by the bishop of Norwich in pursuance of an act of Parliament.[71] He must have liked Terling, since he stayed there during the summer of 1537; he also had a house at Brerechurch, nearer to Colchester, which he suggested Henry VIII might visit in 1540.[72] During this period Audley appears to have begun speculating in lands: he bought Estorpe and Lexden, Essex, from Sir Robert Payton, sold them to Sir Richard Gresham, the lord mayor of London, then bought them back a few months later; he acquired and alienated land in Lamborne;

66. *L.P.*, XIV, i, 220, 403 (5). Audley received £67 for the Saracen's Head; the yeoman was from Essex and had perhaps been in Audley's patronage all along.

67. The phrase is from Audley's will.

68. Essex Record Office, Chelmsford, MS D/DRg 1/91 (I am indebted to the county archivist, Mr. K. C. Newton, for this reference); *L.P.*, V, 166 (1).

69. *L.P.*, X, 1015 (28, 29). One of Cromwell's remembrances had reminded him to have "my Lord Chancellor's bill and warrant" signed: *ibid.*, 929 (ii).

70. *Ibid.*, XI, 385 (1), 519.

71. *Ibid.*, 943 (8, 11); Audley had thanked Cromwell for furthering his suit (*ibid.*, 465) and asked what he would owe the king for it (*ibid.*, 559); 27 Henry VIII, c. 45 (cf. Lehmberg, *The Reformation Parliament*, 230).

72. *L.P.*, XII, ii, 329; XVI, 677.

he exchanged property, no doubt advantageously, with the prioress of Holywell, Middlesex; he owned a house in Calais for a time, and was involved in some trouble with Lord Lisle about it.[73]

Audley's greatest single acquisition came in May, 1538, when he was granted the monastery of Walden, Essex. This, as usual, he had sought from the king through Cromwell; he wrote the secretary:

I beseche your good lordshipp to be my good lord in this sute: yf it shal plese the Kynges mageste to be so good and gracious lord to me, it shal sett forth as moche my pour estymacion as the valu of the thynge. In the besy world I susteyned damage and injory, and this shal restore me to honeste and comodyte.... And where I have promysed you to gyf his highnes v^c markes redy mony, if ye thynke it to litell, order me as his grace may be best plesid, so that I may have dayes for the rest; ffor, on my fayth, I am in dett; besechyng your good lordship to use this my sute as the Kynges highnes shal not thynke nor conceyve me to be importune, ffor I desire more his graces contentacion then eny profight in the world.[74]

In addition to the monastic site itself Audley received five manors and seven advowsons in Essex and other lands in Middlesex, Warwickshire, Oxfordshire, Northumberland, Cambridgeshire, and the Isle of Ely. The annual value of the properties was said to be £372 18s. 1d. (a good bargain for 500 marks!); Audley was released from any payment of rent or first fruits and tenths.[75] Almost immediately he sold or exchanged the outlying lands, trading (for instance) a manor in Warwickshire for land in Rye and Layer de la Haye, Essex.[76] Audley regarded Walden Abbey as his "chiefe and capitall mansion howse," as he noted in his will and as he made clear in his choice of title

73. *Ibid.*, VIII, 334, 410; IX, 820, 897; X, 270; XI, 943 (12), 1417; XII, ii, 411 (14, 15), 1027; XII, i, 887 (1). The sale to Gresham appears to have been genuine and not a fictitious transfer for the purpose of altering the title.

74. Cottonian MS Cleopatra E. IV, fol. 197, B.M., printed in Thomas Wright (ed.), *Letters Relating to the Suppression of the Monasteries* (London, 1843), XXVI, 245–48.

75. *L.P.*, XIII, i, 1115 (23). As usual Cromwell had made a remembrance about the grant: *ibid.*, 878.

76. *Ibid.*, 1115 (44–45, 51).

when created baron, but he seldom spent time there—only a
few surviving letters are dated from Walden [77]—and he does
not appear to have altered the buildings extensively. That was
left for his grandson, Thomas Howard, earl of Suffolk, the
lord treasurer to James I. Suffolk spent £200,000 on an enormous house at Audley End (as the estate came to be called);
on one of his visits King James is said to have remarked, "By
my troth, mon, it is too much for a king, but may do for a
Lord High Treasurer." [78] It was the largest house in England
at the time. Even now, with more than half of the original
structure pulled down, Audley End ranks among England's
greatest stately homes.[79]

    Audley was still not satisfied, and he kept dealing in land
until the last months of his life. He was particularly concerned
with the fate of the abbeys of St. John's, Colchester, and St.
Osyth's, near the coast southeast of Colchester. His first suit
was that the foundations might be allowed to continue, not
as monasteries but as colleges of priests, since many poor people
depended on St. John's for relief while St. Osyth's stood "at
the end of the shire," where there would otherwise be little
hospitality. He added, "as . . . Seynt Jones lakkyth water, and
Seynt Osyes stondyth in the mersches, not very holsome, so . . .
few of reputation, as I thynke, wil kepe contynual houses in
eny of them, oonlez it be a congregation, as ther be nowe." [80]

    When it became clear that the houses were to be dissolved
they suddenly seemed more desirable. Audley now changed
his tune and began seeking the properties for himself, lamenting

    77. *Ibid.*, XV, 351 and 402, both of March, 1540. Addison *(Audley End,* 13) states
erroneously that not one letter is addressed from Walden.
    78. Addison, *Audley End,* 2, 26.
    79. It remained in the family until 1943, when it was taken over by the state in
satisfaction of death duties after two members of the family had been killed in the
war *(ibid.,* 223–4). Its use by Cambridge University was discussed, but university officials
believed it unsuitable (information communicated to the author by Thomas Knox-Shaw,
former master of Sidney Sussex College and treasurer of the University); it is now
operated by the Ministry of Works and is open to the public. On Audley End see
also J. D. Williams, *Audley End: The Restoration of 1762–1797* (Chelmsford, 1966).
    80. *L.P.,* XII, ii, 306, printed in full in *State Papers of Henry VIII,* I, 586–88. Audley
offered Cromwell £200 if he would support this scheme.

that he had nothing so far but the chancellorship, "high but chargeable." He was placed in control of St. Osyth's and forwarded to Cromwell the inventory of its jewels, plate, and other possessions, worth in all more than £1353.[81] Later he acquired the use of St. John's also. But neither estate was actually granted to Audley, and late in 1539 he heard that the king intended to retain St. John's himself. In pain "with a sore and akyng foote" he scribbled another importunate letter to Cromwell. "To forgo al this," he whined, "shalbe no litell losse to my poor honeste and estymacion, consideryng this to be in the contree where I was borne and most part browt up." He begged Cromwell to further his suit for an exchange with the king according to a bill which he enclosed; once again he promised that he would seek nothing more. (Cromwell and Henry must have learned long before that they could not believe that assertion!) His marriage to a marquis's daughter and his desire for children (he had none by his first wife, though his second was to bear him two daughters) demanded greater wealth, and his present holdings were worth no more than £800 a year clear.[82] In March, 1540, he reminded Cromwell of his suit.[83] But for once Audley did not speed. St. Osyth's was granted to Cromwell himself in April, just before the secretary's fall. Even after Cromwell's disgrace it did not come to Audley. Nor did St. John's.[84]

Land transactions continued after 1540, but they were all minor sales or purchases of manors. As before, Audley was consolidating his holdings by disposing of land in other counties and buying property in Essex.[85] There were also a few more grants from the king: the manor of Great Chesterford in Cam-

---

81. *L.P.*, XIII, ii, 764; XIV, i, 1326 (3); XIV, ii, 36; Wright, *Letters*, 239–41.
82. Cottonian MS. Cleopatra E. VI, fol. 222, B.M. (*L.P.*, XIV, ii, 775).
83. *L.P.*, XV, 351.
84. *Ibid.*, 611 (8). The great gatehouses of both abbeys survive.
85. See, *e.g.*, *ibid.*, XIV, ii, 780 (18); XV, 282 (56), 498, 612 (6), 942 (72); XVI, 107 (8), 305 (12), 580 (101), 1056 (53), 1135 (3); XVII, 362 (52), 1012 (43); XVIII, i, 100 (10), 802 (12, 60); Essex Record Office, MSS D/DHt T 313/10, D/DSy 21. Several more private acts of Parliament confirmed Audley's exchanges and holdings.

bridgeshire, just across the county line from Walden, worth
about £56 a year, and the mansion called the Founder's Lodging
at the dissolved monastery of Tilty, Essex, with lands valued
at £28.[86] Further research into manorial records, where they
survive, would be needed to work out the details of Audley's
transactions and to determine his exact wealth, but the general
position is clear enough. In the assessment of the loan in 1542
he was rated at 4000 ducats. Despite all his protestations of
poverty he had become the third richest man in the realm,
surpassed only by the dukes of Norfolk and Suffolk.[87] And
he lived in the grand style, with his own serjeant-at-arms, mes-
sengers, bargemen, and even a troup of players.[88]

As Audley tirelessly sought honor and wealth for himself,
so he sought preferment for a number of his servants and
associates. He was fond of complaining, as we have seen, that
he enjoyed few opportunities for patronage. Perhaps it was
true that, compared to Cromwell, Audley could do little for
his friends; but what he could do, he did avidly. In one of
the earliest recorded instances he sent Cromwell one of his
own rings to gain favor for Sir Roger Cholmeley.[89] Later, over
a period of several years, he used his influence with Lord Lisle,
the deputy of Calais. In 1536 he wrote commending "young
Whethill," whom he wished admitted to the Calais garrison
as a spearman. Lisle hated Whethill, for he and his father had
"ordered me openly at Lantern Gate with words and countenance that I never suffered so much of no degree since I was
sixteen years old," but at Audley's request he agreed to forgive
and forget.[90] The next year Audley obtained the reversion of
a soldier's post at Calais, with pay of 8d. a day, for his servant
John Nicholas, and he asked Lisle to admit Nicholas to the

---

86. *L.P.*, XVI, 678 (36); XVII, 285 (2); cf. XVIII, ii, 100 (10).
87. *Ibid.*, XVIII, App. B, 13. The figures are Chapuys' but are likely to be reliable.
Audley's will is not very helpful, since it does not include valuations of his land. Bequests
in cash amounted to more than £900.
88. *Ibid.*, XIV, ii, 782; XV, 282 (65).
89. *Ibid.*, VII, 833 (probably from the summer of 1534).
90. *Ibid.*, X, 117 (i, ii).

place which had become vacant.[91] In 1538 he sought another place at Calais for another servant, one Richard Griffith.[92] These suits, together with Audley's possession of a house at Calais, may strengthen the possibility that he had himself served in the garrison there when young.

Offices in England proper also fell to Audley's friends. When the Court of Augmentations was established Thomas Pope, one of the chancellor's servants, was named to the lucrative post of receiver general. Cromwell had first sent him to Audley, who found in him "much kindness."[93] During the final illness of John Onley, attorney of the Augmentations, Audley wrote Cromwell supporting the promotion of Robert Southwell, who had served faithfully as solicitor. John Lucas, a "right well learned and discreet" lawyer from the Temple, was his choice for solicitor; Audley preferred him because he was "no common meddler in causes, whereby he may give the better attendance."[94] In 1537 Audley helped John Grenfeld obtain the office of controller of the ports of Exeter and Dartmouth: Grenfeld was a "poor younger brother" with many children and had served the king well in suppressing the Pilgrimage of Grace; he had no advancement but the office of serjeant-at-law, which had proved costly. After a few months Grenfeld was licensed to employ a deputy controller and devote himself to Audley's service, as before.[95] The chancellor also suggested men, "honest and well learned," who should be appointed judges and king's serjeants, as well as serjeants-at-law.[96]

91. *Ibid.*, XII, ii, 411 (20), 623.   92. *Ibid.*, XIII, i, 857.
93. *Ibid.*, X, 573; XV, 351; cf. Richardson, *Augmentations*, 71–2.
94. *L.P.*, XII, ii, 1160. Audley offered Cromwell £10 for wine if he would further the suit. Onley died November 20, 1537, and Southwell was appointed as of November 23 (*ibid.*, XIII, ii, 457). After 1538 Lucas was Audley's deputy as steward of Augmentation lands north of the Trent (Richardson, *Augmentations*, 494), and he and Pope jointly held a reversionary grant of the office of clerk of the crown in Chancery (*L.P.*, XII, ii, 384 [101]). There seems to be no evidence that he was appointed solicitor of Augmentations.
95. *L.P.*, XII, ii, 738–89; XII, i, 384 (37). The earl of Wiltshire had previously offered Grenfeld the stewardship of the monastery of St. Albans, only to find that the king had previously promised it to Norfolk and his son. In 1539 Grenfeld was named steward to Anne of Cleves (*ibid.*, XIV, ii, 609).
96. *Ibid.*, XII, ii, 805. Audley was also influential in the choice of justices of the

Audley enjoyed considerable ecclesiastical patronage, and in a number of cases he tried to secure profitable positions for churchmen whom he regarded highly, or for his own servants. He gave a Welsh benefice to one of his chaplains and was surprised to hear that Cromwell was also interested in the place.[97] He secured the reversion of a corrody at St. Augustine's, Bristol, for his servant Henry Tappe.[98] He sought appointment as a chantry priest at Lapworth, Warwickshire, for one Thomas Garrett.[99] He helped John Hodgkin, the last provincial of the Black Friars, become suffragan bishop of Bedford,[100] and he was influential in procuring the archdeaconry of Leicester for his friend William More, the suffragan bishop of Colchester.[101] It is surprising that Audley did not attempt to secure monastic land for his associates more frequently. The only recorded instance seems to come from 1537, when he sought to have the friary at Sudbury made over to a friend who was willing to pay the price given in the official valuation.[102] Perhaps he could not resist the temptation of seeking every available property for himself.

These successes in patronage were coupled with a few rebuffs. We have already noted several cases in which Audley was forced to yield to Cromwell, most notably that involving the undersheriff of Middlesex. In 1540 the Privy Council wrote Audley insisting that the king's nominee should have the benefice of Gillingham despite Audley's claim that he could make such presentations when they were of limited value. The chancellor was advised further to make denizens of no more

---

peace, whom he could appoint by warrant, but since these positions were unpaid they cannot properly be considered as part of his patronage. An analysis of his appointments might prove interesting; in all likelihood it would tell more about county society than about the chancellor.

97. *Ibid.*, 747. This is not the case of Dr. Vaughan, mentioned above.

98. *Ibid.*, XIII, i, 888 (7). 99. *Ibid.*, XIV, ii, 250.

100. *Ibid.*, XIII, ii, 1245. This letter, in which Hodgkin complained that he had lived in poverty for five years, is misdated in *L.P.*; it must have been written prior to Hodgkin's consecration on December 9, 1537. Cf. *Handbook of British Chronology*, ed. F. M. Powicke and E. B. Fryde (2nd ed.; London; 1961), 271.

101. *L.P.*, XIV, ii, 36. Audley offered to pay £80 to the bishop of Hereford for resigning the archdeaconry and £20 to Cromwell "for his pains."

102. *Ibid.*, XII, ii, 736.

foreign merchants until he had conferred with Henry.[103] The
chief problem, as Audley himself groaned, was that there simply
were not enough posts to go around. One of his servants, John
Greene, was reduced to seeking preferment through Wriothesley because he despaired of ever gaining it from Audley. The
chancellor, Greene said, had to provide for too many of his
first wife's relatives.[104]

     With this evidence about Audley's property and patronage
before us we may return to the charges that he was guilty of
greed and servility. It is hard not to agree that they have some
basis in fact. Certainly Audley sounds, in his letters to Cromwell,
curiously like a spoiled child, always wanting some new toy,
never satisfied with what he has, and jealous enough to keep
for himself everything he can lay his hands on. As the abbot
of Colchester wrote, his thirst would not be slaked if the very
Thames ran with gold.[105] Yet this judgment may be too severe.
High-ranking officers of state are entitled to be well paid for
their services, and in the sixteenth century such rewards usually
consisted of grants from the king and gifts from suitors rather
than ordinary salaries. Though the Tudor age may have seen
a decline in public morality, there is no evidence to suggest
that Audley was guilty of egregious corruption or malfeasance
in office. One may think, in absolute terms, that he acquired
too much: that no one should have enjoyed such wealth while
others starved. But this is a moral argument rather than a historical one. It would be more realistic to inquire how well Audley
deserved what he got. How well, that is to say, did he perform
the tasks assigned to him by Henry VIII?

     This question can be approached in two ways. The first
would involve a study of the Chancery as a bureau operating
under Audley's supervision and a reading of all the cases to
come before him in his role as a judge. These laborious inquiries,
essential as they are to a full understanding of the situation,
must await the commitment of institutional and legal historians.

103. *Ibid.*, XVI, 34.   104. *Ibid.*, XIII, i, 866.
105. *Ibid.*, XIV, ii, 458.

A second approach—and the only one possible here—relies on the comments of contemporaries, tempered by a few other pieces of evidence. The Henrician observers may have been limited in perspective, but clearly their opinions have value; they will have to be set alongside modern analyses even when these become available.

Sixteenth-century critics of Audley charged him with partiality and, less often, inefficiency. Of course Audley was partial: he was partial, at least, to the king who gave him office. When Chapuys reported, in 1533, that Henry had named a chancellor suited to his purpose he was only telling the obvious truth.[106] Especially in the great state trials Audley acted as an agent of the king, conducting actions which were regarded as being essential to the security of the realm. Naturally one feels sympathy for the victims and a certain revulsion for those who brought them to their fate. It is surely worth emphasizing, however, that the driving force in such matters was the sovereign. If Audley had not cooperated, Henry would have found a chancellor willing to do so. The chancellorship, that is to say, was no job for a man of finely honed moral conscience; after More's retirement no man of such scruples would have been appointed, or once named would have remained long in office. So it will not do to shift the blame to Audley's shoulders when it belongs squarely on Henry's. And—before we judge the king himself —we should recall that the later decades of his reign *were* troubled; that political dissenters presented a genuine threat to order and stability; that there was ample medieval precedent for removal of those who opposed the regime; and that even in the great Tudor cases strict legality was preserved.

Contemporary criticism, unlike that of later writers, did not center on these trials. Instead, it alleged that Audley was guilty of favoritism in less exalted matters where, as a judge, he should have acted without bias. Lord Vaux of Harrowden was convinced that Audley was "not mine indifferent good lord,"

106. *Ibid.*, VI, 180.

and he thought that without Cromwell's intervention he would
be "trodden under foot and made a slave." [107] Dr. John London
believed that he was certain to have Audley's disfavor in a suit.[108]
Robert Aske, who was a London lawyer before he took up
the lead in the Pilgrimage of Grace, held a special grudge against
Audley "for playing of ambidexter in granting and dissolving
of injunctions." [109] John Hussee wrote Lord Lisle of a suit in
which the law was "clearly against us" and there was no remedy
unless the king "should stop the course of his common laws."
Yet this miracle occurred: "God wrought in it," Hussee thought,
and on a more mundane level he credited Audley and Cromwell.[110] On several occasions Lisle himself sent Audley gifts and
money to gain favor in suits; once Audley grumbled because
he had not received some wine promised him, and Lisle had
to dispatch it from Calais with haste.[111] When Cromwell fell
the French ambassador, Charles de Marillac, wrote that "for
affairs of justice they have deputed the chancellor, who, among
other virtues, can neither speak French nor Latin, and has
the reputation of being a good seller of justice, whenever he
can find a buyer." [112] But Marillac was scarcely unbiased himself,
and we must dilute his vitriol.

Against such criticisms we should in fairness set two
contemporary encomiums and one of Audley's own letters. The
laudatory testimonials come from fellow administrators who
were in a particularly good position to evaluate the chancellor's
work. Brian Tuke, whom Audley once denied a writ of *liberate,*
took no offense but rather praised the chancellor as "a great
wise councillor that would not I should have two discharges
for one matter, lest I might take double allowance." John Hales,
answering the hypothetical question what jewel or treasure was
most meet for the king, replied, "ten such judges as the lord

107. *Ibid.,* X, 744.   108. *Ibid.,* XII, ii, 429.
109. *Ibid.,* XIII, i, 6.   110. *Ibid.,* 1333.
111. *Ibid.,* VII, 491; XI, 1397; XIV, ii, 390, 535.
112. *Ibid.,* XV, 804.

chancellor is." [113] Audley's own letter, an uncommonly revealing one, concerns a case in which Paulet and Cromwell wished him to set aside an earlier decision. He wrote:

I am content to accomplishe your desires, and yet neverthelesse all thinges considered it standyth neyther with equyte nor justice in this case, beyng betwene party and party for perambulacion of the lymytes. . . . In so moche as the comyssion went forth as I am enformed by assent and Master Countroller beyng privy to the namyng of the comyssioners, . . . yt semyth to me very sore to graunt now a super-sedeas. In good fayth I wryte not this for the favor of eny person, albeyt I may be otherwise jugyd. There is no creature lyvyng shal cause me to do eny thynge wherby the Kynges highnes shuld be wrongyd or onlawfully handelyd, yff I may know yt, but I am thus bold to declare my poor mynde to you both my ffrendes, that you with me and I with you may runne by a just lyne to the Kynges honor and profyght. [114]

Partiality, of course, could extend to religion. Here Audley was criticized too: Cardinal de Bellay called him the deadly enemy of Rome, while one of Catherine of Aragon's adherents prophesied early death for the "false Chancellor." [115] Certainly these writers were correct in asserting that Audley was no papist. Beyond this his religious position is less clearly defined. Was he in fact, as is sometimes thought, particularly favorable to reformers and reformed doctrines?

There is, admittedly, some evidence linking Audley with Protestant causes. A letter to Melanchthon described the chancellor, Cromwell, and Cranmer as excellent men, most friendly to the purer doctrine of the Gospel, and several letters to Bullinger emphasize Audley's regard for the continental reformers. He even offered to care for Bullinger's son personally should the boy come to England. [116]

113. *Ibid.*, XIII, ii, 499; Harleian MS 4990, fol. 44, B.M. (*L.P.*, XVII, App. 1), "An oration in commendation of laws," sent to Sir Anthony Browne to be given to the king.
114. SP 1/73, fols. 98–99, P.R.O. (*L.P.*, V, 1721).
115. *L.P.*, VI, 1572, 923.
116. *Ibid.*, XIV, ii, 423; XV, 383; XVI, 1204.

But most surviving papers cast Audley in a conservative role. In 1535 he caused the English translation of the New Testament to be burned, and he stopped the printing of a book attacking images with the comment that such talk should be damped down until the king might take a final order therein.[117] In 1536, referring to the proposed execution of a heretic, he wrote Cromwell, "if the person be worthy to suffer, it is good to be done for example." [118] Later he examined heretics sent to him by Bishop Stokesley.[119] In the summer of 1537 he complained that the people of Essex appeared irritable and inconstant, and that there was contentious preaching in several parishes; he sought authority to promulgate the conservative Bishops' Book, which he hoped would calm the stir, earlier than planned.[120] None of the clerics whom he helped in obtaining office was a reformer. Audley probably championed William More, not out of religious principle, but simply because More held *in commendam* the abbey of Walden and was willing to surrender it if properly compensated. John Hodgkin, the other suffragan who came under Audley's patronage, remained in office throughout Mary's reign and survived to become one of the consecrators of Matthew Parker in 1559. Like the new archbishop, he "had his rochet on" during the service, an outward sign that he was more conservative than Coverdale, who wore only a black Geneva gown.[121]

In his will Audley left to Magdalen College such orthodox props of his own chapel as copes and sensers. Despite the reformers' belief to the contrary, there is some evidence that he worked for, not against, the Act of Six Articles.[122] The archconservative Pole family did not believe Audley antagonistic to them; it was to the chancellor that Geoffrey Pole turned when

117. *Ibid.*, VIII, 1; IX, 358.   118. *Ibid.*, XI, 369.
119. *Ibid.*, XIV, i, 1001.
120. *Ibid.*, XII, ii, 329. The book was issued officially in September.
121. Thomas Fuller, *Church History of England* (London, 1842), II, 452.
122. In Cottonian MS Cleopatra E. V. fol. 129, B.M. (*L.P.*, XIV, i, 1040) a conservative writer says that Audley had been "as good as we can desire " in the parliamentary debate. Cf. *L.P.*, XIV, ii, 423 for the views of the reformers.

he wanted permission to come to London in 1537.[123] Of course
the rebels in the Pilgrimage of Grace railed against Audley,
as they did against Cranmer and Cromwell, for favoring excessive change.[124] But their leader's phrase, applied originally to
law, might more accurately express Audley true position in
religion. "Playing of ambidexter!" Here is the key: without real
conviction on either side Audley followed the king's lead,
appearing conservative or reformed as seemed most likely to
benefit him personally at any given moment.

Now for the signs of inefficiency. In 1532, early in Audley's
career, some documents sent him to seal were found lying in
the street, and the king was informed that the loss had been
caused by Audley's negligence. Here Audley was probably not
guilty; he blamed one Stokley, a servant to the clerk of the
crown, and succeeded in convincing Cromwell.[125] A more serious matter calls into question the chancellor's legal expertise,
or at least his care in legal matters. About 1535 the Irish officials
drew up a bill suspending Poynings' Law. When Audley saw
it he was dissatisfied, and he prepared his own shorter draft.
This passed the Irish Parliament in 1536, but it proved necessary
to follow it up almost immediately with two amendments touching matters which Audley had not foreseen.[126] The same Parliament was forced to pass a second subsidy act because the first
had been improperly drafted, probably through Audley's negligence.[127] The chancellor seems to have done better by the
legislation for England proper which he helped write, though
here again part of a subsidy act (that of 1534) was deficiently
drafted.[128] Perhaps his greatest legislative achievement was the

123. *L.P.*, XII, i, 829.
124. See, among the very numerous related items, *ibid.*, XI, 902 (2), 1182, 1246.
125. *Ibid.*, V, 1437, 1463.
126. R. Dudley Edwards, "The Irish Reformation Parliament of Henry VIII, 1536
-37," in *Historical Studies*, VI (London, 1968), 81–84.
127. *Ibid.*, 69. The second act alleges that the engrossing clerk caused the error,
but the evidence does not bear out that interpretation. Probably Audley was trying
to shift the blame. A number of letters between Audley and Cromwell testify to his
involvement in the Irish legislative program: cf. *L.P.*, IX, 41, 65, 90, 149; XI, 382
(3).
128. Lehmberg, *The Reformation Parliament*, 208 and n. The act probably originated

Statue of Uses. Its severity we may attribute to Henry VIII, and the political maneuvers preceding its passage to Cromwell; the meticulous attention to detail which led Bacon to call it "the most perfectly and exactly penned of any law in the book" must have been largely Audley's.[129] Unfortunately, surviving drafts generally do not enable us to determine precisely what was done by whom in phrasing the legislation of the 1530's, but some corrections in Audley's hand and some letters which passed between him and Cromwell suggest strongly that the chancellor's role, particularly in technical legal matters, was a significant one. Certainly the great Reformation statutes were conceived with care and did their work well.[130] On balance Audley comes off well; his slips seem to have been those minor ones which any overworked administrator is likely to make.

Our brief inquiry cannot pretend to be definitive. Still, we have assembled some of the evidence, and we should be able to act as better informed judges of Audley's character and stature. What conclusions can we draw?

First, it is clear that Thomas Audley was a man of uncommon ability, willing to labor uncommonly hard. This made him an effective administrator, able to grasp complex situations quickly and to handle many different sorts of duties. Further, he was possessed of a keen perception of personalities and possibilities. As David Lloyd implied, he could often divine the king's reaction even before problems were presented to him, and he could discard solutions which would be unacceptable to the sovereign.

In this very strength lay Audley's chief limitation. He was content to do whatever pleased Henry, not attempting to divert royal policy into nobler channels. He was no innovator, and he strove toward no clear goal. In this he stands in contrast

---

with Cromwell, not Audley, but the chancellor should have examined its technical legal aspects carefully.

129. Sir Francis Bacon, "Reading on the Statute of Uses," in Bacon's *Works*, ed. James Spedding (London, 1857–74), VII, 416.

130. The point is reinforced in Elton's recent study, *Policy and Police: The Enforcement of the Reformation in the Age of Thomas Cromwell* (Cambridge, 1972).

to Thomas Cromwell, who, Professor Elton has recently argued, was guided by a vision of England reformed in body and soul.[131] There is no convincing evidence that Thomas Audley saw that vision, or any other. His greatest achievement was his own rise in wealth and status, not the implementation of any wise policy for the realm.

For this reason Audley cannot be given a place among English statesmen of the first rank. A strong second-rater, he did well for himself, well for the king, well for Cambridge, well for his family and for friends who sought his patronage. His soul, contrary to Fuller's analogy, was not as black as the marble of his tomb, nor his heart as hard. Rather he resembled his monument in being conceived on the grandest scale and wrought in the most fashionable taste of the time. Shrewd and servile, effective and energetic, prudent and partial, grasping and generous, he was the embodiment of much in Tudor society.

131. *Ibid.*, 424.

Mortimer Levine

The fall of edward, duke of buckingham

In the beginning 1520's Henry VIII sat firmly on his throne. Thanks to the dispatch of Edward IV's nephews—John de la Pole, earl of Lincoln, in 1487, Edward, earl of Warwick, in 1499, and Edmund de la Pole, earl of Suffolk, in 1513—no Yorkist claimant remained who could be considered a serious threat to the Tudor dynasty.[1] The future of that dynasty was in doubt, however. When Catherine of Aragon in February, 1516, gave birth to Princess Mary, her first child likely to survive, the king was confident that "the sons will follow."[2] When Catherine was delivered of a stillborn child in November, 1518, Henry did not know that this was to be her last pregnancy. Nevertheless, the situation was hardly conducive to continued sanguineness. The king might regard his daughter as his heir

1. Richard, the last of the de la Poles, pretended to the crown, but he was an exile in a France now allied to England.
2. John S. Brewer, James Gairdner, and Robert H. Brodie (eds.), *Letters and Papers, Foreign and Domestic, of the Reign of Henry VIII* (21 vols. in 33 parts; London, 1862–1910), II, 438, hereinafter cited as *L.P.*

presumptive, but it was questionable whether England would accept a little girl as his successor. His death by natural or other cause would present a real opportunity for someone else to attempt to emulate Richard III. It is uncertain how deep was Henry's concern about the succession before it was aroused by his passion for Anne Boleyn, but the fear that some person or group was compassing his death was never remote from him.

Sometime in 1520 or early 1521 panic apparently came to the king. Although writing was "somewhat tedious and painful" to him, he took the trouble of writing in his own hand a confidential letter to his lord chancellor, Cardinal Wolsey. He instructed Wolsey to "make good watch on" Charles Brandon, duke of Suffolk, Edward Stafford, duke of Buckingham, Henry Algernon Percy, earl of Northumberland, Thomas Stanley, 2nd earl of Derby, Henry Stafford, earl of Wiltshire, and "others which you think suspect to see what they do with this news." [3] We do not know what "this news" was, but, considering the action that Henry was to take in the spring of 1521, it seems likely that he feared a conspiracy relating to the crown. It is difficult to account for the naming of Suffolk, Henry's brother-in-law and close friend, except on the ground that the king was in a state of panic, perhaps stirred up by somebody else. Suffolk, despite his dukedom, was as much a creature of the Tudors as Wolsey. Unthinking loyalty to Henry VIII was the trademark of this mediocre man. Potentially the most dangerous man named by Henry was Edward of Buckingham.

Royal blood flowed in the veins of the man who proudly styled himself as "the right high and mighty prince, Edward, Duke of Buckingham." [4] Through his Beaufort grandmother, Buckingham descended from John of Gaunt, duke of Lancaster and fourth son of Edward III. Through the Staffords he was

3. British Museum, Additional MS 1938, fol. 44. *L.P.*, III, 1, places this letter in early 1519, but the footnote therein practically rules this out. J. J. Scarisbrick, *Henry VIII* (Berkeley and Los Angeles, 1968), 120, doubtless is correct in dating it as 1520 or early 1521.

4. B.M., Cotton MS Titus B I, fol. 179.

the heir of Thomas of Woodstock, duke of Gloucester and youngest son of Edward III. This last, unlike either the Yorkist or Beaufort descent of Henry VIII, was one of unquestionable legitimacy. In 1502 loyal servants of the crown had preferred Buckingham or Edmund de la Pole to the ten-year-old Prince Henry as a successor in the event of Henry VII's untimely demise.[5] In 1519 the Venetian ambassador had written that the "extremely popular" Buckingham "might easily obtain the crown" if Henry VIII died "without male heirs." [6] Moreover, Buckingham was a great magnate of the fifteenth-century type with fortified castles and hundreds of armed retainers.[7] His annual landed income of over £6,000 [8] probably made him England's richest nobleman. He had made marriage alliances with great families much in the manner of the fifteenth-century Nevilles. He himself married a Percy; he matched his son with Ursula Pole, a granddaughter of Edward IV's brother George, duke of Clarence; he married his eldest daughter to Thomas Howard, earl of Surrey and later 3rd duke of Norfolk, and his two younger daughters to Nevilles. Furthermore, of the three named after Buckingham in Henry VIII's letter, Northumberland was his father-in-law and Wiltshire was his brother.

Whether due to baseless fear, a real conspiracy, or someone's instigation, Henry VIII decided to strike at Buckingham. In early April, 1521, the unsuspecting duke received a royal command to come to London; when his journey took him beyond the point where escape was possible it dawned on him that his destination was death.[9] Henry's original intention seems to have been to have Buckingham tried in Parliament,[10] but

5. James Gairdner (ed.), *Letters and Papers Illustrative of the Reigns of Richard III and Henry VII* (2 vols.; London, 1861–73), I, 233.

6. *L.P.*, III, 143.

7. Lawrence Stone, *The Crisis of the Aristocracy, 1558–1641* (Oxford, 1965), 201, 217; Albert F. Pollard, *Wolsey* (London, 1929), 201.

8. *L.P.*, III, 511.

9. John S. Brewer, *The Reign of Henry VIII from His Accession to the Death of Wolsey*, ed. James Gairdner (2 vols.; London, 1884), I, 384–85.

10. *L.P.*, III, 453.

when a Parliament finally met in 1523 its only duty in this regard was to pass an act of attainder against an already executed man.[11] Maybe it was decided that a trial of the popular duke in Parliament might prove too sticky. At any rate, Buckingham was tried in mid-May, 1521, by Thomas Howard, 2nd duke of Norfolk, who was designated lord high steward for the occasion, and nineteen other peers.[12]

The institution which came to be known as the Court of the Lord High Steward was first used by Henry VII in 1499 to try Edward, earl of Warwick, for high treason. Since Warwick had long been a prisoner in the Tower, he could not credibly be accused of making war on the king and, as was usual in the fifteenth century, be tried for treason under the law of arms in a constable's court. And a trial of the unfortunate young earl, whose real crime was his Yorkist descent, in Parliament might well have been troublesome. In any event, a court of peers presided over by a specially appointed steward of England was devised to try Warwick. A fictitious precedent and a genuine but merely coincidental one probably were used to give this bastard court the appearance of antiquity. Since Warwick cooperatively pleaded guilty, his trial was hardly a real test of the court. Nor was the obscure trial of a lord for felony in 1503 which doubtless ended either in acquittal or pardon. It was Henry VIII's 1521 trial of Buckingham for high treason that definitively established the Court of the Lord High Steward: a court that has been described by its historian as "a fraudulent device for the degradation of the nobility generally . . . intended to supersede and altogether deprive them of trial in Parliament." [13]

The case against Buckingham rested exclusively on the

11. 14 & 15 Henry VIII, c. 20; *The Statutes of the Realm* (11 vols.; London, 1810–28), III, 246.

12. *Appendix II to the Third Report of the Deputy Keeper of the Public Records* (London, 1842), 230, 233, hereinafter cited as *Deputy Keeper's Report.* I have checked the keeper's report of the trial against the original in the *Baga de Secretis* (Public Record Office, King's Bench 8/5) and found his translations cited below to be adequate.

13. L. W. Vernon Harcourt, *His Grace the Steward and Trial of Peers* (London, 1907), 379–80, 399, 428–43.

depositions of three servants: John Delacourt, the duke's chaplain, Robert Gilbert, his chancellor, and Charles Knyvet, his recently discharged surveyor. Buckingham, howsoever his popularity in the nation at large, was hardly beloved by his retainers and tenants. Certainly Knyvet, probably Gilbert, and perhaps Delacourt had reason to be influenced by a desire for revenge in deposing against the duke.[14] Moreover, there is evidence indicating that Henry VIII, who was convinced of Buckingham's guilt from the start, personally handled the interrogation of witnesses, assisted only by Thomas Ruthal, bishop of Durham.[15] Such royal attention might well serve to intimidate inconsequential men into giving desired testimony. None of this means that the case against Buckingham consisted merely of fabricated accusations; it surely suggests that the accusations should not all be taken at face value.

The general charge against Buckingham was "intending to exalt himself to the Crown of England," and imagining and compassing "to deprive and depose the King . . . and also to effect his death and destruction."[16] The 1523 attainder act implies that the 1521 court found that he had "imagined and compassed traitorously and unnaturally the destruction of" Henry VIII's "most royal person" at "divers times" and "traitorously committed and did divers and many treasons against" the king.[17] Compassing or imagining the king's death was high treason according to the Act of Treasons of 1352,[18] the standing treason statute, and, as indicated by its wording and confirmed by subsequent judicial interpretations, no overt act was required to establish the offense. Moreover, acts or words of little or no relevance could easily be brought within the meaning of compassing or imagining by means of judicial construction.[19]

14. Brewer, *Henry VIII*, I, 378–81.   15. *L.P.*, III, 453, 468.
16. *Deputy Keeper's Report*, 230.   17. *Statutes of Realm*, III, 246.
18. 25 Edward III, st. 5, c. 2; *Statutes of Realm*, I, 319–20.
19. J. G. Bellamy, *The Law of Treason in England in the Middle Ages* (Cambridge, 1970), 122–24, 136–37, 212–13.

Obviously the finding of a court selected by a royal master determined on conviction requires some scrutiny.[20]

The only direct testimony that Buckingham compassed and imagined Henry VIII's death was supplied by Knyvet. This involved an alleged conversation that Knyvet had with the duke on November 4, 1519—Buckingham's accusers consistently displayed a remarkable capacity for recalling the exact dates of alleged past happenings. The duke indicated that he expected to be committed to the Tower due to the king's having blamed him for retaining Sir William Bulmer in his service. If this happened, "the chief actors therein"—presumably Henry and Wolsey—"should not profit by the same," for Buckingham would do what his father had intended to do to Richard III: "to wit that his father had made his suit to come into the presence of King Richard, having about him a concealed dagger, and that his father intended, when he should be kneeling before King Richard, to rise suddenly and plunge the dagger into the body of the said King Richard." [21] This conversation certainly could have occurred. Buckingham had unlawfully retained Bulmer, a royal retainer pledged to serve none but the king. Bulmer was brought before the king and his Council, and Wolsey "then and there gave him 'a lesson to be remembered.' " [22] Buckingham had cause to expect Henry's full wrath to be turned on him. It is possible that he uttered the treasonable words to a then trusted servant. If so, however, they may well have reflected bravado rather than serious intent.[23] At any rate, the sole source for the alleged words was a discharged surveyor.

20. The record of Buckingham's trial, as is usual for sixteenth-century cases, consists mainly of his indictment plus the court's verdict and judgment. Such a record is necessarily rather thin and quite one-sided in its offerings of "factual" evidence. All the historian can do is to point out this limitation and attempt to reconstruct from what he has.

21. *Deputy Keeper's Report*, 231–32.

22. William H. Dunham, Jr., *Lord Hastings' Indentured Retainers, 1461–1483* (New Haven, 1955), 101. Bulmer was also sent to the Fleet. Henry E. Huntington Library, Ellesmere MS 2654, fol. 24.

23. Of course, bravado could easily and legally be construed as treasonous by a sixteenth-century court which did not have to bother about the niceties of meaning when its purpose was to convict.

Another serious charge against Buckingham probably came from Gilbert, though somewhat strangely it does not appear in his recorded deposition.[24] This was that on May 10, 1517, the duke sent his chancellor to the king and his Council to obtain a license to retain men in the counties of Hereford, Gloucester, and Somerset, "and that he might also transmit arms and warlike equipments at his pleasure to Wales." The duke's alleged purpose was to "strengthen himself against the King that he might thereby destroy and subdue the King and take upon himself the crown." Gilbert tried to procure such license from Henry on May 20, 1517, "and at other times." [25] The charge had a dangerous plausibility, for Buckingham's father, Duke Henry, had launched his rebellion against Richard III from his Welsh holdings. Duke Edward, however, could hardly have regarded his Welsh marcher lordships as a suitable base from which to make war on Henry VIII. On November 26, 1520, he instructed Gilbert to inform Wolsey of his intention to visit his lordships in Wales in February, 1521. He wanted to collect a "knowledge" payable to his wife on her first visit to the lordships and to levy his rents, farms, and casual revenues, "which will not be levied unless we be there present; neither justice administered, as our council and officers report unto us; and for that it is well known to all the King's commissioners that have been there . . . that we cannot be there for our surety without three or four hundred men." Gilbert was to ask Wolsey to intervene to obtain Henry's license for the expedition.[26] The license was not forthcoming, but Buckingham's understandable desire to secure his position in his hostile Welsh lordships was something that could be construed in his trial as evidence of treasonable intent.

Gilbert definitely supplied the most cryptic of all the charges against Buckingham. On February 20, 1520, the duke told him that he "would delay, putting off his intentions until a more

24. Printed in full in Brewer, *Henry VIII*, I, 391–92.
25. *Deputy Keeper's Report*, 231.
26. B.M., Cotton MS Titus B I, fol. 182; *L.P.*, III, 392.

convenient time, and that the thing would be well done if the noblemen of the kingdom would mutually declare their minds to one another, but that many of them were afraid so to declare their minds and therefore this spoiled all." The duke further said that all Henry VII had done "had been done in wrong" and that he had "always murmured against what" Henry VIII "had done." He concluded that he was "such a great sinner, that he was certain he wanted the grace of God, and therefore he knew well that he should be the worse for it whenever he began to do anything against the King."[27] What Buckingham intended to do and whether it was treasonous was not revealed, but his alleged conversation, the conclusion of which makes little sense unless he had a death wish, had a treasonable sound.

The matter presented first and at greatest length in the duke's indictment was his relations with Nicholas Hopkins, a monk who claimed to have the gift of prophecy. The evidence here apparently came mainly from Delacourt. On April 24, 1512, Buckingham sent his chaplain to Hopkins. The monk, after swearing Delacourt to secrecy, told him to declare to the duke that he "should have all" and "should endeavor to obtain the love of the community of England." Three months later Hopkins sent a similar message to Buckingham via Delacourt. On April 26, 1513, there was an exchange of letters between the duke and the monk in which the latter predicted that "the King should have no issue male of his body." On April 16, 1515, Buckingham went in person to Hopkins, who informed him that he would be king. The duke's "treasonable" response was "that he would be a just prince if the same should happen." It should be observed that all of these contacts took place when Henry VIII lacked issue and Buckingham was his most logical successor, which should have made it somewhat difficult to construe them as treasonous. Anyway, on March 20, 1519, when Princess Mary was in her third year, Buckingham paid a second visit to Hopkins, who once more told him that he would be king. He then told the monk that it was well that he had sworn

27. *Deputy Keeper's Report*, 231.

Delacourt to secrecy, for "if the King got any knowledge thereof, he, the Duke, would be utterly ruined."[28] Buckingham himself, however, may have been responsible for setting in motion the disclosures that led to his utter ruin, for Knyvet testified that on May 10, 1520, the duke revealed to him the secret of Hopkins' prophecy.[29] A petition made by Knyvet indicates that shortly thereafter he "warned himself out of the service of the said Duke."[30] Buckingham's alleged relations with Hopkins certainly were foolish, especially after Mary's birth, but they do not constitute proof of treasonable intent. Nonetheless, his judges evidently construed them as high treason from their start. April 24, 1512, the date of Buckingham's first alleged contact with Hopkins, is specified in the 1523 attainder act as the date when he first imagined and compassed the king's death.[31]

We have now covered the principal charges against Buckingham. Most of the other charges appear to have been mere embellishments. There was one, however, which, though it could hardly have been made to fit the general charge even by means of judicial construction, may have carried some weight. Gilbert deposed that on September 20, 1509, which was but five months after Henry VIII's accession, Buckingham told him "that he had a certain writing, sealed with the great seal, containing a certain Act of Parliament, by which it was enacted that the Duke of Somerset, one of the King's noble progenitors, was legitimated." Buckingham also said "that he once intended to give the said writing to King Henry VII" and then added "that he would not have done so for £10,000."[32] The document referred to was a parliamentary enactment ratifying Richard II's patent legitimizing the Beauforts. Henry IV, in confirming Richard II's patent, had added words barring the Beauforts from the royal succession. Knowledge of the parliamentary confirmation of the original patent, which doubtless prevailed in

28. *Ibid.*, 230–31.   29. *Ibid.*, 232.
30. *L.P.*, III, 513.   31. *Statutes of Realm*, III, 246.
32. *Deputy Keeper's Report*, 231.

law over Henry IV's debarring addition,[33] would certainly have been useful to Henry VII in justifying his title to the crown. The document, however, was of no great import to Henry VIII, who had a far better claim through his mother, Elizabeth of York, the eldest daughter of Edward IV. Whether Buckingham actually possessed the document cannot be determined, but the allegation that he concealed it may have been more than an immaterial addition to his indictment. It has recently been argued convincingly that Edward IV used a charge of concealing an alleged exemplification under the great of seal of Henry VI entailing the succession to clinch the case of high treason against George, duke of Clarence.[34] It is at least possible that those who tried Buckingham knew of Edward's action and regarded it as a precedent establishing the concealment of a document relating to the succession as high treason.

As for Buckingham's defense, the record of his trial only tells us that he pleaded not guilty and put himself upon his peers.[35] According to a contemporary chronicler, he alleged "many reasons to falsify the indictment." He also asked that the witnesses be brought forth. They were and their depositions were read.[36] In any event, it is most unlikely that the duke was given the opportunity to cross-examine his accusers, which would have been an extraordinary privilege. A Year Book report indicates that he did raise a substantial plea of law, to wit, that no overt act of treason was alleged against him. The court called on Chief Justice Fineux to respond. Fineux made a distinction between felony and treason: "there could be no felony without some act done, but to intend the death of the King was high treason, and such intention was sufficiently proved by words alone." [37] This ruling reflected the development of

33. Stanley B. Chrimes and A. L. Brown (eds.), *Select Documents of English Constitutional History, 1307–1485* (London, 1961), 166–67.

34. J. R. Lander, "The Treason and Death of the Duke of Clarence: A Reinterpretation," *Canadian Journal of History*, II (No. 2, 1967), 1–28.

35. *Deputy Keeper's Report*, 233.

36. Edward Hall, *The Triumphant Reigne of Kyng Henry the VIII*, ed. Charles Whibley (2 vols.; London, 1904), I, 224.

37. Harcourt, *His Grace the Steward*, 438, 469–70.

the law of treason since 1352 and anticipated Thomas Cromwell's Treasons Act of 1534.[38] More immediately, it relieved
Buckingham's peers of any legal qualms they might have had
about sending him to his death.

Buckingham's condemnation by the Court of the Lord High
Steward was inevitable but hardly justified. It was based on
the allegations of witnesses of surely questionable veracity. Even
if the allegations were generally true, about all that was proved
against Buckingham was that he was careless and/or foolish
in speaking and listening.[39] Wolsey apparently deemed the evidence presented at the trial insufficient to convince interested
foreign parties of the duke's guilt. Sir Richard Wingfield, no
doubt on Wolsey's instruction, told Charles V that the charges
were "as well justly as duly proved against the . . . Duke and
also by himself before his death confessed." [40] The claim that
Buckingham confessed was a distortion. When the duke was
sentenced he boldly said: "I shall never sue to the King for
life." On the scaffold he became appropriately meek, and said
that "he had offended the King's Grace through negligence
and lack of grace, and desired all noblemen to beware by him,
and all men to pray for him, and that he trusted to die the
King's true man." [41] This was no actual confession of high
treason; it was simply the customary preexecution speech made
by the victims of Tudor judicial murders.[42]

If a half-truth was offered to Charles V, an outright falsifica-
tion was devised for Francis I. Wolsey instructed the English
ambassadors in France to tell Francis, whose son and heir had
been affianced to Princess Mary since October, 1518, that Buckingham had recently been "detected of diverse treasons by himself thought and imagined as well against the King's person

38. On which see Geoffrey R. Elton, "The Law of Treason in the Early Reformation,"
Historical Journal, XI (1968), 230–36.
39. Foolish or careless speaking, like bravado (above, note 23), was sufficient at
law to support an indictment for treason.
40. B.M., Cotton MS Vitellius B XX, fol. 250; *L.P.*, III, 532.
41. Hall, *Triumphant Reigne*, I, 225–26.
42. On which see Lacey B. Smith, "English Treason Trials and Confessions in the
Sixteenth Century," *Journal of the History of Ideas*, XV (1954), 476–90.

as against his succession, and specially against the Princess, with whose alliance in the house of France he was greatly miscontented and grieved. And these things being openly and manifestly proved and at the last by himself confessed, he was by the due order of the King's laws condemned and put to the execution of death according to his demerits." [43] It was true enough that Buckingham, whose dislike of the French was notorious, shared the aversion of most Englishmen to Mary's match with the dauphin, which held the prospect of a Frenchman someday ascending the English throne.[44] But it was an out-and-out lie to say that the duke was detected of imagining treasons especially against Mary and that this was openly proved and in the end confessed by him. Not a trace of this is to be found in the records of Buckingham's indictment, trial, and execution; in fact, one looks there in vain for a single direct reference to Mary. Clearly Wolsey found misrepresentations preferable to the actual evidence as means to convince foreign rulers who, unlike the English people, did not have to accept the finding of the Court of the Lord High Steward as beyond question.

If Buckingham's guilt was more than doubtful, it remains to be explained why he was brought to destruction. Polydore Vergil, no friend of Wolsey, set what was to become the popular view when he maintained that the duke's fall was the work of the cardinal.[45] And Wolsey was not without reason to want to get rid of Buckingham, what with the duke's scorn for the baseborn cardinal, jealousy of his authority, and disapproval of his policies.[46] A modern defender of Wolsey, however, has presented two main arguments against his responsibility for Buckingham's ruin. The first is an unsigned and undated letter to Wolsey in which the writer reminded the cardinal that he had previously sent word to Buckingham via Gilbert that

43. B.M., Cotton MS Caligula D VIII, fol. 39: *L.P.*, III, 515.
44. Brewer, *Henry VIII*, I, 376, 398–99.
45. Denys Hay (ed.), *The Anglica Historia of Polydore Vergil, A.D. 1485–1537* (London, 1950), 263–65, 279–81.
46. Scarisbrick, *Henry VIII*, 120.

"although he used to rail upon your Grace, yet that he should take heed how that he did use himself towards the King's Highness." [47] This would be rather impressive evidence that the cardinal actually tried to save the duke, that is, if Buckingham did anything against the king to merit the warning and if Wolsey did not inform Henry VIII of the warning. The second argument is that Wolsey seems to have played no active role in Buckingham's prosecution, the interrogation of witnesses evidently having been conducted by Henry.[48] Of course, if Wolsey had convinced Henry of Buckingham's guilt and he wanted to do the interrogating, the king was obviously the more effective prosecutor, and it was better for the cardinal, whose participation might be suspect, to stay out of the business.

Moreover, there are matters in which Wolsey's conduct in relation to Buckingham is suspect. On April 3, 1518, Richard Pace wrote to Wolsey from Abingdon, where Henry was staying, expressing the king's "most hearty thanks" for his letter suggesting the danger of visits by "great personages" and indicating that such visitors were being informed secretly "to bring with them but a very small company." Pace further told Wolsey: "This day arrived here the Duke of Buckingham." [49] The cardinal may well have known of the duke's impending arrival and could have written his letter with the purpose of arousing the king's suspicions about that particular great personage who liked to travel with a large retinue. Wolsey could also have been responsible for instigating Henry's previously referred to panic letter instructing him to "make good watch on" specified noblemen. This might explain the naming of Suffolk with Buckingham, his relatives, and Derby.[50] Over the years Suffolk had been alternately in and out of favor with the cardinal,[51] who may have regarded his personal closeness to the king as a potential threat to his own position. It also may be of some significance here that Henry did not name Norfolk, England's third duke,

47. Brewer, *Henry VIII*, I, 379.   48. *Ibid.*, I, 383–84.
49. PRO State Papers 1/16/ fol. 211; *L.P.*, II, 1256.
50. See above, 33–34.
51. Walter C. Richardson, *Mary Tudor, the White Queen* (London, 1970), 176–78, 194, 203, 221.

who had long been on very good terms with Wolsey.[52] Then there is the case of Sir William Bulmer, which Wolsey apparently initiated and prosecuted with vigor.[53] A desire to impress on Henry that it was Buckingham who had enticed away a royal retainer may have had something to do with Wolsey's zeal. And finally there is the inclusion in Buckingham's indictment of Gilbert's charge, omitted in his deposition, relating to the duke's "treasonable" purpose with regard to Wales. Wolsey knew of Buckingham's proposed Welsh expedition [54] and would have been the logical one to construct it into the serious charge that appeared in the indictment. Although it certainly cannot be proved that Buckingham's fall was the work of Wolsey, that possibility cannot be dismissed lightly—an innocuous but unavoidable conclusion.

Modern historians usually prefer another explanation of Buckingham's fall, to wit, its cause was state necessity. One approach here might be called the object lesson thesis. Henry and Wolsey wanted to remove the possibility of a conspiracy by discontented noblemen, probably the majority of the nobility, who hated the cardinal for his low birth and for excluding them from their due share of influence in the state, and who might be tempted to take advantage of the national aversion to the French alliance. Buckingham would have been the logical leader of such a conspiracy. That the duke probably lacked the ability, courage, and even inclination to assume such a role did not matter. His execution served to cow the nobility into quiescence.[55] There may well be some truth in this view, but, if so, one wonders why the final step of execution was deemed essential. Henry VII's treatment of Edmund de la Pole offered a rather effective alternative: Buckingham could have been kept in the Tower with the dread sentence hanging over him and thereby served as a continuing object lesson to his fellow noblemen.

Perhaps the most likely state necessity explanation has

52. Melvin J. Tucker, *The Life of Thomas Howard, Earl of Surrey and Second Duke of Norfolk* (The Hague, 1964), 132–33, 136.

53. See above, 37 and *n*. 22.

54. See above, 38.   55. Brewer, *Henry VIII*, I, 397–99.

already been implied in our opening paragraph, that is, the possibility of Henry VIII's death before he had a reasonably mature heir, preferably a male one, to succeed him. Richard III's usurpation stood as a terrible precedent in that event. Considerations of blood, rank, prestige, and wealth in land and men all pointed to Buckingham as the man best qualified, maybe the only one with the potential at all, to play Richard III's role. If Buckingham was eliminated in the interest of removing such a threat to little Mary's succession, those responsible for his end at least had the extenuation of acting for what they believed to be a worthy *raison d'état*.

The threat, however, may have been more apparent than real. Buckingham was well aware of the fate of Richard III, whose royal blood and personal resources were superior to his own. The duke was proud of his Stafford heritage, part of which was a tradition of loyalty rare among great families. The Staffords had been nearly alone among such families in consistently supporting Lancaster in its wars with York. Buckingham's great-grandfather and grandfather both died fighting under the banner of Henry VI. Though his father, Duke Henry, made an expedient accommodation with the Yorkists after the extinction of the direct Lancastrian line, he was executed in 1483 for leading a rebellion in behalf of Henry Tudor, the collateral heir of Lancaster. As for Duke Edward himself, Henry VII apparently regarded him as almost a member of the royal family and as nearer to the throne than any but his own sons. Never did that king, who was ever fearful for the future of his dynasty, waver in his trust of Buckingham. Nor did Henry VIII ever question the duke's loyalty until the time of his panic letter to Wolsey. Queen Catherine was the duke's friend of twenty years and probably the only one who pleaded with the king to spare him.[56] Catherine, whose knowledge of the ways of Renaissance politics came from long and often sad experience, obviously did not consider Buckingham a threat to her daughter's succession. Trusting Buckingham in the event of

56. Garrett Mattingly, *Catherine of Aragon* (London, 1950), 37–38, 161.

Henry VIII's untimely death was a gamble, but it could have been a gamble worth taking, for Richard III's was not the only precedent.

In 1422 Henry VI ascended the throne at the age of eight months. That England did not fall apart completely during Henry's long minority was largely due to the stabilizing influence of his powerful uncle and protector, John, duke of Bedford.[57] A long minority for Mary promised to be even more perilous for England than Henry VI's had been. The biblical warning, "woe to thee, O land, whose king is a child," was doubly pertinent when the child was a girl. There were Poles and Courtenays of Yorkist descent who, though too weak to act on their own, might find noble and popular backing for attempts to seize the crown. What was needed to give a minority for Mary real hope of stability and survival was a John of Bedford: a loyal regent of the blood royal with the prestige and power to command the respect of both nobility and people. Wolsey, whose position depended on Henry VIII, would not be a satisfactory alternative. Nor would Suffolk, whose royal marriage did not overcome his common origin and mediocrity. Nor would Norfolk, who, though abler than Buckingham, lacked royal blood and whose only indirect connection with it was his son's marriage to Buckingham's daughter. Buckingham, whatever his defects and whatever the risk involved, was the only possible approximation of John of Bedford. His destruction removed an important and irreplaceable potential prop for a minority that only the accident of Henry VIII's longevity prevented from coming into being.

The consequences of Buckingham's fall, ignoring its effect on his dependents and on the holding of a considerable amount of real estate, ranged from the trivial and temporary to the significant and ominous. Wolsey was rid of an enemy, but the cardinal had no reason to fear anyone but the king. Catherine of Aragon perhaps excepted, the one most opposed to Wolsey's

---

57. For a convenient survey of Henry VI's minority indicating Bedford's role see V. H. H. Green, *The Later Plantagenets* (London, 1966), 288–312.

policy of alliance with France was gone, but during the months that followed Buckingham's execution the French alliance was abrogated, Mary became engaged to Charles V, and England made war on France. The nobility was indeed taught an object lesson, but that was not the only lesson learned. Henry VIII now knew how easy it was to destroy an overmighty subject of royal lineage. Such knowledge had to suggest to him that the royal power to destroy individuals, no matter what their greatness, was well-nigh unlimited. Noblemen were not alone among the great in being menaced; queens, cardinals, great ministers, and even saints were unsafe. Some years after Buckingham's execution, Thomas More, one of Henry's future victims, warned Thomas Cromwell, another such victim, of how dangerous it would be "if the lion knew his own strength." [58] What More did not realize was that Henry VIII had already learned about his strength in the spring of 1521. This was the great and terrible meaning of the fall of Edward, duke of Buckingham.

58. Richard S. Sylvester and Davis P. Harding (eds.), *Two Early Tudor Lives* (New Haven and London, 1962), 228.

Arthur J. Slavin

LORD CHANCELLOR WRIOTHESLEY AND REFORM OF AUGMENTATIONS: NEW LIGHT ON AN OLD COURT

I

Among the Wriothesley deeds in the Hampshire Record Office are a few manuscripts not dealing with the estates or family affairs of the earldom of Southampton.[1] The paper most interesting to students of government and politics is one entitled "The erectyon and establishmente of the Courte of the Kinges Revenues."[2] Part of its interest derives from the fact that the historians of the Court of Augmentations wrote in ignorance of its existence and thus without the light it alone sheds on some problems touching that court's reorganization in 1546–1547.[3] This manuscript, printed here for the first time, also

1. Hampshire Record Office, Winchester, holds two collections. One, 5M53, contains nearly a thousand documents, chiefly muniments, but some letters and other papers reflecting on Sir Thomas Wriothesley's Henrician career. A smaller deposit, 5M51, consists of 149 pieces relevant to the properties of the Southampton earldom.

2. HRO, 5M53/967.

3. The chief work is Walter C. Richardson, *History of the Court of Augmentations* (Baton Rouge, 1961), 111–59. See also Geoffrey R. Elton, *Tudor Revolution in Government* (Cambridge, 1953), 223–30.

throws some light on the fall of Lord Chancellor Wriothesley in 1547.

It thus has two claims on our attention. These will appear more cogent, however, in relation to two other manuscripts. One is the unprinted patent of creation for the second Court of Augmentations, issued in January, 1547.[4] The other is a manuscript fragment of a scheme touching reforms in revenue administration, of uncertain date.[5] I will show below the exact character of this fragment and suggest a date for it. More to the point, by establishing the character and circumstances of drafting of the Hampshire Record Office paper, I will show how certain political problems were created by the reform of revenue administration.

In order to do so in the least cumbersome way, I shall use an abbreviated system of reference for the three relevant reform documents. The patent I shall call MSC, while labeling the Hampshire paper MSB and the Exchequer fragment MSA. By means of certain comparisons and contrasts, I will show MSB to be in Wriothesley's hand and of 1546 vintage. I will further show that its creation was in part a design of the lord chancellor, by which he hoped to materially enhance the power of his office, at the expense of the autonomy of Augmentations. These demonstrations will make it clear that Wriothesley actively participated in the work of reform, with the consequence of making unacceptable the now prevalent view of his passivity in this respect.[6]

II

Only lack of familiarity with Wriothesley's career could induce the view that the chancellor would bow to the opinions of others expert in finance. Wriothesley is now best remembered as the

---

4. PRO, C 66/790, membranes 15–28, in part five of the patent roll, 38 Henry VIII. There is an inadequate calendar of its contents, in *L.P.*, XXI, ii, 771 (1). My transcript of the patent extends to 104 typed pages.

5. Preserved in the Miscellanea of the Exchequer: PRO, E 163/11/49. The class belongs to records of the king's remembrancer.

6. Stanford E. Lehmberg, *Sir Walter Mildmay and Tudor Government* (Austin, 1964), 14–17. See also Richardson, *History*, 137.

facile and ambitious clerk of Thomas Cromwell who rose to high office through cleverness and lack of scruple.[7] He was better cast when, still a student at Cambridge, he took the part of Palestrio, in Plautus' *Miles Gloriosus*. With him in his role as the inventive servant of Periplectomenus, played by his tutor Stephen Gardiner, was William Paget, who was Meliphidippa, a clever maid of all works.[8] The future bishop and his pupils were more than a match for the braggart soldier, which Gardiner would recall some twenty years later, when the three privy councillors were less able to govern circumstances and the rising hero Sir Edward Seymour: "We be now in a world where reason prevaileth not, learning prevaileth not, covenants be not so regarded but the least pretense sufficeth to avoid the observation of them. This is another manner of matter than when I played Periplectomenus, you Meliphidippa, and my Lord Chancellor Palestrio. And yet our parts be in this tragedy that now is in hand." [9]

Leland, who saw the performance, recalled it favorably.[10] Gardiner, however, in 1545, was right to say Wriothesley then had a more difficult part than that of Palestrio. He had acquired office and fortune before 1544, having served for four years as principal secretary of state, with first Sir Ralph Sadler and then Paget as his partner.[11] In that year, he had come into the keepership of the great seal, when Lord Audley had grown too ill to discharge its then bitter burden of crown wars and crown debts. His appointment as lord chancellor followed quickly on the lesser tenure, however.[12]

7. There is no good study of Wriothesley, pending the completion of my book, tentatively titled "Politics and Power." The current view is summarized in W. K. Jordan, *Edward VI: The Young King* (Harvard, 1968), 57–59, 64–65, 99–100, but especially in the section on Wriothesley's fall, 69–72, where he is passed off as "an inveterate intriguer," "an opinionated and thorny man," as well as "self-seeking" and "somewhat unscrupulous."

8. J. A. Muller, *Stephen Gardiner and the Tudor Reaction* (London, 1926), 10–11.

9. PRO, SP 1/210/fo. 127; Gardnier to Paget, November 13, 1545.

10. *Principium, ac illustrium alignot et eruditorum in Anglia virorum Encomia, Trophaea, Genethliaca, et Epithalamia* (London, 1589), 49.

11. See the brief treatment in A. J. Slavin, *Politics and Profit* (Cambridge, 1966), 49–56; and Elton, *Tudor Revolution*, 309–13.

12. PRO, C 54/436, membrane 3, records the surrender by Audley on 21 April

His work in the highest lay office was less secretarial than political, less juridical than financial, however. Both circumstances and his past career were in that well matched. The whole of his training before 1544 had conspired to make Wriothesley expert in the crown's finances. As Cromwell's man in 1538 he was already sufficiently the master of revenues to survey them and report on them in a state paper.[13] Earlier, Wriothesley had taken an active role in suppressing monasteries and weighing their wealth.[14] While in the secretary's place, he gained a wide knowledge of the finances of Henry VIII's campaigns against Scotland and France.[15] And between 1544 and 1547 he and Paget were in effect an ex officio committee on finance, acting for the privy council.[16] This domination derived in part from the absence of the lord treasurer, the duke of Norfolk, who was directly involved in the wars.

The responsibility was a mixed blessing. On the plus side, the two old friends had behind them more than two decades of friendship. This helped immensely in what was an unpleasant task. Crown credit was in very bad straits, as their agent in Flanders, Stephen Vaughan, repeatedly showed them.[17] The wars had sadly depleted available resources and had forced on Wriothesley unpleasant inventions, including the revival of benevolences, happily asleep since Wolsey's experience of them in 1524–25.[18] Moreover, as letters between Wriothesley and Paget demonstrate, the precarious state of crown finance had led both men to accept the necessity of far-ranging reforms.[19]

1544 and Wriothesley's creation as keeper on April 22, when he got the great seal from the king. Audley died on May 3, at which time Henry named Wriothesley "lorde chauncellor of Englande," *ibid*, membrane 4.

13. B.M., Cottonian MSS Cleopatra E. IV, fol. 341.

14. PRO, SP 7/1, is a volume of 85 letters addressed to Wriothesley ca. 1535–38, chiefly bearing on monastic wealth.

15. F. C. Dietz, *English Government Finance, 1485–1558* (Urbana, 1920), 152–58.

16. *L.P.*, XIX, i, 272; XX, i, 892, 1099, 1194, 1214; XXI, i, 197, 399.

17. *L.P.*, XX, i, 1194, 1214; see the study of Walter C. Richardson, *Stephen Vaughan* (Baton Rouge, 1953).

18. For Wriothesley's experiments with "loans" of this type, see *L.P.*, XIX, i, 368; XX, i, 17, 52, 125(5). He was more successful than Wolsey, since the combined yield in 1544–45 was £129,551: PRO, E. 34/4/86, E. 370/2/23.

19. *L.P.*, XX, ii, 212–13, 222, 231, 268, 272, 302, 358, 425, 453, 472, 697, 709, 713, 729, 746, 752, 769, covering half of 1545 only, reflect this.

Wriothesley knew well enough that substitutes for reform were mere make-weights. One could not forever mulct the bishops,[20] float loans at Antwerp,[21] sell crown lands,[22] borrow from or coerce war profiteers,[23] and debase coins.[24] The chancellor was himself intimately familiar with these devices and their limitations. His service had made of him a man acutely aware that the cost of war was the ruin of Henry VIII's solvency and the erosion of political confidence and personal amity. While he had reason to be thankful for the mint, since recoinage there was his "holy anchor" in troubled financial seas, he knew even it was not bottomless. Serious underestimations of war costs by Paget and the generals had swept it clean, along with the chamber treasury.[25] Their barrenness made him "weary of life," when even his subtle mind was strained to encompass new devices to find money for the king's use.[26] He chafed at each new demand, and on one occasion bade Paget no more "bid me run as though I could make money. I would I had that gift but one year for his majesty's sake." [27]

III

The consequence of their experiences drove Wriothesley and Paget to actively support the appointment of a commission to examine the state of the revenues. The commission headed by Wriothesley included Sir William Paulet, Gardiner, and both principal secretaries, Paget and Sir William Petre.[28] It had the assistance of Walter Mildmay, and continued the work begun

20. *L.P.*, XIX, ii, 212, 751.
21. Wriothesley himself gave personal bonds for their repayment, among others to the Vivaldi and Bonvisi agents: *L.P.*, XIX, i, 360, 759, and also 630, 725, 733, 822.
22. *L.P.*, XIX, i, 278 (4), XX, i, 125 (12).
23. Charles Wriothesley, *A Chronicle of England . . . from 1485 to 1559*, ed. W. H. Douglas (2 vols.; London, 1875–86), I. 151, 153.
24. On the debasement, see J. D. Gould, *The Great Debasement* (Oxford, 1970); for the chancellor's crucial role in supervising the mint see the papers by him: *L.P.*, XIX, i, 272(2), 513(5). His brother-in-law, Sir Edmund Peckham, was high treasurer of the mint.
25. *L.P.*, XX, ii, 324, 336, 354, 358, 425, 746 and 769, XXI, ii, 172.
26. *L.P.*, XX ii, 366, also 221, 241, and 211–13.
27. *L.P.*, XX, ii, 746.
28. *L.P.*, XXI, i, 1166 (71), June 30, 1546.

in December, 1545, by Sir Richard Rich and Sadler.[29] Its ostensible purpose was to ascertain what the king owed and what was owed to him, although calling in debts was to be less central to its work than had been true of Rich and Sadler's work. The work of the group actually began in April, 1546, well before the patent itself was made. And some political strain was apparent. First of all, it is worth notice that Rich and Sadler were omitted, despite the fact of their considerable expertise, the outgrowth of their earlier careers and the December commission, which had not been terminated.[30] Moreover, as the commissioners went about their business in London, the king was on progress and increasingly subject to the influence of an emergent triumvirate, consisting of Paget, Hertford, and Sir John Dudley.[31] The year had been hard on Gardiner, who, with Tunstall, had been forced to negotiate disadvantageous land exchanges.[32] Seymour was the chief instigator and beneficiary of the deals involving Tunstall.[33] Dudley had publicly humiliated Gardiner, in council.[34] And just as the reform commission concluded its work, charges were laid against the powerful Howards. These brought Surrey to his death, while Norfolk awaited final sentence in the Tower.[35]

Such political circumstances were extremely discomforting to the lord chancellor. Wriothesley had himself run afoul of Hertford in 1544, when he had prevented the earl from getting certain Buckinghamshire estates from the crown at a price below their assessed value.[36] He had also been involved in the affair of Hertford's countess, who had been implicated in certain

29. The earlier commission was dated December 14, 1545: *L.P.*, XX, ii, 1068 (28). See Richardson, *History*, 112–15.
30. Richardson, *History*, 114.
31. Slavin, *Politics and Profit*, 151–57.
32. PRO, SP 1/197, fos. 228–29; also *L.P.*, XXI, ii, 487–88, 493, 647 (10).
33. PRO, SP 1/197, fol. 228.
34. *L.P.*, XXI, ii, 347; Dasent, *Acts of the Privy Council*, I, 546.
35. B.M., Cottonian MSS. Titus B I, fo. 94, undated, Norfolk to the Council, see also, *CSPSp*, VIII, 371, Van der Delft to Mary of Hungary, December 24, 1546.
36. Longleat, Wiltshire, The Seymour Papers, IV, fols. 41–42d., 43–44d., 49–50d., 53–54d., 56–57d., 60–61d., 66–69d., and 70–71d., letters ca. March 6–April 15, 1544, from John Berwick to Seymour.

heretical opinions, in the persecutions which surrounded the trial and death of Anne Askewe.[37] The disgrace of Gardiner, Tunstall's senescence, and the Howard calamity had in fact completed a revolution in power and given the lead to Hertford, Lisle, and Paget.[38] Thus Wriothesley, who was more conservative in religion than those rising stars, found himself isolated in Council at an awkward time.

IV

What was especially awkward for Wriothesley in the autumn of 1546 was the emergence of a plan of reform that touched the interests of the Chancery. The commission of which he was head had understood the necessity of general reform and grasped the nettle. The plurality of revenue courts had resulted in an administration that was bureaucratic, expensive, and top-heavy in salaries. There were numerous overlaps in jurisdiction and authority among the intricate hierarchies of Augmentations, General Surveyors, Wards and First Fruits and Tenths. To diminish the king's charges in administering his revenues, it was decided to amalgamate Augmentations and General Surveyors. A gain in both efficiency and economy was intended, and to further this, it was suggested that the new agency be autonomous.[39]

What this meant in practical terms was a scheme to give an enlarged jurisdiction to Augmentations. This jurisdiction would make use of a great seal and privy seal peculiar to the court and not dependent on traditional warranting procedures for the exercise of the full powers of Augmentations. The result would be to completely bypass Chancery in matters touching every sort of process in which the king's grace distributed the profits of former monastic lands, their leases and offices.[40]

37. *L.P.*, XXI, i, 1181 (5). Earlier, Chapuys had heard of Hertford's "violent and injurious" words addressed to Wriothesley: *L.P.*, XXI, ii, 756.

38. See Van der Delft's reports: *CSPSp*, VIII, 150, 320.

39. Elton, *Tudor Revolution*, 225, stresses the decline of the chamber and court of general surveyors, in explaining the amalgamation, while Richardson, *History*, 112–21, emphasizes the need for corrective measures, in view of the general fiscal crisis.

40. MSC, membrane 15.

Wriothesley learned of this first in a letter from Mildmay, warning that the proposed court would encroach upon Chancery fees, by passing all business under its own seals.[41] The chancellor had apparently been too busy with the details of the wars, diplomacy, and the gathering political crisis, and had thus not followed the commission's work closely. Once apprised of the scheme, early in October, he reacted vigorously. This we know from his letter to Paget, dated at Ely Place, on October 16, 1546.[42]

The crux of the matter lay in the king's intention. Wriothesley could not believe that Henry would knowingly derogate from the dignity of Chancery and the great seal. These had been pillars of the monarchy since the Conquest. To establish utterly foreign channels of grace will undo the offices of honest men, long the king's servants, and also cause confusion and a decay of the law. So great is the danger that he hastens to send two Chancery officers, John Hales [43] and John Croke,[44] in order to further explain the calamity faced by the king's ministers in Chancery. For his own part, the chancellor sees in the scheme a blow to the favor he had enjoyed. And he begs Paget to persuade the king against this course of action.

In the midst of the scramble for offices in the new court, this challenge made by the lord chancellor could not have been welcome. Yet on the basis of the received account, we get no clear idea of how determined was Wriothesley's opposition.[45] According to that account, this was the course of events before January 1, 1547. During November and December, the liquidation of the old courts went forward. Mildmay supervised the reorganization, not without some qualms. There had been no patent or statute making legal the transformation. The transfer

41. *L.P.*, XXI, ii, 273.
42. PRO, SP 1/225. fol. 243.
43. Clerk of the Hanaper; see A. J. Slavin "A Sixteenth Century Struggle for Property and Profit," *B.I.H.R.*, XXXVIII (1965), 31–47.
44. One of the six clerks; he became an authority on chancery practices and wrote about its orders. See B.M., Lansdowne MSS 163, fols. 143–44.
45. Richardson, *History*, 136–38.

of revenues was in fact without legal foundation. Even the issuance of the patent dissolving the old courts and erecting the new one some deemed insufficient, on the grounds that what had been made by parliament could not be undone by patent.[46] Hence the introduction of a draft bill in Lords on January, 15, the intent of which was the provision of a retroactive authority for the dissolutions and creation of January 1.[47] Supposedly, this bill, which passed as far as engrossment in the Lords under the guidance of Wriothesley and Paulet, failed to become law only because of the king's death on January, 28.[48] The result was to give rise to new doubts as to the legality of grants under the seals of the second Court of Augmentations.[49]

Here, we must pause to consider some doubts raised by this account. There is something jarring in the idea that only the king's death prevented the passage of the reform statute. The second session of Henry's last parliament did pass one act *magna cum celeritate*—that which doomed the Howards.[50] This was done with haste, between the 18th of January and the 24th. Wriothesley signified the king's assent by commission, alleging Henry was too ill to be present, but wished passage, without delay; this last, on the 27th.[51] Why had Wriothesley not been able to push through the bill touching Augmentations, which was in some respects of greater urgency? Crown finances, for which he had special responsibility as head of the reform committee, were in a mess. Warrants directed to the new Court of Augmentations were being cancelled by Mildmay, because

46. These objections were cited in the preamble of Edward VI's retroactive enabling act: 1 Edward VI, Chap. 8, and also in the new act in Edward VI's last year; 7 Edward VI, Chap. 2. See *Statutes of the Realm*, IV, 13–14, 164–65.
47. *The Journal of the House of Lords*, I, 284 b, 290 a.
48. Richardson, *History*, 138.
49. The matter was especially complex, since it touched entitlement to fees and also the validity of quittances given to accountants. The issues were aired retrospectively in the March Parliament of 1553: *Journal of the House of Lords*, I, 435 a; and *Journal of the House of Commons*, I, 25a, 26a.
50. *L.P.*, XXI, ii, 753. The original act is not among those printed.
51. *Journal of the House of Lords*, I, 283–91, for the whole session, with the readings of bills less expeditiously handled.

they lacked authority, "being not yet established by Act of Parliament." [52]

The official record is too slender to help us. The commitment of the bill to Wriothesley is suggestive, however. After all, it was the chancellor himself who opposed the new arrangements. In the light of this hostility, may it not be the case that his custody of the bill inhibited its career? This surmise is plausible on its face. In what follows, I hope to establish a prejudice in favor of it. For between the letter to Paget and the presentation of the government's draft bill, the lord chancellor had done some drafting of his own.

V

The hand of MSB is Sir Thomas Wriothesley's. That of MSA, which Professor Richardson attributed to him, while also making of it a possible rough draft for the abortive Augmentations bill of 1547, is not. [53] The two scripts exhibit similarities of the sort ordinary in mid-Tudor secretary hands. These extend even to the majuscules, where we expect fewer. Tudor writers took delight in their embellishment, and, in the characters R, T and P, MSB and MSA diverge seriously. There are also other traits of contrast. MSA is a more vertical and detailed hand than MSB, which is more open and cursive. It also has a definite right-hand slant conducive to speed. Again, the MSB writer employed fewer pen lifts, even to the point of making ovals with a single stroke, against the two used in MSA. MSB also regularly employs ligatures, in typing supralinears to their followers.

The whole appearance of this hand is that of shortcuts for speed. It eschews every artifice and the decorative use of strokes of varying weights. The drive for efficiency is summed up in majuscule P. The MSA hand uses an initial semioval, where MSB prefers a left-hand loop and tail only. Stylistic differences of this range make it impossible to attribute the two documents to the same writer. Furthermore, the same tests applied to

52. *L.P.*, XXI, ii, 647, no. 14.   53. Richardson, *History*, 138.

known specimens of Wriothesley's hand, selected over the period 1535–47, induce the opinion of identity between them and MSB.[54]

There are also good reasons to separate MSA from MSB in time. The jurisdiction of MSA extends only to monastic lands that are in the crown's hands.[55] It is hard to credit an assignment of MSA to 1547, when any scheme for Augmentations would necessarily have taken into account the 1545 act touching the chantries. Both MSB and MSC provide for a variety of lands falling to the crown, whether by gift, bargain, exchange, attainder, escheat, or according "to the forme of thacte of Charentries."[56]

It follows from this that MSA must derive from some year before 1545, while MSB can only have been written between the passage of the chantries act and the issuance of the patent of January 1, 1547. I think G. R. Elton has correctly assigned MSA to a hand written by one of Cromwell's clerks, probably between 1536 and 1542.[57] Its contents are relevant to some tightening up of administration in the first Court of Augmentations and exerted some influence on the reform of law pertaining to crown lands in 1542.[58] We may thus set to one side MSA satisfied that it was no proposal made by Wriothesley relevant to the events of 1546–47.

I think we may also argue for a closer dating of MSB. I would assign it to the period October 15, 1546—January 1, 1547. My reasons for doing so are already apparent, but some attention to the contents of both MSB and MSC will make them explicit. Before doing that, it will promote understanding, if I comment on the organization of the first Court of Augmentations, especially its seals and their use.

Cromwell's energetic creation of revenue courts were not in effect the revolution in government associated with his minis-

54. This I rest simply on my constant work with Wriothesley's hand, dating from 1965.
55. MSA, paragraphs 5 and 6.
56. MSB, section 2; and MSC, membrane 15.
57. *Tudor Revolution*, 207.   58. *Ibid.*, 207, n. 3.

try. Professor Elton himself stressed the lack of new principles at work in them.[59] And Professor Richardson has demonstrated at length their debt to the procedures of the Lancaster Duchy Chamber.[60] In fact, both First Fruits and Tenths and Augmentations were devices whereby Cromwell intensified the personal nature of his government. They gave to him the measure of control over royal finance he attained in the secretariat, by his joint tenure of the principal secretaryship and the privy seal.

The tasks of handling the crown's accession of ecclesiastical wealth could be solved only by an agency combining the financial methods of the Chamber, the judicial powers of an equity court, and the political initiatives of a secretariat. This last required the setting up of a court of record, autonomous in its own sphere, both in its ability to judge its officers and clients and its control over the wealth it administered. Toward those ends, the Augmentations was from the beginning equipped with its own seals, both great and privy. Its chancellor had authority to make leases for twenty-one years *without warrant*. He could make no reversions without special warrant, however. Nor could he utterly alienate lands in fee simple or knight's fee. Otherwise, he could dispose of much former monastic land and many offices. The chancellor and council of the court needed no warrants other than the king's commandment, in making conditional gifts, grants, and leases. The court's privy seal was adequate in issuing process, with express prohibitions against Exchequer interference. Clearly, the intention was to make agencies capable of actions independent of Chancery and Exchequer.[61]

VI

It was against this independence that Wriothesley bent his bow in 1546. Every one of the clauses of MSB which was not merely

59. *Ibid.*, 202.   60. *History*, 38–40.
61. Elton, *Tudor Revolution*, 204–207.

descriptive of some action or jurisdiction was a shaft directed at a single target: To transfer from Augmentations to Chancery ultimate authority over acts of grace and certain processes.

Not content to protest the assault on his court and office, the chancellor attacked a wide front. MSB proposed to deny the title of chancellor to the head of the new court.[62] Against the chancellor and two general surveyors of MSC,[63] Wriothesley set three coequal "generalles" of the royal revenue.[64] He thus indicated his desire not merely to preserve the dignity of Chancery but to roll back the allocation of his title to the heads of an inferior court, despite nearly eleven years of contrary practice.

Touching their jurisdiction, he proposed allowing them power to hear only such cases wherein the king was party. This is of some interest. The 1547 patent made no such restriction.[65] Wriothesley's proposal ran thus: "All other matters Betwene partie and partie they shall not medle w^t all But leave them to the commen Lawes of the Realme." [66] The two statutes that later sanctioned Augmentations processes did just what Wriothesley had earlier suggested but had failed to carry.[67] His defense of the common law we must say more about later.

Having thus sought to elevate the reputation of Chancery and protect the common law regarding contests over property, Wriothesley turned to less august matters. MSB would allow Augmentations only limited rights in its disposal of crown leases. Leases worth twenty nobles or more yearly were to follow the old course of the seals: signet, privy seal and great seal.[68] Only lesser leases could pass by action of an Augmentations warrant. Sections six through twelve in MSB recommend routines of audit and internal control in the court's regime.

62. Section 3.
64. Section 3.
66. Section 4.
63. Membrane 15.
65. Membrane 21.
67. The original statutes of 1536 and the amplifying law of 1542 had implied no power in causes between parties, except in a very circumscribed way: *Statues of the Realm*, III, 572–73 and 886–88. Compare 27 Henry VIII, Chap. 27 and 33 Henry VIII, Chap. 39, with 1 Edward VI, Chap. 8, and 7 Edward VI, Chap. 2.
68. Section 5.

In section thirteen, however, Wriothesley is again at pains to circumscribe the use of the one seal he would allow the court, a privy seal. Any certificate made for the purpose of levying royal debts must be addressed to the lord chancellor of England. He would then proceed by writs of extent "for the levying . . . as is used by the Clerke of the statute of the Staple. . . ." MSC contained no such safeguard. The court's freedom in collecting debts and making payments not in excess of £200, on its own warrants, was later a source of much corruption. Such powers had formerly been exercised by the whole council or its committees, acting under special warrant.[69]

It followed from these restrictions that letters patent under the great seal of England would be required to complete every major action touching the king's favor. Bills signed by the king and directed to the "generalles" had in turn to be made into Augmentations warrants directed to Chancery, "for the making oute thereof of lettres patentes under the greate seale of Englande."[70] MSC knew no such restrictions, and, where the "great seal" is mentioned, by it is meant the one proper to Augmentations.[71]

One other front on which Wriothesley fought deserves mention. MSB prescribes the finding of offices concerning attainders. These are not to be found in Augmentations but where they had traditionally been found, by the clerks of the Petty Bag in Chancery. They would then certify the offices "in to this courte." [of Augmentations].[72]

What was at stake in these struggles was a vast array of fees arising out of the application of seals. Since the only great concession made to Wriothesley's proposals was that leases worth more than ten marks yearly had to pass the old depart-

69. Richardson, *History*, 160–245.   70. Section 14.
71. Membranes 18, 19, 21, 23, etc.
72. Section 17. This stipulation is on the patent, which suggests another victory for the chancery. Why Wriothesley would have complained, had the proposed patent not infringed the rights of his court, is hard to understand. See membrane 17. Common Pleas must have misliked its loss of exclusive rights to enter concords of fines, when such concords made in Augmentations were deemed as lawful (membrane 20), but we have no record of protest.

mental seals, something was salvaged.[73] More was lost, however. The major share of instruments passed only the great seal of Augmentations: leases, surrenders, indentures, appointments, tenements, liberties, grants of lands, offices, and franchises. For each one of them, the fee was 13s. 4d., of which the chancellor got half.[74] In 1549 some 2,991 patents passed the court's great seal.[75] However great a source of income was thus lost to Wriothesley was not the issue. He was rich in lands and official incomes. His dependents and clients in the lesser Chancery offices had more cause for regret. The clerk of Augmentations, Richard Duke, made £597 4s. in 1549 from the fees of drafting and enrolling those patents Wriothesley had tried to divert to Chancery. Moreover, the crown lost by the arrangements made in 1547.[76]

VII

MSB was the stuff of politics. In his concern over the proposed reform of Augmentations, Wriothesley had had three objectives in mind. He had sought to protect the dignity and fees of his own court and its officers. He had sought to guard the crown against the dangers he recognized in the too great autonomy of the new court. He had too great an experience of office and officeholders to think the proposed arrangements would work to the crown's advantage in the coming years of minority government. Motives selfish and generous were doubtless mixed in hidden proportions in his protests and proposals. It is not necessary to make a plaster paragon of the worldly, ambitious chancellor. He saw in the future a large place for himself. By putting his own office squarely athwart the administration of so much of the crown's revenue as Augmentations had at its disposal, he was in effect seeking power for himself.

73. Membrane 18. 74. *Ibid.*
75. Richardson, *History*, 244.
76. On duke's fees, see E. 315/251, fol. 69d., 257, fol. 101; 258, fol. 108. The commission to survey the revenue in 1552 calculated that £ 314 6s. 8d. was the profit of the great seal of Augmentations, one of the facts it alleged in recommending *all* grants pass under the great seal of England: B.M., Harleian MSS 7383, fol. 72.

He certainly opposed Hertford's claims to be protector, when others had neither the courage nor the ambition to do so, in the February days that sealed Somerset's coup.[77] In that wider struggle, he lost as well, matching a great defeat with those sustained in his struggles to reshape Augmentations.

Yet more was at issue than his personal power. Wriothesley's third purpose was to protect Chancery and the common law against the thick growth of administrative law. Here, we trench on one of the great ironies of Tudor politics. On March 7, 1547, the lord chancellor was deprived of his office, allegedly because of acts *ultra vires*.[78] His specific offense was said to be the issuance of a commission under the great seal without sufficient warrant. This was a groundless charge and grew out of Somerset's determination to brook no opposition in his regency.[79] The general occasion of his degradation was a complaint from certain students of the common law, that Wriothesley had practiced in Chancery the "great hinderaunce, prejudyce and decaye of the saide Commen Lawes." [80]

There is more to be said than that about his fall, but it belongs to another episode in the career of this remarkable governor. He was by experience and temperament a man eager for power and shrewd in its use. In 1547, however, he was overmatched. The zeal of his struggle in the matter of Augmentations was a harbinger of his dismissal from office. Had I the space, I might convince you he was less a danger to the realm

77. Professor Jordan finds no evidence for Wriothesley's opposition: *Edward VI*, I, 58, casting doubt on the tradition maintained by Bishop Burnet *(History of the Reformation of the Church of England,* ed. N. Pocock [7 vols.; Oxford, 1865], II, 40). He is in error. B.M., Additional MSS 48126, fol. 15a, an eyewitness report of the coup against Somerset, in 1549, has this to say about Wriothesley: "by cause his being lord chancellor. . . . at the death of Henry VIII was sure against any to be made protector, whereupon he was put from his office and made to submit himself. . . ." Andrew Malkiewicz, who published most of this account and established its reliability, omitted fols. 15a–b and 16; see *E.H.R.*, LXX (1955), 600–609.

78. The Council acted on an "original determination" of charges, given by a commission named for that purpose. It is in B.M., Harleian MSS 284, fols. 9b–10a. The "judges" were Richard Rich, John Walter, Thomas Moyle, Richard Cholmeley, John Chylde, John Gosnold, and Richard Keilaway. For Wriothesley's plea before the council and his submission, see *Acts of the Privy Council*, II, 48–59.

79. Harleian MSS 284, fol. 9a.; see n. 77 above.

80. The students' supplication is among the documents in *A.P.C.*, II, 47–50.

than the "Good Duke." [81] Instead, I am content to recall that
Professor Richardson's study of Augmentations reveals that by
1554, when Wriothesley was long since bait for worms, the
challenges he made to the "reforms" of 1547 became government policy.

The erectyon and establishmente of the
Courte of the Kinges Revenues*

1. First yt is ordered that all thonours Castelles seigneoryes
Manours Landes tennementes and hereditamentes which Be
at this pnte in the surveys of the seuall courtes in thaugmenta-
cons and S^{r}veyours genal shalbe holly and entirely incorporate
in this courte which co^{r}te shalbe called/ The Courte of the
Kinges Maiesties Revenues
2. To this courte shall acrewe and growe all Landes and
possessions that shall com to the Kinges Ma^{te} By gift Surrendre
By entre according to the fourme of thacte of Chauntereys/
By Bargan and sale from any psoune By exchaunge attanidre
and exchete/ And if the Kinges Ma^{te} shall geve sell or exchaunge
w^t any pson or Body politique any of the Landes invested in
the said co^{r}te there shalbe reserued a tenur /e/ By Knightes
seruice in capite and an yerely rent of the tenth pte of the
vallue of the said landes/
3. In this courte shalbe three psounes which shalbe the
chef and Principall officers of it and shalbe called the genalles
of the Kinges Ma^{tes} revenues whoo shall haue suche Auctoryte
and be bound to doo as hereafter shalbe declared And in the
same courte shalbe a Threasourer which shalbe next the said
genalles/ A M^r of the Wooddes/ An attourney/ A Sollicitour/
Audito^{r}s Receyvo^{r}s twoo Clerkes and twoo Messengers/

81. See Jordan's treatment in *Edward VI*, I, 70–71. He merely follows Froude, Pollard,
Richardson, and Eric Kerridge, who are quite wrong in· this matter. In my book,
I will cite ample archival evidence, showing the propriety of Wriothesley's commission
to allow masters in chancery to hear and determine cases in his absence. Here, it
is enough to adduce his patent, which authorized him to do so *"juxta suas discretiones,"*
and his charge from Edward VI, which continued this right: c. 54/453, m. 33.
    *Bold-faced and superscript characters are used here to represent common ellision
signs used to write the Tudor secretary hand.

Thauctoritie and office of the ge*na*lles

4. First they shalbe the Iudges of the courte and sha*ll* here
and determyn all matters touching the said Revenues Wherein
the Kinges Ma^{te} is only a **p**tie/ A*ll* other matters Betwene partie
and **p**tie they shall not medle w^tall But Leave them to the *com*en
Lawes of the Realme/

5. They or twoo of them sha*ll* haue auctoryte to make leases
of the Mano^rs Landes etc. w^tin the Iurisdicion of the said courte
for twenty and oon yeres reserving tholde and accustomed
rentes or more the same to passe vnder the greate seale of
Englande in lyke fourme as is nowe vsed in the courte of the
ge*na*ll S^rveyo^rs/ That is to saye if it be aboue twenty nobles
yearly to passe vnder the Signet and privy seale and if it be
under/ By Imedyate Warrant or bill signed from the said ge-
*na*lles or twoo of them which leases shalbe enrolled By oon
of the Clerkes of the said courte/

6. They and every of them sha*ll* haue fu*ll* powre and
auctoryte to take recognizaunces of every Receyvo^r/ Bailif/ Col-
lecto^r and a*ll* others By what name so*eu* they be called and
of their sureties which haue or shall haue charge of any receipt
of any of the possessions hereditamentes or proffittes wthin
the lymyttes of this co^rte to thentent the Kinges Ma^{te} may
be truely aunswered of his revenues that sha*ll com* to theyr
handes and for the true serving of his Matie in their se*ua*ll
offices which recognizaunces the said ge*na*lles shalbe bound
to take for his maiestes suretie of every suche Receyvo^r Baylif
ect. w^tin six monethes at the ferthest after the **p**fet erecion
of this courte and likewise of a*ll* others that shalbe admytted
officers after wthin six monethes/ after they shall entre into
their offices/ which recognisaunces oon of the Clerkes of the
said courte sha*ll* enro*ll* to remayn of recorde in the said courte/

7. They and every of them shall haue powre and auctorite
to take knowlege By ffyne or dede enrolled of all persounes
that shall sell geve surrender or exchaunge Landes w^t the Kinges
Ma^{te} for his graces Bettre and more *p*fett assuraunce in the
same/

8. The said ge*na*lles shalbe Bounde to kepe the courte at

Westm^r or where it shall please his Ma^{te} to haue his courtes Kept During the ffowre vsue*ll* Termes/ at which tymes they shall here and discusse matters in controversie touching the possessions of the said courte where the kinges Ma^{te} is partie onely And also they shall deuise for the calling in of the Kinges Ma^{tes} debtes/ ffor the Better doing wherof they sha*ll* haue auctorytie to mak suche good rules and ordres as vppon occasion to their wisdomes shalbe tho*u*ght convenente in corrobora*c*on and suppliment onely of thordres prescribed in this erection and ynnowise repugnante to the same/

9. They sha*ll* also Be Bounde to take yerely betwixte the ffeaste of the Natiuitie of o^r lorde and the tenth of ffebruary nexte following/ all Thaccomptes of the Receyvo^{r}s the said office and where they shall fynde that any of the said Receyvours ha*th* converted any of the Kinges Ma^{tes} treash^r By him receyued to his owne or any other mannes vse w^{t}out specill Warrante from the Kinges Ma^{te} or twoo of the ge*n*alles at the leste or shall appeare to them more negligente in their offices then were mete to be suffered they shall haue auctorytie to co*m*yte e*uy* suche receyvo^r to warde and after to depryve hym of his office and also to assesse fyne of him to the Kinges ma^{tes} use or otherwise to p*u*nishe hym at their discreatyons/

10. They shalbe bounde Betwene the tenth of ffebruary and the ffeast of Ester thenne next following to tak thaccompte of the Threasourer of the said office/ and to *p*sente a Declaracon of the same yerely for the yere passed to the Kinges Ma^{te} Betwene Ester and whitsontide w^t a note also what landes or possessions hath grow/*e*/n to his Ma^{te} in that yere/ and what hath in lyk m*an* go/*e*/n from his hieghnes owte of the said co^{r}te the same yere/

11. The said generalles shalbe bound whenne any thing shall growe to the Kinges Ma^{te} in the said courte/ or be by his Ma^{te} sold or otherwise disposed owte of the same to certifye the particulers therof/ and from whome yt c*á*m or to whom it was geven sold or exchaunged wthin ffowre Monethes next after yt Be there passed to thaudite of the circuit where e*uy* suche landes or possessiones do lye to thentente he may entre

the same in his Due place for the more **p**fection of thaccompte of his charge and circuite/

12. They or twoo of them shall haue auctorite to signe Billes for re**p**acions and Buildinges of the Kinges Ma^{tes} hono^rs lordships ect. wch shalbe sufficient warrante to the treasourer for the paym*et* of the same

13. They shall haue auctoryte vnder their handes and the *pv*ey seale of the co^rt to make Certificat to the lorde Chauncello^r of Englande for the making owte of writtes of extente for the levying of the Kinges Ma^{tes} debtes as is vsed By the Clerke of the statute of the Staple and like order shalbe obserued for the liberates as in thextentes uppon the said Statute of the staple/

14. They shall haue auctoryte uppon Billes signed By the Kinges Ma^{te} and dyrected to them to make warrante vnder their handes or twoo of theym to the lorde Chauncello^r of Englande for the making owte therof of lres patentes vnder the greate seale of Englande/

15. They or twoo of them shall haue auctoryte to com [?] recognisaunces uppon the paymente or **p**formance of [the] con-ditions/

16. There shalbe a prevy seale spea*lly* made of the said office for the making owte of suche processe as they shall think mete for the calling in of Accomptes debtes or any others having to doo in the said co^rte which shall remayn in the custody of the said ge*n*ales/

17. Item all offices to be founde concernyng any Attaindre to be certified in to this courte By the clerkes of the pety Bag owte of the Chauncery/ And all offices founde virtute officii of any thing wthin this courte to be Imediatly returned in to the said co^rte and not elleswheare/

Thauctoryte and charge of the Threasourer

18. The Threasourer shalbe oon of the Counsaill of the ccourte Bounde to kepe his office in london/ or where it shall please the Kinges Ma^{te} to haue his plees kepte

19. He shall receyve the Kinges Ma^tes revenues and onely
of the genall Receyvours of the same to whom he shall geve
sufficiente accquttaunces therof which shalbe their discharges/
and he shall r[?] the said office By any recognizaunce or speci-
altie/

20. He shall paye no pencons or Anuyties But suche as
shalbe appoynted specially By warrante from the Kinges Ma^te
or from the genalles

21. He shall make his Accompte Before the genalles Betwene the tenth of ffebruary and Ester thenne next following

J. R. Lander

The hundred years war and edward iv's 1475 campaign in france

In the later Middle Ages success in warfare depended upon a threefold combination: a king who was an able military leader, an enthusiastic ruling class (both aristocracy and gentry) prepared to fight and command the armies, and a people willing to bear the cost through taxation. Traditionally, most historians have held that the reign of King Henry V fulfilled this recipe for success, that war against France was popular and continued to be popular throughout the century. Consequently Edward IV was politically astute when, in 1475, he set out to revive the glories of his usurping predecessor.[1] A closer examination of events, however, hardly supports the age-old glamour of the St. Crispin's Day tradition and the campaigns following the Battle of Agincourt.

Of Henry V's military genius there is no possible doubt,

---

1. The standard biography of Edward IV states that the king's subjects showed "their willingness, even eagerness" for war with France. C. L. Scofield, *The Life and Reign of Edward IV* (2 vols.; London, 1923), I, 452, II, 10.

but though the campaigns and conquests of the last five years of his reign were brilliantly successful, opinion about him was already deeply divided before his death. Some warriors worshipped him as the splendid hero-king who led his victorious lords to victory to recover his just rights as the legitimate heir to the kingdom of France: sentiments carefully fostered after the king's death by his devoted brother, Humphrey, duke of Gloucester, who commissioned an official biography in praise of the noble dead from the Italian humanist, Tito Livio da Forli.[2] The London chronicles also maintained this laudatory tradition;[3] the tradition of the hero whose fame captivated Henry VIII, when he too, young, romantic, and reckless, against all the dictates of political and financial common sense, lunged into war to recover his "French inheritance."[4]

This carefully fostered tradition, enriched, embellished, and immortalized by William Shakespeare, has tended to obscure rather more brutal and prosaic facts. An examination of some contemporary sources throws serious doubts upon Henry's wisdom in embarking upon a policy of war with France to enforce what he regarded, under feudal laws of descent, as his personal claim to a foreign territorial inheritance. It throws even more doubt upon how far, even during his own lifetime, the popularity of his achievements amongst large sections of his subjects survived the cost of their attainment.

Richard II, realistic at least in this, knew that the Hundred Years War had become an intolerable drain upon the resources of the English monarchy: so much so (or he may have been merely indifferent to his "French inheritance") that, with the

2. Titi Livii Forojuliensis, *Vita Henrici Quinti*, ed. T. Hearne (Oxford, 1716).

3. R. Fabyan, *The New Chronicles of England and France*, ed. H. Ellis (London, 1811), 578–89; *The Great Chronicle of London* (also written by Fabyan), ed. A. H. Thomas and I. D. Thornley (London, 1938), 91–123.

4. J. J. Scarisbrick, *Henry VIII* (London, 1968), Chap. 2. A compilation, in English from Tito Livio da Forli, and to a lesser extent from other writers, including information which the anonymous author had obtained from the earl of Ormonde was composed in 1513. Henry VIII himself commissioned the work, and the translator, in turn, calls upon him to emulate Henry V. See C. L. Kingsford, *The First English Life of Henry V* (Oxford, 1911), and *English Historical Literature in the Fifteenth Century* (Oxford, 1913, reprinted New York, 1964), 64ff; J. Scarisbrick, *Henry VIII*, 23, n. 3.

exception of Calais, he was ready to abandon it to John of Gaunt to hold directly as a vassal of the king of France.[5] Other people also shared his views for some of the knights in a Great Council held at Westminster, summoned for September 30, 1414, on the very eve of the war's renewal, though they expressed themselves in a moderate way, obviously felt that Henry's diplomatic demands were extravagant and they were certainly not enthusiastic for war.[6]

Moreover, none of the Lancastrian kings had the slightest financial sense, and Henry V badly misjudged his capacity to pay for a prolonged war. Henry's income was considerably less than that of his great-grandfather, Edward III, but he, unfortunately, without his great-grandfather's income also thought in strategic terms which were much more costly.[7]

Owing to almost insatiable demands for English wool from the weavers of Flanders and Italy, Edward III had been able to pay approximately half the cost of his French campaigns out of an immensely high export tax upon this article—an indirect tax borne in very great part by the foreign consumer.[8]

5. J. J. N. Palmer, "Articles for a Final Peace between England and France, 16 June 1393." *Bulletin of the Institute of Historical Research*, XXXIX (1966), 180–85, and "The Anglo-French Peace Negotiations, 1390–96," *Trans. Royal Hist. Soc.*, ser. 5, XVI (1966), 81–94.

6. *Proceedings and Ordinances of the Privy Council of England*, ed. Sir H. Nicolas, (6 vols.; London, 1834–37), II, 140–42; Sir J. H. Ramsay, *Lancaster and York* (2 vols.; Oxford, 1892), I, 187.

7. As Mr. K. B. MacFarlane noted, in the fourteenth century "It was very far indeed from being total or continuous war. Until Henry V decided upon piecemeal conquest it was a war of raids in which the English chose the time and place of their descent upon France. If sufficient troops or transport were not available, the raid could be called off. In fact it often was." "England and the Hundred Years War," *Past and Present* (No. 22, 1962), 5. For the expensive nature of Henry V's new strategy and campaigns see the comments of the experienced veteran, Sir John Fastolf. *Letters and Papers Illustrative of the Wars of the English in France During the Reign of Henry VI*, ed. J. Stevenson, (2 vols. in 3, Rolls Ser.; 1861–64), II., Pt. 2, p. 579. Festolf's report, made in 1435, commented in particular, upon the methods of Henry's brother, John, duke of Bedford, after the king's death, but Bedford had merely continued Henry's own strategy. For the decline of Lancastrian income from that of the level of Richard II, see A. Steel, *The Receipt of the Exchequer, 1377–1485* (Cambridge, 1954), Chaps. 2–5.

8. MacFarlane, *Past and Present*, 3–9.

By Henry V's time the English domestic cloth industry was absorbing a high proportion of English wool,[9] and cloth exports could not be taxed at the same high rate or they would not have sold abroad.[10] The king was, therefore, forced back into politically much more explosive demands for direct taxation. Late fourteenth- and fifteenth-century Englishmen had become adamantly resistant to realistic assessments for taxation [11] and Henry's reputation quickly fell as a result of his demands for money. Already in 1417, at the beginning of his most expensive campaigns, the king was deeply disturbed that the clergy, resenting his heavy taxation, *tepide causante,* were ceasing to pray for the success of the war.[12] In 1420 the Commons refused any further grant of money,[13] and in the following year Adam of Usk's Chronicle broke off with the vehemently disparaging words:

"Our Lord the King, rending every man throughout the realm who had money, be he rich or poor, designs to return again into France in full strength. But, woe is me! mighty men and treasure of the realm will be most miserably foredone about this business. And in truth the grievous taxation of the people to this end being unbearable, accompanied with murmurs and with smothered curses among them from hatred of the burden, I pray that my liege lord become not

9. *Ibid.* MacFarlane points out that "Edward III and Richard II together received well over three million pounds from this source (i.e., export duties on raw wool, wool fells, and hides), Henry VI perhaps as little as £750,00 between 1422 and 1453, an annual average of less than half that of his fourteenth-century predecessors." After reaching a peak in the 1350's and early 1360's these exports began to decline rapidly. See E. M. Carus-Wilson and D. Coleman, *England's Export Trade, 1275–1547* (Oxford, 1963), 122–23.
    10. The export tax on wool was about 33⅓ percent, that on cloth no more than 2 or 3 percent.
    11. A. R. Myers, *English Historical Documents,* IV, 1327–1485 (London, 1969), 379–81. See also Adam of Usk's remarks upon the almost blasphemous iniquity of taxation. He commented on the sinking, by a storm, of a fleet under Sir John Arundel in 1379 "causa infortunii sui pecuniis clero et populo exactis non inmerito imponebatur." *Chronicon Adae de Usk, A. D. 1377–1421,* ed. Sir E. Maunde Thompson (2nd ed.; London, 1904), 8, 149.
    12. *The Register of Henry Chichele, Archbishop of Canterbury, 1413–1443,* ed. E. F. Jacob (4 vols.; Oxford, 1943–47), IV. 176. Also E. F. Jacob, *Essays in the Conciliar Epoch* (2nd ed.; Manchester U. P., 1952), 59, n. 2.
    13. Ramsay, *Lancaster and York,* I, 288.

in the end a partaker, together with Julius, with Asshur, with Alexander, with Hector, with Cyrus, with Darius, with Maccabeus of the sword of the wrath of the Lord!" [14]

Dr. M. R. Powicke has recently attempted to gauge the popularity of the war among the supposedly militarily minded classes by an analysis of the contingents which the aristocracy and the gentry led into Normandy [15] —a sure enough method since "the armies of the fifteenth century were composed of companies of irregular numbers serving under captains who first recruited and then commanded them." [16] Under this system a captain raised a number of men-at-arms and archers, a proportion of three archers to one man-at-arms generally being regarded as the most effective combination, and Dr. Powicke rightly took this as a useful standard of efficiency.

His conclusions demonstrate clearly enough that doubts about Henry's war policy grew very quickly, and the original enthusiasm for it did not long survive. In 1415 twenty peers recruited and led just over one-half the total forces. In the same campaign knights led all the larger nonnoble companies, knights who tended to be prominent men in their local communities and who served in Parliament. Prominent local gentlemen of the same type also raised the smaller contingents, and a high proportion of prominent local men, esquires and gentlemen, either served alone or with one companion or follower: a group who Dr. Powicke sees as "the essentially non-military country squire setting off to do his duty in the wars."

In the campaigns of 1417 to 1421 the picture changed.

14. *Chronicon Adae de Usk*, 133, 320. The manuscript breaks off at this point, the remainder being lost.

15. For the contents of the next five paragraphs see M. R. Powicke, "Lancastrian Captains," in *Essays in Medieval History Presented to Bertie Wilkinson*, ed. T. A. Sandquist and M. R. Powicke (Toronto, 1969), 371–82.

16. Powicke, "Lancastrian Captains," 371. For the change from the feudal levy to this type of army recruited under indentures between the king and captains see A. H. Burne, *The Agincourt War* (London, 1956); C. Oman, *A History of the Art of War in the Middle Ages* (2nd ed.; London, 1924), II; F. Lot, *L'Art militaire et les armées* (Paris, 1949); R. A. Newhall, *The English Conquest of Normandy* (New Haven, 1924), and *Muster and Review* (Cambridge, Mass. 1940); M. R. Powicke, *Military Obligation in England* (Oxford, 1962.)

The contribution of the titled aristocracy fell from one-half to just over one-third. There was a larger proportion of small contingents (less than twenty men) and their leaders were less likely to be knights than they had been in the days of Agincourt. Moreover the captains of Agincourt did not lead the campaigns of conquest in the years 1417 to 1422. Although the great dukes and earls still remained prominent as contingent leaders, no single parliamentary baron now led a company to the wars. Moreover, only 31 out of 177 contingent commanders during these years were veterans of Agincourt—and even of this remnant of 31, only 25 went on to serve in the armies of Henry VI. This failure to maintain a sizeable corps of experienced captains suggests a fundamental weakness in the English forces, and, as Dr. Powicke states, the whole trend shows "a decline, not cataclysmic but noteworthy in the involvement of the politically leading class after the high point of the Agincourt campaign."

One last revival of interest occurred in the "Coronation March" of 1430 to 1431, but, at the same time the contingents were now of lesser quality, for the proportion of archers to men-at-arms had begun to increase. In the companies led by the great nobles the ratio increased only slightly: from three to one, to four to one. In most of the lesser companies it rose a little higher, but in some of the greater nonnoble companies it rose to the very high ratio of sixteen to one, and a few companies became little more than bands of archers. As Dr. Powicke again remarks, this significant deterioration "probably represents a drying-up of the source of men-at-arms rather than a deliberate military policy and, as such, reflects the growing disenchantment of the English middle-class with war in France."

After the "Coronation March" this deterioration continued, and the change in the increased ratio of archers to men-at-arms became a typical feature of Henry VI's reign. Moreover, the involvement of the prominent men of the countryside declined to such a degree that only "the persistent interest of *the court aristocracy* in the war was all that kept the English effort alive," and even this all but disappeared in the closing campaigns of the war. Long before the final collapse in the 1450's the idea of a military career must have been distinctly passé. Contemporary English chroniclers showed so little interest in the later stages of the war that when the Tudor historian Edward Hall came to write about them he had to cull most of his information from Monstrelet, Waurin, and other Burgundian and French authors.[17]

Nor could Henry V and his successors make up for this growing lack of enthusiasm amongst the politically prominent by appealing to a wider national feeling. As we have already seen, some of the knights in a Great Council gave voice to misgivings about war in 1414, and in the Parliament of December, 1420 (the same Parliament which refused any further grant of direct taxation), the Commons' debates showed considerable constitutional fears about the future if the king carried through his plans. They demanded his early return to England and the reaffirmation of a statute of 1340 guarding against any subjection of the people of England to their king qua king of France.[18] Moreover, Henry was forced to deny any intention of appointing a joint chancellor for both England and France. Also, as I have pointed out elsewhere,[19] Henry could not afford to whip up any kind of aggressive nationalistic feeling in England for that would have boomeranged in France where he claimed his "rights" not as a foreign conqueror but

17. B. J. H. Rowe, "A Contemporary Account of the Hundred Years War from 1415 to 1429," *English Historical Review*, XLI (1926), 504–13. Moreover, at the Winchester Parliament of 1449, when the situation of the English possessions in France was desperate, we are fortunate in possessing an authentic account of a parliamentary debate, a rare document at this period. At the king's command Reginald Boulers, the abbot of St. Peter's, Gloucester, appealed to both Lords and Commons for aid for the duke of Somerset, lieutenant of France, but all that came of the appeal was a discussion in the Lords which showed very little sense of urgency and the meager grant of a half subsidy by the Commons. See A. R. Myers, "A Parliamentary Debate of the Fifteenth Century," *Bulletin of the John Rylands Library*, XXII (1938), 388–404. Mr. Myers discusses the situation in great detail.

18. *Rotuli Parliamentorum* (6 vols.; London, 1783), VI, 125, 127 (hereinafter cited as *Rot. Parl.*).

19. J. R. Lander, *Conflict and Stability in Fifteenth Century England* (London, 1969), 62.

as a Frenchman—as the legitimate descendant and representative of the French royal family: a concept around which, after the king's death, his brother John, duke of Bedford, developed an intensive propaganda campaign in Normandy, emphasizing in a flood of political literature and symbolic objects the equal status of English and French under a king descended from the blood royal of both realms. Moreover, by 1426 the government also found it necessary to issue propaganda to justify to the English public Henry's title to the throne of France.[20] Henry V's takeover of France was, both in legal theory and in practice, the warlike enforcement of a legal right denied, not the conquest of one people by another. Although an unknown number of Englishmen received grants of estates in Normandy, Frenchmen who swore an oath of allegiance were left in possession of their estates,[21] and apart from small settlements at Harfleur, Honfleur, and Caen, Henry made no attempt to anglicize the population of Normandy,[22] and John, duke of Bedford, left the civilian administration as far as possible in Norman hands.[23]

Henry V, therefore, held only one major card—his undeniable military genius. It was not enough to ensure the success of his plans. In the absence of any ardent nationalistic spirit he was forced to rely on the enthusiasm of the ruling segment of English society to fight for (and upon the populace to pay for) the warlike enforcement of his legalistic claims. However great their ancestors' enthusiasm for such projects had been in the fourteenth century, theirs rapidly vanished, and they

20. J. W. McKenna, "Henry VI of England and the Dual Monarchy: Aspects of Royal Political Propaganda, 1422–1432." *J. of the Warburg and Courtauld Institutes,* XXVIII (1965), 145–62.

21. Although most of the greatest proprietors fled at least three-quarters of the landowners stayed on their estates. Henry V's invasion of Normandy was certainly not "the Norman Conquest in reverse" which some writers have imagined.

22. W. T. Waugh, "The Administration of Normandy, 1420–1422," in *Essays in Medieval History Presented to Thomas Frederick Tout,* ed. A. G. Little and F. M. Powicke (Manchester, 1925), 352.

23. B. J. H. Rowe, "The *Grand Conseil* Under the Duke of Bedford," in *Oxford Essays in Medieval History Presented to Herbert Edward Salter,* ed. F. M. Powicke (Oxford, 1934), 207–234.

quickly ceased to relish the part which the king's plans had assigned to them.

It is now time to turn to Edward IV, to try to assess his policy and actions by the same criteria. Edward has come down to posterity with the reputation of a great general. His reputation, however, seems to be based solely on the fact that he never lost a battle: a consideration that hardly decides the question one way or the other. His success may well be due to the fact that his opponents were as comparatively inexperienced as he was himself. Edward never faced a veteran continental commander and the battles of the Wars of Roses (when they were not mere skirmishes as some of them were) were hardly notable for the strategic or tactical skills of their protagonists.[24] Even Edward's famous pursuit of Queen Margaret to Tewkesbury "was tenacious rather than able." [25]

Nor does enthusiasm in the country appear to have been at all conspicuous. William Worcester, more or less the spokesman of the remnant of the dispossessed war captains of the previous generation, had in the 1450's written his *Boke of Noblesse* [26] and had made a collection of documents about the war [27] to encourage Henry VI and his advisers to renew it. Worcester revised the *Boke* in the early 1470's, touched it up again, and presented it, together with the collection of documents, to Edward IV on the eve of the 1475 campaign.[28] His enthusiasm for war by this time, however, may well have been no more than an echo from a vanished past. By contrast, an anonymous writer of ca. 1470, or slightly later, in discussing Henry V hardly mentions the French war after the triumph of Agincourt, and ends his brief account of the reign with the somewhat frigid words, "[Henry] departed this life at Bois de

24. J. R. Lander, *The Wars of the Roses* (London, 1965), 20–21.

25. C. A. J. Armstrong, "Politics and the Battle of St. Albans, 1455," *Bulletin of the Institute of Historical Research*, XXXIII (1960), 25.

26. William Worcester, *The Boke of Noblesse*, ed. J. G. Nicholss (London, 1860).

27. Lambeth MS 506, printed in *Letters and Papers Illustrative of the Wars of the English in France*, ed. Stevenson, II Pt. 2 p. 521–742.

28. K. B. MacFarlane, "William Worcester, A Preliminary Survey," in *Studies Presented to Sir Hilary Jenkinson*, ed. J. Conway Davies, (Oxford, 1957), 210–13.

Vincent in Paris, after having ably reigned nine years and five months."[29] The Second Anonymous Croyland Continuator, traditionally, though perhaps dubiously, described as one of Edward IV's councillors,[30] remarked that in the Parliament of 1472–75,

The principal object of the King was to encourage the nobles and people to engage in the war against France: in the promotion of which object, many speeches of remarkable eloquence were made in Parliament, both of a public and private nature, especially on behalf of the duke of Burgundy. The result was that all applauded the King's intentions, and bestowed the highest praises on his proposed plans; and numerous tenths and fifteenths were granted, on several occasions, according to the exigencies of the case, in assemblies of the clergy and such of the laity as took any part in making grants of that nature. Besides this, all those who were possessed of realty and personal property, all of them, readily granted the tenth part of their possessions. When it now seemed that not even all the grants before-mentioned would suffice for the maintenance of such great expenses, a new and unheard of impost was introduced, everyone was to give just what he pleased, or rather just what he did not please, by way of benevolence. The money raised from grants so large and so numerous as these amounted to sums, the like of which was never seen before, nor is it probable that they will ever be seen in times to come.[31]

No other English writer of the day has left any account of contemporary opinion,[32] and although the Croyland Con-

29. "The First Anonymous Croyland Continuator," in W. Fulman, *Rerum Anglicarum Scriptorum Veterum* (Oxford, 1684), 514.

30. Sir G. Edwards, "The Second Continuation of the Croyland Chronicle: Was It Written in Ten Days?" *Bulletin of the Institute of Historical Research*, XXXIX (1966), 117–29.

31. Fulman, in *Rerum Anglicarum Scriptorum Veterum*, 557–58.

32. Admittedly the English sources for this period are pitifully meager. Foreign sources, however, are almost equally uninformative, e.g., *The Calender of State Papers and Manuscripts Existing in the Archives and Collections of Milan*, ed. A. B. Hinds (London, 1912), frequently mentions English war policy but except for references to resistance to taxation and descriptions of the Benevolence (177, 184, 193–94) mentions public opinion only twice. In December, 1473, Christopher Bollati, the Milanese ambassador to the French court, wrote home that "King Edward is not so eager to make war on the King of France as his subjects" (177), and in August, 1474, he wrote of the duke of Burgundy stirring up "the English people to make war on France" (183). The Milanese state papers are, however, crammed with the wildest rumors about English affairs and should be used only with the greatest caution. Miss C. L. Scofield (*Edward*

tinuator describes accurately, if somewhat vaguely, the *course* of proceedings in the Commons, the Rolls of Parliament themselves and the transcript of a speech preserved at Christ Church, Canterbury, show that his testimony to the enthusiasm of the members gives, to say the least, somewhat wide bounds to truth. These sources show that enthusiastic, warlike feeling was hardly conspicuous. Both royal propaganda and debates seem to have been conducted in a low key, quite different from the earlier appeals of King Henry V—with an emphasis squarely and firmly placed upon defense rather than upon agression.

This emphasis upon defense may be easily explained by the development of Anglo-French relations since the loss of Normandy and Guienne in the early 1450's. As the Wars of the Roses developed they became more than a series of domestic crises. Neither Lancastrians nor Yorkists scrupled to call in foreign help when they could get it, and the rapid upheavals of English politics upset the calculations of statesmen in distant parts of Europe—and they still particularly affected France. Even after 1453 the king of France still dreaded a renewed English invasion, and within a few years fear of Burgundy became an even greater obsession with him. From about 1456 to the death of Charles the Bold in 1477, the mutual suspicions of Burgundy and France developed into a bitter diplomatic contest in which no holds were barred—a contest in which both sides alternately dreaded and wooed the English.

In 1462 Louis XI of France, alarmed once more at the prospect of an Anglo-Burgundian alliance, countered by supporting the exiled Margaret of Anjou, only to abandon her cause at the end of the year when the Burgundian threat to his kingdom had diminished. France and Burgundy then com-

---

IV, II, 53–54) states that in 1473 James III of Scotland proposed to Louis XI that for the sum of 10,000 crowns he should keep Edward at home "by attacking him if that proved to be necessary, or by promising to protect him against his subjects if they should rise in revolt when he gave up his expedition to France." This does not, however, prove that the war policy was popular. It may merely indicate the probability of fury against what would then have appeared to be fraudulent war taxation.

peted for an English alliance. Charles the Bold unsuccessfully tried to persuade Edward to join the League of the Public Weal against Louis XI. Later it was a temporary success on the part of France which drove Charles to marry Margaret of York, and in 1468 Edward IV was threatening to invade France. Reacting strongly, Louis (probably as early as 1468) toyed with the idea of bringing together Queen Margaret and the earl of Warwick: the almost fantastic plan which led to their successful invasion of England in 1470—and to their ultimate failure because, Louis, going too far, pushed their puppet Lancastrian government into plans for an invasion of Burgundy. Duke Charles, until then coldly unsympathetic to the woes of his exiled English brother-in-law, Edward IV, in self-defense quickly supported plans for a counterinvasion. After his return Edward tried to come to terms with Louis XI, and his attempts at rapprochement, though unsuccessful, may well have been sincere.[33] At any rate they failed and the suspicion-laden diplomatic maneuverings of the 1460's began all over again. Amongst other things, Louis tried to egg on the Scots to invade England, tried to keep up disturbances in Wales, where in 1471, Jasper Tudor still held out, and gave some help to that irreconcilable Lancastrian, the earl of Oxford, to whose treasonable activities rumour persistently linked Edward IV's brother, the duke of Clarence.[34] We should, therefore, most probably, see the campaign of 1475, not as a revival of the genuinely aggressive policies of Henry V, but as a reaction to this background of deep, intense suspicions and fears, a somewhat defensive reaction to the development of Anglo-Burgundian-French relationships over the past two decades.

From the beginning of the Parliament of 1472–75 Edward made intensive efforts to popularize his war policy with the Commons. At some point he presented them with a "declaration

33. Edward apparently thought of a French alliance as early as the middle of 1472. Scofield, *Edward IV*, II, 16–17.
34. Miss Scofield's very detailed account brings out this atmosphere of suspicion, duplicity, and constant diplomatic flux extremely well. *Ibid.*, 1–151.

in writing" on the subject and informed them of his intentions "dyvers tymes" through speeches by the chancellors.[35] Unfortunately, the Rolls of Parliament at this period rarely record the full text of speeches, but the Roll does very briefly summarize an oration made, on February 1, 1474, by the chancellor, the bishop of Durham, on the dual themes of good and stable government at home and the recovery of France.[36]

More fortunately, however, the same themes are dealt with and the connection between them made absolutely explicit in the full text of a speech (in English) preserved in the Letter Books of Christ Church, Canterbury.[37] This oration (obviously one of the "many speeches of remarkable eloquence" mentioned by the Croyland Continuator) was most probably delivered in the first session of the Parliament (October 6–November 30, 1472).[38] It is indeed eloquent—and it is long, very long, covering no less than eleven printed pages. The most significant, and perhaps surprising, thing which emerges from its considerable

35. *Rot. Parl.*, V, 111. The declaration is mentioned in the subsidy bill of the sixth session of the Parliament (January 23–March 14, 1474) as having been delivered to the Commons "afore this tyme." It is also mentioned in the seventh session, *Ibid.*, 150. The same bill of the sixth session also informs us of the chancellor's speeches. There were three chancellors in the course of this Parliament—Robert Stillington, bishop of Bath and Wells (April, 1471–July, 1473), Laurence Booth, bishop of Durham (July, 1473–May, 1474) and Thomas Rotheram, bishop of Lincoln (May, 1474–May, 1483).

36. *Rot. Parl.*, VI, 88–89. "Ut idem Cancellarius recitavit, inter alia fuerunt, ad bonum regimen infra Regnum plantand', idemque Regnum per ministrationem justicie stabiliend', ac personas in ociositate nimium degentes per medium guerre exterius in labore ponend', necnon jus Regium in Regno Francie recuperand'."

37. *Literae Cantuarienses*, ed. J. B. Sheppard (3 vols.; Rolls Series, London, 1887–89), III, 274–85.

38. Mr. J. B. Sheppard, the editor of *Literae Cantuarienses*, assigned the year 1474 as the probable date of the speech, but as Miss C. L. Scofield (*Edward IV*, II, 44, n. 1) has pointed out, this date is disproved by internal evidence. The speech mentions that Edward was hoping for a treaty with the Hanseatic League, and such a treaty was signed on February 28, 1474. It also refers to instructions given by the duke of Burgundy to the Lord Gruthuyse and there is a statement that "last summer" the duke of Burgundy had been on French territory. Both these things can be dated to the summer of 1472. Moreover, the speech refers to Denmark and Scotland threatening England, but treaties were made with these countries respectively on May 11, 1473, and July 30, 1474. (Scofield, *Edward IV*, II, 50, 102). Miss Scofield suggested that the archbishop of Canterbury made the speech, but there seems to be no evidence for this beyond the fact that the text is preserved in the Canterbury archives. It could have been made by the chancellor, Robert Stillington, bishop of Bath and Wells.

emotional rhetoric, however, is its markedly *defensive* tone. The king's title to the crown of France is not even mentioned until almost the end of the fifth page. And even then it is rapidly disposed of in fourteen lines as part of a long argument that attack is the best form of defense.[39]

The speech begins with a peroration that internal peace and tranquility are the means by which a country waxes to abundance and riches. Although the king's recent "moost victorious prowesse"[40] has extirpated the worst causes of dissension "extorcions, oppressions, robberies and other grete myscheves" still abound.[41] The severest justice would be insufficient to repress the perpetrators of such deeds without a remedy worse than the disease, that is, "within fewe yeres such distruction of people necessarie to the defence of the lande" that enemies would be tempted to invade it. In other words many of the country's thugs are part of its ruling class. They cannot without peril be destroyed, but their exhuberant surplus energy must be diverted into socially less abominable channels.

Moreover, the Scots and the Danes are threatening England, and the subtle and crafty enterprises of King Louis XI of France have for long been, and still are, a constant danger

39. *Literae Cantuerianses*, 279. After a long passage on the danger of foreign attack the speech goes on, "it is thought to the Kyngs Highness most expedient, that rathe than he shuld abide the defence of the werre atte home, and leve his lande in the jeopardie that Rome stode in by the comyng of Hanyball out of Carthage, and, like as Scipio, when the Romanes were in dispair of their defence in their owne contre ageynst Hanyball, departed fro Rome and went to Cartage and victoriously behad him there, to the grettest comforte of the Romaynes that he came fro; right soo our Souverayne Lord thynketh that [he], considered his just and rightwys title whiche he hath to the corone and reame of Fraunce, whereof a grete partie was but in late daies in the possession of Englissh men, seeyng also that he hath largely doo his parte in requisicion of justice or of some resonuble recompence in that partie, as is aboveseid, coude doo thynges better for the recomforte, sewertie and welthe of his subgetts, than, now havying noon other remedie, to entre and begynne in his owne querell a werre in tho parties ageinst the seid adversarie, for the recoverie not oonly of the duchies of Normandie and Guyenne, but also of the corone of Fraunce . . . ."

40. A euphemistic reference to Edward's victories over the Lancastrians at Barnet and Tewkesbury and his restoration in 1471.

41. This statement is made the more plausible by the fact that the Commons themselves complained of such things in certain parts of the country in the session of October–November, 1472. *Rot. Parl.*, VI, 8–9.

in spite of Edward's efforts to reach a friendly agreement with him.[42] Therefore, war abroad, taking the agressive line, is demonstrably the surest guarantee against invasion and the road to internal order and prosperity. Moreover, for the first time in Edward's reign, the state of the country and the king's foreign alliances combine to make this policy feasible.

Pelion is then piled upon Ossa in the way of subsidiary, negative arguments to make this long appeal more attractive— possession of the French coast would make the English Channel safer for English shipping and reduce the intolerable financial burden of keeping the sea. Many gentlemen, younger sons, and others could be rewarded with land, "men of werre that have none other purveaunce" could be settled in garrisons and live by their wages: the type of men who, otherwise unoccupied, would cause mischief at home. Then, in an appeal to history, the chancellor reminds the king's subjects that since the Norman conquest internal peace has never for long prevailed "in any King's day but in suche as have made werre outward."

These long, emotional, at times even eloquent appeals are, in the end, distinctly negative. The gist of them—fight in France to avoid more trouble at home, reduce (in the end) the king's expenses, and make something for yourself in the process—are a very far distant cry from Henry V's aggressive clarion calls to conquest. He, after all, would never have slipped in his claim to the French crown as a short aside in a long argument about defense. The claim to the throne had been the very core of his policy.[43] It looks as if Edward IV realized that he must use all the arts of propaganda at his disposal to whip up an aggressive spirit in a blasé and indifferent people.

Efforts to raise taxation for the campaign show an equally indifferent, if not a definitely hostile, spirit toward the king's plans. In November, 1472, instead of the standard levy of a fifteenth and tenth on personal property granted by both houses

42. See above, 84.
43. This is not, of course, to say that Henry V never used the appeal for defense; he did, but it was never the central theme of his propaganda.

of Parliament, the Lords voted a special tax of one-tenth of their incomes from lands, annuities, and offices, and the Commons separately granted a similar tax from nonaristocratic revenues to pay the wages of 13,000 archers for one year,[44] for which a sum of £118,625 was needed. Both houses were obviously in a suspicious mood, for both made their grants with the grudging stipulation that the money was to be returned to the taxpayers if the army was not mustered by Michelmas, 1474, and both houses added other, intensely humiliating conditions. They refused to trust the king with the money. It was not to be paid into the royal Exchequer. Instead the Lords instructed the collectors of their grant to pay the proceeds to the archbishop of Canterbury, the bishop of Ely, the prior of the Hospital of St. John of Jerusalem in England and John Sutton, Lord Dudley. They, in turn, were, for safekeeping, to commit the money to the dean and chapter of St. Paul's Cathedral to hold until such time as Parliament authorized its release to the king. The Commons, in their bill, ordered the commissioners appointed to supervise the collection of their tenth to place the money in provincial repositories—local castles, towns, houses of religion, and other suitable places—again until Parliament authorized its use. Either the Lords and Commons bitterly grudged the money or they doubted the sincerity of Edward's war policy.[45] Possibly both.

   In the next session of the same Parliament, in April, 1473, the Lords confirmed their grant of the tenth and now allowed the proceeds to be paid into the Exchequer. According to Sir James Ramsay, the Exchequer Tellers' Roll for Michelmas, 1472, reveals that the Lords' tenth had produced only £2,461.3.4.[46]

44. Both bills state that the grants were made for the "defence" of the realm by means of war abroad. *Rot. Parl.*, VI, 4–6, 6–8. There were several precedents earlier in the century for this form of taxation, See H. L. Gray, "Incomes from Land in England in 1436," *English Historical Review*, XLIX (1934), 607–39.

45. Parliament had made a grant for war on France in 1468, when, owing to political complications at home, no campaign had followed. In 1472 Edward was forced to remit the still unpaid portion of this grant and any claim he had to a grant made for archers to Henry VI as far back as 1453. *Rot Parl.*, VI, 6.

46. *Ibid.*, 42–43; Ramsay, *Lancaster and York*, II, 393–94.

If the figure is complete they must have underassessed themselves in a big way.

The Commons' tenth was to have been levied by the Feast of the Purification of Our Lady (February 2), but by April no certificates of collection had come in from the local tax commissioners appointed under the terms of the Commons' grant. Because no records were available from previous taxation of this kind, it was impossible to calculate what the tenth would yield.[47] As the king's preparations called for money urgently, the Commons now granted (in addition to the tenth on incomes) a standard fifteenth and tenth on the value of movable property. Yet they still restricted the new grant to the payment of the archers' wages, and in view of their own admission that the king's needs were urgent, illogically still withheld it in the local repositories until the proclamation of the army musters.[48]

Delay followed upon delay, expedient upon expedient—and all of them unsatisfactory. In the seventh session of the Parliament, in July, 1474, the government revealed to the Commons that by the previous January the commissioners had returned most of the certificates for the original levy of the tenth on incomes, from which it appeared that their assessments amounted to £31,410.13.1½.[49] To exert pressure upon recalcitrant districts, the Commons then allotted specific numbers of archers (558 in all) to be supported by those areas from which the commissioners had so far returned no certificates of assessment.[50] Moreover, upon hearing that the fifteenth and

47. Records survived from the income tax of 1436 (See above, n. 44), but Parliament and the government were either unaware of them or chose to ignore them.

48. *Rot. Parl.*, VI, 39–41. The collectors were to certify to the Chancery within twenty-two days after the Feast of St. John. (Probably either the Nativity of St. John, June 24, or the Decollatio of St. John the Baptist, August 29).

49. Slightly more, in fact, than the yield of the standard fifteenth and tenth which, at this time, was about £31,000.

50. In compensation £5,383.15.0 was to be deducted from the contributions of other shires and districts. The districts were Cheshire, Northumberland, Cumberland, Westmorland, the bishopric of Durham, the town of Newcastle upon Tyne, the city of Lincoln, the wapentake of Ewcrosse in Yorkshire, and the hundred of Wormelowe in Herefordshire. In the past some of these northern areas had often been exempted from taxation for war against France owing to their obligations for the defense of the Scottish border.

tenth had not yet been collected they somewhat oddly granted another in its place [51] and extended the time limit for the sailing of the army to the Feast of St. John the Baptist (August 29, 1476).

The government also revealed that the combined sum for the tenth and the fifteenth and tenth from those shires where the commissioners had made assessments would not exceed £62,094.0.4. The king, therefore, asked the Commons to make up the balance of the money needed to pay the archers' wages—£51,147.3.7½. This they granted, but only on condition that it should be raised from sections of the community normally untaxed—from the Order of St. John of Jerusalem in England (except for the prior himself) and from "the Goodes and Catalles of such persones not havyng any or but littell Lond, or other frehold, nor to the XVe and X^e afore tyme but litell or not charged, in ease and relyef of other persones to the said Xth part and other charges afore tyme gretly charged, specially at this tyme to be chargeable and charged." To make things firmer, definite sums were allotted for collection in each county. In other words the Commons now attempted to shift part of the burden of war payments off the shoulders of the customary classes of taxpayers and onto those of an exempt religious order and those of the poor. Once again the grant was to be void if the king exceeded the time limit for the expedition.[52]

Even after this, worse was to come, and worse was to be revealed. The Roll of the seventh, and last, session of the Parliament, held from January 23 to March 14, 1475, tells a horrifying story of inefficiency, resistance, and corruption.

"And howe be it that grete part of the said Xth part in every Shire, Cite, Towne and Burgh, is levied by the Collectours thereof, it is so, that some of the Collectours have not delyvered the sommes by theym receyved to the place lymyted and appoynted by the said Commyssioners, but have converted it to their owne use, and some that have receyved it, and not so delivered it, bee nowe dede, and some of

51. "a XVe and X^e for and yn the name and place of the forsaid XVe and X^e."
52. *Rot. Parl.*, VI, 111–19.

the said Xth part both be delyvered by the Collectours therof to the place lymyted by the said Commyssioners, and the Governours of the same place have converted it to their owne use, and some of the said Commissioners have receyved parcell of the said Xth part, and will not delyvere it to the Kyng's Commissioner, ordeyned by the Kyng to be receyvour therof, and some persones to whom parcell of the said Xth part have be delyvered by the Collectours, therof, saufly to be kept to the Kyng's use, will not make payment therof to the receyvour of the same, and some persones that with strong hand have taken parcell of the said Xth parte oute of the place where it was put to be kept by the said Collectours, accordyng to the said Graunte. . . ." [53]

Twenty-six months after the first war grant had been made, the king still had no money in his hands except the meager proceeds of the Lords' tenth on incomes. Everything else was still in a welter of confusion. The Commons at last, however, released to the king what money had been collected. Admitting also that their attempt in the previous session to shift part of the burden onto the Order of St. John and onto the poor had been overingenious and the money (owing to difficulties in the assessment of new taxpayers) could not be collected in time for the expedition,[54] on March 15 they granted one and one-third fifteenths and tenths to raise the outstanding £51,147.4.7½.[55]

Edward, in the end, through Parliament, had raised nearly the equivalent of four normal fifteenths and tenths—almost as much as Henry V had raised in a similar period[56]—but

53. *Ibid.*, 121.

54. It was to have been delivered to the Exchequer on Ascension Day, but as the Commons now admitted, "The fourme of the Levie by your Commissions to be made of the said LIMcxlvii li iiijs vijd. ob.q. is so diffuse and laborious . . . cowed not by that tyme be convenyently levied." New assessments had to be made by commissioners given powers of investigating incomes, while the standard fifteenth and tenth could be collected against longstanding, traditional assessments.

55. Estimated to yield £53,697. The fifteenth and tenth was to be paid by the quindene of Easter, the third by the Feast of St. Martin in winter (November 11), *Rot. Parl.*, VI, 149–53. Between 1473 and 1475 the clergy were also taxed, the convocation of Canterbury granting three and a half tenths, that of York two. Ramsay, *Lancaster and York*, II, 401.

56. Henry V had received six fifteenths and tenths between Martinmas 1413 and Martinmas 1417. Ramsay, *Lancaster and York*, ii, 401.

with infinitely more trouble than Henry had ever encountered and against far greater resistance to payment. Even now, after all this time, haggling, and confusion, money for the campaign was still so short that Edward, taking immense personal trouble, begged, cajoled, flattered, and bullied contributions from some of his richer subjects and sent out commissioners to do likewise with others, placing the collected in the hands of a trusted official of the royal household—the notorious first Benevolence.[57]

57. A fair amount of scattered evidence confirms the impression, derived from the Rolls of Parliament, of unwillingness to pay and tardiness in paying. In March, 1473, before the second parliamentary grant was formally made, John Paston the younger, writing to his brother, Sir John, who was apparently an M.P., said "God send yow ... rather the Devyll in the Parlement House ... we sey, then ye shold grante eny more taskys." In May, 1475, Margaret Paston alleged that heavy taxation had depressed prices and wrote, "The Kyng goth so nere us in this cuntre, both to pooer and ryche, that I wote not how we shall lyff." *The Paston Letters*, ed. J. Gairdner (4 vols.; Edinburgh, 1910), III, 82, 135. See also 126. On April 21, 1475, the king sent a signet letter to the collectors of the subsidy in Nottingham urging the quicker collection of money, pointing out that payments for the second quarter's wages of troops, due at Easter, were in arrears. *Records of the Borough of Nottingham* (11 vols.; London, 1882– 1956), II, 387–88. See also British Museum, Harleian MS 543, ffs., 148–49.

For the Benevolence, see *The Great Chronicle of London*, ed. A. H. Thomas and I. D. Thornley (London, 1938), 223; the Second Anonymous Croyland Continuator in Fulman, *Rerum Anglicarum Scriptorum Veterum*, 558, and E. L. Gray, "The First Benevolence" in *Facts and Factors in Economic History Presented to J. F. Gay*, ed. A. E. Cole, A. L. Dunham and N. S. B. Gras (Cambridge, Mass., 1932), 90–113. In London in January, the mayor was ordered to present all persons with incomes of £10 a year, or personal property worth £100. As late as June 17 (less than three weeks before the expedition sailed) the property qualification was reduced to 100 marks and the mayor and aldermen were ordered, with the help of the two chief justices and the chief baron of the Exchequer, to obtain a grant from everybody in the city who had not yet contributed. This latest levy, however, seems to have produced only £282. The mayor and aldermen passed on both orders to the livery companies, and the mercers alone presented 119 people between January and July. *Acts of Court of the Mercers' Company, 1453–1527*, ed. L. Lyell and F. D. Watney (Cambridge, 1936), 78–80, 84; Scofield, *Edward IV*, II, 127–28.

The Great Chronicle of London (244–45) commenting upon a later benevolence under Henry VII notes the advantages of this method of raising money: "The Kyng'is grace was well contentid with the lovyng demeanure of his subgectys. And soo he hadd good cawse ffor [by] thys waye he levyed more money, Then he shuld have doon with ffowyr ffyfftenys, and also wyth less grudge of hys comons, ffor to this charge payd noon but men of good substaunce, where at every ffyfftene ar Chargid pore people, which make moor grudgyng for payying of vjd., than at this tyme many did for payyng of vj noblys."; The same reluctance to provide money for war with France was notable under Henry VII. See G. R. Elton, *England Under the Tudors* (London, 1955), 24.

We may now turn to the other preparations for the campaign and to the composition of the army. In spite of the immensely frustrating financial difficulties already noted, the government lavished great care on these preparations.[58] Military leaders also carried on their recruiting in good time. Some were already organizing their contingents in the middle of 1474. Sir Richard Tunstall, for example, entered into indentures in August to provide ten spears and one hundred archers,[59] and the majority of the contingent leaders had their indentures drawn up and sealed by the end of December.[60] They were retained for one year and they were to be paid their first quarter's wages at Westminster on January 31, 1475, the date upon which they were to muster and upon which their service formally began. Compared with Henry V's preparations, Edward IV's were made in very good time. In Henry's day, February had been the usual month for drawing up indentures for the year's campaigning. In 1415 they had been drawn up as late as the end of April, and some even later.[61]

Although the campaign was bloodless [62] and ended in a peaceful settlement, there is no reason to believe that from

58. Military stores were being collected and workmen impressed from the end of 1472 and such efforts were intensified from the middle of 1474 onwards. *Calendar of Patent Rolls*, 1467–77, pp. 362, 365, 366, 372–73, 379, 395, 398, 462, 474, 479, 492, 494–96, 515, 524, 525–27. Great care was taken over the supply of ordnance, bows, bowstrings, and arrows. *Ibid.*, 462, 492. Over 10,000 sheaves of arrows were brought back after the campaign was over. J. Calmette and G. Périnelle, *Louis XI et l'Angleterre* (Paris, 1930). Pièces Justificatives, No. 63. Three London merchants who were apparently prepared to speculate in army supplies were licensed to requisition all things needful everywhere in England except on ecclesiastical lands. Scofield, *Edward IV*, II, 118. Large supplies of food were purchased and instructions issued for transporting it overseas. *Cal.Pat.Rolls*, 1467–77, pp. 515, 516, 527, 529, 532, 537.
59. T. Rymer, *Foedera*, etc. (17 vols.; London 1704–17), XI, 817–18.
60. Exchequer Various Accounts, P.R.O., E.101/71/5/956–70, E.101/71/6/971–988, 990–1,000, E.101/72/1/1001–1030, E.101/72/2/1031–1045. Only 4 out of the 94 surviving indentures for men-at-arms and archers were sealed after the end of December, P.R.O., E.101/72/2/1046, 1048, 1057, 1058.
61. R. W. Newhall, *The English Conquest of Normandy* (New Haven, Conn., 1924), 24, n. 109; J. H. Wylie and W. T. Waugh, *The Reign of Henry V* (3 vols.; Cambridge, 1914–29), I, 455–56, 466.
62. Except for a skirmish between an English foraging party and some Frenchmen near Noyon in which about fifty Englishmen were said to have been killed. Scofield, *Edward IV*, II, 132.

the first Edward intended it to be a mere military parade. Louis XI of France certainly regarded the English threat seriously. During the early months of 1475 he was most agitated, in a state of acute nervous anxiety. In his pious and yet worldly way, he did everything he could by both prayer and diplomacy to break the alliance between Edward IV and Charles the Bold, and to induce Charles to agree to a truce. The bloodless dénouement was mainly due to Charles's irrational folly in carrying on his war against the Swiss, continuing the siege of Neuss, and ignoring his treaty obligations towards Edward.[63] Edward, let down by his temperamental ally, took the wise, if unheroic, course of leaving France in return for a large payment and an annual pension. Yet the long preparations for the campaign, Edward's immense labors in raising money and war stores, Louis' anxiety to break the Anglo-Burgundian alliance all point strongly to the supposition that everybody concerned expected a hard campaign. We are, therefore, surely justified in supposing that Edward intended to lead overseas the largest and finest army he could assemble and transport to France.

At this point government records can provide a good deal of information on both the nature of recruitment and on the quality of the troops ultimately assembled. There are three sets of easily accessible records dealing with the forces engaged: (1) a declaration of payments made at Canterbury in June, 1475, by the tellers of the Exchequer to leaders of troops for the second quarter of their engagement, preserved in the College of Arms and published in facsimile by Mr. Francis Pierrepoint Barnard in 1925; (2) a number of indentures, preserved in the Public Record Office, drawn up between the king and the various contingent leaders; and (3) the Exchequer Tellers' Rolls, also preserved in the Public Record Office.

The indentures are incomplete. There were at least 192 contingent leaders, but only 95 of their indentures have sur-

63. *Ibid.*, II, 114, 122−24, 126, 129, 131−35. Miss Scofield is, in general, hostile to Edward in discussing this campaign. Her testimony on this point is, therefore, all the more weighty.

vived.[64] Although they supply interesting details of the conditions of service, they are, therefore, useless for any discussion
of the numbers engaged. Again, at first sight, the College of
Arms Roll seems to be a most impressive document, but a closer
examination shows it to be inaccurate and incomplete.[65] We

64. See above, n. 60. There are eight indentures dealing with specialized services,
transport, artillery, etc. Exchequer, Various Accounts, P.R.O., E.101/71/6/989; E.-
101/72/2/1051−56. E.101/72/2/1049 is an interesting example of a subcontract: an inden-
ture between the duke of Clarence and James Hyde, esquire, to bring five archers
to the duke's retinue and to serve himself as a man-at-arms. Clarence agreed to pay
Hyde from March 19, 1475, and he was to be ready for muster by that date.

65. F. P. Barnard, *Edward IV's French Expedition of 1475: The Leaders and their Badges,
Being MS. 2. M.16. College of Arms* (Oxford, 1925). The roll bears the title "A declaracion
Aswell of Capitegnes theire Speires and Archers Reteigned wyth our Sou[er]eigne
lord Kyng Edward the iiij^th in his s[er]uise of Guerre into his Duchie of Normandye
and his Realme of ffraunce as of theire wages for the second q[ua]rter paid by John
Sorell and John ffitzherberd Tellers of the Kynges mony in his Receyt at Canterbury
the moneth of Jun the xv yere of the Reigne of our said sou[er]eigne lord Kyng
Edward the iiij." Thomas Bulkeley, an official of the Exchequer of Receipt, was sent
to Canterbury on the royal council's advice to take charge of the money sent there
for the payment of the troops. He and six others stayed there for four weeks to
guard the money. P.R.O., Warrants for Issues, E.404/76/4/112, Tellers' Rolls, E.405/60,
m.2d, E.405/61, m.5d.

   The roll begins with a summary of the numbers of men-at-arms and archers led
by dukes, earls, barons, bannerets, knights, and others, and the numbers of artificers
and tradesmen, together with the payments made under each heading. Grand totals
of both numbers and money are then given. Detailed entries from which this summary
was partially compiled then follow, giving the names of the individual dukes, earls,
barons, bannerets, and knights with the numbers of their individual contingents. On
the right side of each entry is a drawing of their coats-of-arms. But with the knights
these generous details unfortunately end.

   The roll is incomplete because (a) a number of contingent leaders must have been
paid their wages elsewhere than at Canterbury. For example, the roll states that 173
esquires and gentlemen led contingents whereas the Tellers' Rolls supply the names
of 194. Also, although the roll includes the names of the marquess of Dorset, Lord
Clinton, and Sir Simon Mountford, it gives no figures for either the men-at-arms
or archers in their contingents, and no figures for archers for Sir Thomas Burgh,
Sir Richard Brandon, Sir Richard Corbett and Sir John Crokke—all of which figures
the Tellers' Rolls supply. There are also a good many other omissions.

   The arithmetic of the roll is highly inaccurate even by medieval standards. (1)
The totals in the first section of the roll very often differ from the addition of the
detailed figures in the second section of the roll from which they were ostensibly
compiled and (2) in the first section of the roll itself the grand total of the archers
gives an excess of more than 1,500 over the figures from which it is supposed to
be made up.

   The College of Arms Roll is, therefore, useless for my particular purpose. The
relationship between the Tellers' Rolls and the College of Arms Roll remains obscure.
The College Roll may have originated as an attempt to calculate the cost of the second
quarter of the expedition—but if so, it can hardly be considered a very successful
attempt.

are, therefore, forced back upon our third source, the Tellers' Rolls.[66] These seem to give a reasonably full record of those taking part in the campaign. Unfortunately, however, although the rolls always supply the numbers of men-at-arms and archers which each commander led, they generally give no more than the mere names of these commanders—which often makes very difficult a precise identification of some of the leaders below the knightly class.[67]

Edward's preparations did, in fact, produce a total of at least 11,451 combatants—the largest army which had so far crossed the English Channel during the fifteenth century.[68] An analysis akin to that which Dr. Powicke made for the contingents of the earlier part of the century can now be used

66. There are three Tellers' Rolls with entries relating to the payment of troops (a) Michelmas Term, 14 Edward IV, P.R.O., E.405/59, ms. 8r. & d; 9r. & d; (b) Easter, 15 Edward IV, P.R.O., E.405/60, ms. 1r. & d; 3r. & d; 4r. & d; 5r. & d; and E.405/61, ms. 1r. & d; 2r. & d; 3r. & d; 4r. & d. Although E.405/61 is incomplete it contains most of the entries for the Easter Term relating to the war. To this degree it duplicates the entries on E.405/60. Rymer printed most of the entries concerning men-at-arms and archers from E.405/61 but he misdated it Michelmas Term, 14 Edward IV, and stated that the payments recorded were made during the first quarter. The Roll itself has no headings and is not dated. Internal evidence, however, proves that it was compiled during the Easter Term, 15 Edward IV, as there is an entry on m.5d. recording a payment to John Fitzherbert for going to Canterbury with money to pay the troops for the second quarter. Fitzherbert went to Canterbury for that purpose in June and stayed there for four weeks (see above, n. 65). The payments recorded were therefore for the second quarter; the matter is put beyond doubt by the fact that the payments tally with those recorded on E.405/60 which is dated Easter Term, 15 Edward IV. Rymer's caption, *Foedera*, XI, 844–48, indicates that the roll is an Issue Roll, but it is in fact a Teller's Roll.

67. Many of these, however, can be more precisely identified by comparison with the returns of the knights of the shire, lists of sheriffs, appointments of justices of the peace, and other local officers.

68. The fighting men who went to France in the Agincourt campaign had numbered not more than 9,000. In 1417 there were something like 10,000 mobile troops, increased by reinforcements during 1418 to over 13,000. E. F. Jacob, *Henry V and the Invasion of France* (London, 1947), 85; Newhall, *The English Conquest of Normandy*, 192–94, 204–206. Edward, therefore, took to France a bigger army than any which Henry V had been able to muster at the beginning of a campaign. Allowing for noncombatants the whole host was probably much greater. P. de Commynes, *Mémoires,* ed. J. Calmette and G. Durville (3 vols.; Paris, 1924–25), II, 10–11, states that there was a numerous body of camp servants, although there was not one page in the whole army. If the army contained the same proportion of noncombattants as Henry V's the numbers crossing to France would have to be quadrupled. There were in addition 2,000 archers sent to the duke of Brittany under the command of Lords Audley, and Duras and Lord Dynham commanded a fleet with 3,000 men to protect the crossing. Scofield, *Edward IV*, II, 122, 124, 127.

to suggest both the quarters from which Edward IV obtained support for his war policy and the comparative quality of the forces which he was able to recruit.

As the table at the end of this article shows, the army divides into two parts: firstly, contingents led by men who were part of, or had very close connections with, the royal court, and, secondly, contingents led by men who had no such strong court connections, men whose following we may regard as the response of the countryside to the war effort.

The leaders of the court section of the army comprised peers who were closely related to the king and queen or holding appointments in the royal household, officials of the household, and a few officials from other government departments. This group, between them, led approximately 63 percent of the men-at-arms and 66 percent of the archers. The second group, consisting of peers who had no strong connection with the court and a number of nonnobles ranging from prominent bannerets to quite obscure countrymen, produced only 37 percent of the men-at-arms and only 34 percent of the archers.

The most prominent amongst the military leaders were the "court" peers—11 peers led 516 men-at-arms and 4,080 archers,[69] the most conspicuous contingents of all the individual contingents being on average three times larger than those of the "country" peers in the second category: 12 "country" peers producing 231 men-at-arms and 1,619 archers.[70] Members

69. The duke of Clarence (brother to the king), duke of Gloucester (brother), duke of Suffolk (brother-in-law), duke of Buckingham (married to the queen's sister), marquess of Dorset (stepson), Earl Ryvers (brother-in-law), Sir Anthony Grey of Rythyn (married to queen's sister and heir-apparent of Edmund, earl of Kent), Lord Stanley (steward of the Household), Lord Hastings (chamberlain), Lord Howard (treasurer of the Household, October, 1468–December, 1474), Thomas Howard, his son and heir and an esquire of the Body. (I have included in this category the eldest sons of two prominent peers, since they appear logically to fit here better than with any other group.)

70. The duke of Norfolk, the earls of Northumberland, Pembroke, and Ormonde, Lords Cobham, Ferrers, Fitzwarren, Sir John Fenys (son and heir of Lord Dacre of the South), Grey of Codnor, John Grey (son and heir of Lord Grey of Wilton), Lysle, Scrope. Once again two heirs of peers have been included. Lord Clynton is named in the College of Arms Roll, but the roll gives no figures for him. He does not appear in the Tellers' Rolls and, therefore, presumably did not take part in the campaign. Two Scottish lords (the earl of Douglas and Lord Boyde), in exile at Edward's court, also took part in the campaign. These have been separately classified (see table).

of the court aristocracy were thus overwhelmingly important as recruiting agents for the campaign. To add to the recruiting of the court circle, the household officials produced 50 contingent leaders with a total of 270 men-at-arms and 2,587 archers, 9 other officials,[71] 29 and 134 respectively. By contrast the whole country in general produced 108 nonnoble leaders who raised only 220 men-at-arms and only 1,693 archers—individual contingents roughly no more than one-third the size of those which the officials led.

Of these nonnoble "country" leaders 5 were bannerets and 13 were knights, that is men whose fairly prominent social position speaks for itself. Of the rest, the Tellers' Rolls designate 52 of them as esquires, 6 as "gentlemen," and there are 32 others to whom no description is attached—most of them (though not all) falling below even the rank of gentlemen. Of these 90 (responsible between them for only 136 men-at-arms and 972 archers), as many as 70 led only archers: 27 of the 70 as few as three archers or fewer. As to their standing in their county communities, only 8 were (at some time or other) both members of parliament and justices of the peace, 3 certainly, and possibly 6 were justices of the peace, and another may have been a member of Parliament.[72] Eighteen bannerets and knights and fifteen other prominent men. So below the ranks of the peerage[73] the coun-

71. John Crabbe (servant of William Hatteclyff, the king's secretary), Peter Curteis (keeper of the Great Wardrobe), Thomas Downes (clerk of the Ordnance), Geoffrey Gate (marshall of Calais), Robert Radclyff (master porter of Calais), John Sturgeon (master of the Ordnance), Thomas Swan (clerk of the Ordnance), William Tymperley (servant of John Morton, master of the Rolls of Chancery), Thomas Ustwayte (servant of John Gunthorpe, king's almoner, secretary to the queen and clerk of Parliament).

72. (1) M.Ps. and J.Ps.—James Blount, esquire, Derbyshire; Thomas Cokesay (no descr.), M.P. Gloucestershire, J.P. Warwickshire; Egidius Daubeney, esquire (created Lord Daubeney, 1486), Somerset; Thomas FitzWilliam, esquire, Lincolnshire; John Fortescue, esquire, Herts.; Walter Hungerford, esquire, Wilts.; William Meryng, esquire, Notts.; John Risley, esquire, Middlesex. J.P.s—John Blount, esquire, Derbyshire; Halnath Malyverer, esquire, Devon; Robert Palmer (no descr.), Devon; Possibly J.P.s—Thomas Fenys, esquire, Sussex; William Redmyle (no descr.), Somerset; Brian Talbot (no descr.), Lincolnshire. And Thomas Mauncell, esquire, may possibly have been M.P. for High Wycombe.

73. The participation of some gentry may, however, be concealed since they raised men for peers, e.g. Sir John Paston raised a group which seems to have been absorbed into Lord Hastings' contingent. *The Paston Letters*, III, 122. See also above n. 64.

try in general produced only thirty-three men really notable in their own local communities, plus seventy-five minor figures, all but a few of which led only a handful of archers. Hardly an impressive figure for the entire country: in fact, a miserable total which seems to indicate that most people were indifferent, if not hostile to the war policy.

Another of Dr. Powicke's criteria was the ratio of archers to men-at-arms. In 1475 this was astonishingly high. Nowhere was the highly desirable figure of three to one attained. In only two small contingents did the figure approach this standard and amongst the bannerets of the royal household it rose as high as ten to one. For the army as a whole it was over seven to one.

Therefore, by means of intensive propaganda, immense efforts in raising money, and in other preparations the government, despite indifference or even hostility to the war, managed to put a large army into the field. It is, however, doubtful if, in addition to size, the government also managed to produce quality. Since the army was never put to the test of fighting, one should not be dogmatic about its efficiency, but the probabilities would seem to lie strongly against military distinction.

As we have seen, after 1430 the quality of the English forces in France had notably declined, and even such permanent military organization as then existed had disappeared with the loss of Normandy and Guienne. The campaign of 1475 was, therefore, based upon an improvised organization called into being for a particular occasion and hurriedly disbanded with its passing, mounted by a generation with little or none of the professional experience and expertise which prolonged warfare brings with it. All over Europe, at this time, such particular mobilizations, after long periods of peace, were generally amateurish affairs. Commynes commented upon this very strongly when, in 1464–65, Charles the Bold of Burgundy embarked upon his first military expedition in the *Ligue du Bien Public:* "car je ne croy pas que de douze cens hommes d'armes ou envyron qu'ilz estoient, qu'il en y eust cinquante qui eussent sceu coucher une lance en l'arrest. Il n'y en avoit pas quatre cens arméz de cuyrasses et sy n'avoyent pas ung seul serviteur armé, *à cause de la longue paix,* et que en ceste maison ne tenoit nulles gens de soulde pour soullager le peuple de tailles."[74]

Commynes, again, basing his statement upon observation of Englishmen serving as mercenaries in continental armies, both before and after the campaign, thought that they became excellent soldiers with experience, but, having little knowledge of foreign warfare and being unpracticed in seige methods, they were more or less useless when they first crossed the seas. He thought that Charles the Bold was most unwise to carry on the seige of Neuss since the English army was no longer formed of the experienced soldiers who had fought in France with so much valour in earlier days, but all raw soldiers, unacquainted with French affairs, whom he should have been at hand to guide during their first campaign.[75] Commynes' words seem to be true enough. It was now twenty-two years since the last English soldier had been thrown out of Guienne in 1453. Most of the battles of the Wars of the Roses were insignificant by continental standards, fought by nonprofessional soldiers, the seiges being minor affairs.[76] Apart from the garrison of Calais, which was not, after all, a field army, the only standing force available was the king's bodyguard of two hundred archers, formed in 1467.[77]

74. Commynes, *Mémoires,* I, 27. See also the similar description, I, 13. For similar remarks upon other occasions, I, 176–77, 177–78, 188–89. In 1478 he also made similar observations upon the weakness of the Florentine forces under threat of attack from the Papal and Neapolitan armies. See II, 272–73.

75. Commynes, *Mémoires,* II, 8, 15, 120–22, 134. He seems to ignore the seiges of the northern and Welsh castles in Lancastrian hands in the 1460's, but these, except for Harlech, were very short affairs compared with continental seiges and his opinion is undoubtedly correct.

76. See Lander, *The Wars of the Roses,* 20 ff. See above, n. 75.

77. The garrison of Calais was 1,120 in war, reduced to about 780 in peace time, but none of it was available for this campaign. The only other large permanent forces at this time, those of the Wardens of the Scottish Marches, can be neglected for this purpose since they obviously could not be taken out of the country. According to the pseudo-William Worcester, Edward IV formed a bodyguard of "CC Valettos probos et valentissimos sagittarios Anglie, ordinando quod quilibet eorum haberet viij.d. per diem, equitando et attendendo super personam suam propriam." *Letters and Papers*

Figures of Combattants*

	Number of Contingent Leaders†	Men-at-Arms	Archers	Avg. No. per Leader Men-at-Arms	Avg. No. per Leader Archers	Ratio of Archers to Men-at-Arms
1. *Household*						
(a) Bannerets	7	69	720	10	103	10
(b) Knights‡	5	39	370	8	54	7
(c) Esquires	28	107	910	4	32	8
(d) Gentlemen	2	2	7	1	3½	3½
(e) Others	7	10	80	1½	11½	8
(f) Gentlemen of the House of the Lord King‡	1	43	316	43	316	7½
(g) Archers of the King's Chambers			184			
Total of 1	50	270	2,587			
2. *Peers*: Royal Relations and holding Household Appointments	11	516	4,080	47	371	8–
3. *Other Officials*	9	29	134	3	15	5
Total of 1, 2, 3	70	815	6,801			
4. *Other Peers*	12	231	1,619	16	135	9–
5. *Other: Nonhousehold*						
(a) Bannerets	5	32	272	6	54	8½
(b) Knights	13	52	449	4	35	9
(c) Esquires	52	91	672	2	13½	7–

(d) Gentlemen	6	5	32	1	5	5
(e) Others	32	40	268	1	8	8
Total of 4 and 5	120	451	2,312			
6. *Scottish Lords*	2	8	60	4	30	7½
Total of 4, 5, 6	122	463	3,372			
Total of 1, 2, 3, 4, 5, 6	192	1,278	10,173			

Total **Men-at-Arms** (including leaders) and Archers	11,451
Add Technical Personnel (transport, miners, carpenters, medical, etc.)	387
Grand total	11,838
Plus secretaries, councillors, royal servants, possibly another 10 or 12 percent	1,182
	13,020

NOTES

*Small numbers may be omitted from all these sources. E.g., the city of Salisbury sent and paid 54 men under Sir Edward Darrell. R. C. Hoare, *The History of Modern Wiltshire* (4 vols.; London, 1843), IV, 195–96. It is possible that other cities may have acted in the same way.

†These figures are also included in the column "men-at-arms," and therefore are not included again in the total figures.

‡Sir John Elrington, the cofferer of the Household, led a contingent as a knight as well as leading the gentlemen of the Household of the lord king.

The army of 1475, unlike Charles the Bold's army of 1464–65, seems to have been well enough armed because preparations had been underway for a long time. Its fighting quality, however, was a different matter entirely, and a verdict upon it must, at best, be left in doubt.

As we have seen, the response from the countryside to the king's call to arms was hardly fervent, and the proportion of men-at-arms to archers in the army was woefully low. It may well be that from about 1430, certainly from 1453 onwards, the numbers of men trained for this role had declined.[78] As William Worcester bitterly lamented the English were no longer the martial race they had formerly been.[79] It is, perhaps, no exaggeration to claim that the majority of the aristocracy and gentry were no longer enthusiastic for continental war, nor particularly fitted for it, and that Edward IV's claim to be waging defensive war was true. The old enthusiasm (such as it had been) for the king's claim to the French throne had long since departed and the campaign of 1475 was not so much a fervid renewal of ancient glories as a defensive reaction of the government to the complications and dangers of the international situation in northwestern Europe as it had developed since 1453.

Illustrative of the Wars of the English in France, Stevenson (ed.), II, Pt. 2, p. 788. This bodyguard, considerably expanded, was most probably represented in the campaign forces by the "Archers of the King's Chamber" (See table). It has not, however, been possible to trace a definite connection between them, though Worcester's phraseology and that of the Tellers' Rolls makes such a connection highly probable.

78. It may be objected that the provision of a large ratio of men-at-arms to archers may have been deliberate policy, but this seems implausible. The fact that the parliamentary grants mention only archers proves nothing for no army could be composed of archers alone. Since war tactics in northern Europe do not seem to have changed since the earlier part of the century, the logical deduction seems to be as Dr. Powicke suggested (see above, 77), a drying up of the supply of men-at-arms.

79. Worcester, *The Boke of Noblesse,* 77–78.

DeLloyd J. Guth

NOTES ON THE EARLY TUDOR EXCHEQUER OF PLEAS

The Exchequer bewilders and frustrates anyone who has ever had to deal with it. Medieval and Tudor monarchs, their councils, and their subjects, regularly sought to regulate and reform it. Modern historians have enough trouble simply trying to make sense of its records. In *Tudor Chamber Administration 1485–1547,* Walter C. Richardson gave an unflattering but clear description of the arcanum of Exchequer fiscal process.[1] That book has been invaluable, particularly because of the ease with which it introduces students to historical evidence and the complexities of administrative history. Regardless of the Exchequer's relative position amongst royal institutions in Tudor England, none can match the variety and detail found in the four hundred and more Exchequer classes, even if sheer quantity of surviving boxes, bundles, files, rolls, and volumes puts it second to the Chancery group in the Public Record

---

1. Walter C. Richardson. *Tudor Chamber Administration 1485–1547* (Baton Rouge, 1952), especially Chap. 2.

Office.[2] For English history, medieval and early modern scholars must tour parts of Exchequer-land but it remains a sparsely settled, uncharted labyrinth. Most of what we currently know about late medieval Exchequer practices is not the result of systematic forays into its records. Rather, historians use Elizabethan and seventeenth-century treatises, reading them backward chronologically in hopes of clarifying earlier administrative process.[3] These treatises were written while the Treasury was emerging as a separate department of state, divorcing royal (public) finance from the Exchequer, in a manner reminiscent of the chamber techniques described by Professor Richardson. But why rely on later treatises when, for any period after the twelfth century, we can extract and reconstruct from plea rolls and related documents? The Selden Society and prodigious scholars such as Tout, Tait, Cam, Willard, H. G. Richardson, and Sayles carefully illuminated medieval institutions from their extant records. Their scholarly counterparts for late medieval and early modern institutions have been emerging more recently, encouraged and led by Professors W. C. Richardson and G. R. Elton.[4] Despite

2. *Guide to the Contents of the Public Record Office*, Vol. I: Legal Records, etc. (London, 1963), 45–113. A masterly sketch of the financial and legal records is in G. R. Elton, *England 1200–1640* (Ithaca and London, 1969), 45–66.

3. Nineteenth- and twentieth-century writers usually rely on Thomas Fanshawe (or Peter Osborn?), *The Practice of the Exchequer Court with Its Several Officers* (London, 1658) and Thomas Madox, *The History and Antiquities of the Exchequer of the Kings of England . . . from the Norman Conquest . . . to the End of the Reign of Edward II* (2nd ed.; 2 vols.; London, 1769). Also, Christopher Vernon, *Considerations for regulating the Exchequer* (London, 1641); Richard Crompton, *L'Authoritie et jurisdiction des Courts de la Maiestie de la Roygne* (London, 1594); and William Brown, *The Practice in the Court of Exchequer* (London, 1725). Sir Julius Caesar collected numerous treatises and notes in James I's reign, and manuscript references are given in Richardson, *Tudor Chamber Administration 1485–1547*, pp. 35, 503. Contemporary copies of other treatises survive, several in North American libraries, e.g., a ca. 1636 copy of "A Compendium . . . what every officer of his Ma'tie Exchequer ought to doe," probably written by Thomas Wilson, now in Columbia University Library, Special Collections: Montgomery MS 430.6942/G7922 (brought to my attention by Jacob M. Price).

4. Some examples, in print or yet unpublished, are M. Hastings (on Common Pleas), M. Blatcher (on king's Bench), R. S. Schofield (on taxation and the Exchequer), W. J. Jones (on Chancery, and the judiciary), B. P. Wolffe (on royal revenues), and R. A. Marchant (on church courts), T. G. Barnes (on county government in Somerset, and Star Chamber), H. E. Bell and J. Hurstfield (on the Court of Wards), Charles Gray (on copyhold in royal jurisdictions), P. Williams (on conciliar government in Wales). They have opened gates and provided fresh direction into institutional studies.

growing numbers of researchers in sixteenth- and seventeenth-century records, and except for invaluable county monograph series, historians remain remarkably ignorant about how institutions functioned from one decade to the next. We know surprisingly little about the actual business of the Exchequer, the courts of law, city and town government, manorial and parochial polity, and economic groups in the Tudor era.

This article will focus attention on one common-law jurisdiction during the reign of Henry VII: the Exchequer of Pleas. A quantitative analysis of the complete plea roll for 22 Henry VII (Michaelmas 1506–1507) [5] will be presented, describing and defining the various stages in litigation. This plea roll is complete and typical of court activity for several decades before and after. By reconstructing a court's activity for one year, while looking backward and forward for signs of change, we can capture momentarily a glimpse of part of the law, its enforcement, and its social function. Broader patterns and deeper insights would emerge if we studied a court's activity over a decade or longer. And much more could be learned about the litigants if we used corroborative evidence from ecclesiastical and local records. This article can only point in one direction by limited example, raising more questions than it can answer. Ultimately we will see how narrow and relatively insignificant this law court had become by the early Tudor period.

Professor W. C. Richardson documented the expansion of Chamber administration under Henry VII and his son. The Chamber, from within the king's household, replaced the more bureaucratic Exchequer of Receipt as repository for royal revenues.[6] Chamber command of administration was complemented by expanded judicial and accounting functions within the royal council. The former function became judicialized as courts of Star Chamber and Requests. At the same time parliamentary statute authorized royal prerogative

5. Public Record Office, E13/184. All tabulations and specific cases for the Exchequer of Pleas in 1506–1507 come from this plea roll. See *Guide to the Contents of the Public Record Office*, I, 92–94.

6. B. P. Wolffe, *The Crown Lands 1461–1536* (New York, 1970), provides a meticulous and excellent reinterpretation of royal financial practice.

responsibility for audits of royal officials and debtors that formerly resided in the Exchequer of Account. By Henry VII's reign fiscal control had slipped from Exchequer hands; and we need not be surprised if judicial activity in the Exchequer also declined, probably reflecting the impact of the Chamber-Conciliar expansion.

The Exchequer, most ancient of royal courts derived from the *Curia Regis,* possessed a common-law jurisdiction that traditionally enforced royal financial right. Here the crown could prosecute alleged violators of parliamentary (penal) statutes and royal proclamations, summon its recalcitrant or lazy debtors to account, and protect crown interest in lands, emoluments, and chattels. Here, also, all Exchequer officials could sue and be sued. Four or five barons sat in judgment at common law. By tradition and statute, the chief baron had to be expert in the common law, while in precedence he stood just beneath the two chief justices. The puisne, or associate, barons usually had legal training but it was most likely obtained at the Inns of Chancery where they could prepare for Exchequer experience in auditing accounts, because that was their major responsibility. Clerks employed by the Exchequer acted as attorneys for the hundreds of royal accountants and litigants. Actions came before the barons by information, bill, original writ, or inquisition but not by indictment or presentment.

The barons heard actions and accounts, necessitating memoranda enrollments. After the Exchequer Ordinances of the 1320's, the barons' record was divided between two memoranda rolls and one plea roll. By Henry VII's reign, the lord treasurer's remembrancer enrolled legal process involving lands (at least before Chamber hegemony); the king's remembrancer enrolled process and pleadings in litigation concerning extraordinary, fluctuating revenues such as forfeitures, amercements, escheats, and estreats.[7] To be sure, both memoranda rolls might contain pleas before the barons and are sometimes

7. *Guide to the Contents of the Public Record Office,* I, 49, 60–63, 75, for a brief differentiation between the LTR (E368) and KR (E159) memoranda rolls.

mistakenly called plea rolls. Such pleadings, where the king logically and legally was plaintiff, came in actions on accounts and in penal actions involving alleged violations of parliamentary statutes. But the Exchequer had only one plea roll, that of the so-called Exchequer of Pleas *(Scaccarium ad placita)*, where certain actions between persons, minus the king, might be resolved. These "common pleas" involved Exchequer officials and accountants, either as plaintiffs or defendants. The distinction in all litigation before the barons, then, was one of record-keeping: royal pleadings *(placita coronae)* enrolled on the memoranda rolls, and actions to which Henry VII was not direct party *(communia placita)* placed on the (Exchequer of Pleas) plea roll. The barons probably heard both crown and common pleadings in any one sitting, with the sorting out of enrollments between memoranda and plea rolls left to the engrossing clerks. The Exchequer's clerk of the pleas, a subordinate to the king's remembrancer, centrally supervised the receiving and ordering of the lawsuits. And the several underclerks to the clerk of the pleas would be regularly retained by plaintiffs and defendants as attorneys before the barons.

There are 1,499 plea rolls which record activity in the Exchequer of Pleas jurisdiction from 1235 until 1875, with virtually complete survival after 1500. Physically the rolls are alike, differing only in the number of membranes. For 22 Henry VII (1506–1507), thirty-nine parchment membranes, long and narrow (approximately 8" x 36"), stitched together at the top, rolled up when in storage, make the plea roll.

Sixty-nine legal actions are enrolled on both sides of each membrane for the legal year Michaelmas 1506 through Trinity term 1507. In addition, the final membrane on the roll (entitled *Waranta coram Baronibus de Scaccario apud Westmonasterium ad placita)* lists the attorneys admitted in specific actions. After matching this list to those sixty-nine enrolled actions, there are sixteen more actions cited in the attorneys' list that are not enrolled in the plea roll. These "extra" actions probably began before 22 Henry VII, remained pending throughout that year, and the attorneys' appearances were recorded to prevent their parties' loss. If we allow these latter actions, identified only by the admission of attorneys, then the 22 Henry VII plea roll has a total of eighty-five actions. Of course, in exceptional instances where litigants appear in person, not by attorney, we do not have this doublecheck. In analyzing the plea roll, then, distinction will be made between enrolled actions (sixty-nine) and total actions (eighty-five).

To give further context we can tabulate the king's remembrancer's memoranda roll for the same year. We need not look to the lord treasurer's memoranda roll because by 1506 it merely enrolls process for accounts, not actual pleadings. The king's remembrancer's memoranda roll contains 127 actions, all pleas of the crown, attempting to secure judgments against alleged violators of royal revenue rights (mainly smuggling to avoid royal customs).[8] The comparative numbers of total actions are: [9]

	Michaelmas 1506	Hilary 1507	Easter 1507	Trinity 1507	
Plea roll	35 (26)	21 (18)	18 (17)	11 (8) =	85 (69)
Memoranda roll	61	24	20	22	= 127

This gives a complete view of recorded Exchequer pleas, royal (127) and "common" (85), for the year 1506–1507; a look at the rolls for the rest of Henry VII's reign shows little variation in quantity and distribution. However, placing the Exchequer activity in broader context puts it a distant third for common-law jurisdictions. In Henry VII's reign we can safely estimate the *annual* number of actions in the Court of Common Pleas at over 10,000 and in the king's Bench at over 2,500.[10]

8. Litigation enrolled on the KR memoranda rolls during Henry VII's reign has been analyzed by DeLloyd J. Guth, "Exchequer Penal Law Enforcement 1485–1509" (Ph.D. thesis, University of Pittsburgh, 1967).

9. Total actions for the 1506–1507 plea roll are given, with the number of enrolled actions per term given in parentheses. The KR memoranda roll figures for E159/285 are from Guth, "Exchequer Penal Law Enforcement 1485–1509," Appendix C, 285. Richardson, *Tudor Chamber Administration 1485–1547*, p. 259, comments about increases in Exchequer judicial business complementing the decline in financial activities but the plea rolls and the memoranda rolls do not show any dramatic changes.

10. I have used my own estimates in conjunction with harder figures given for Common Pleas in 1482–83 and for king's Bench in Michaelmas term 1488, found

Plea rolls are frustratingly formal documents to use, rarely allowing a peek behind the facade of "the facts" inserted into an enrollment formula. For the 22 Henry VII Exchequer of Pleas, the analysis can expose these facts: plaintiffs, defendants, types of complaints, pleadings, resolutions. But little can ever be known about the litigants, their fortunes, or even their opinions of the Exchequer. As with twentieth-century police blotters, a human being becomes a name only. But if we know merely names for those populating plea rolls, we can at least learn more about the institutions.

In analyzing records of litigation, whether modern police or medieval civil prosecutions, an endless number of categories and questions arise: who complains, who is ordered to answer, what varieties of complaints are made, and how effective is the entire process? How much delay exists from one stage to another: alleged offense, legal complaint, defendant's appearance, pleading, resolution of issue (especially if joined and then resolved by jury trial), judgment, execution? What distribution of roles is there for laymen, lawyers, and officials? How many actions are resolved and in what manner? And then if one tries to move beyond the hard facts, questions become more speculative but also more socially significant. In what other ways, in and out of the law and law courts, can individuals confront each other, tranquilly or otherwise, and mitigate the clash of interests? How do procedures affect the goal of conflict resolution? To what extent does the mere threat of litigation act continuously for or against equitable resolution of conflicts within the court's jurisdiction? Does public confidence exist in the court's ability to protect right and to remedy wrong? Such questions define the patterns and complexities needed to perceive how law actually functions within society and what it actually accomplishes. This article can barely begin to answer the numerous questions posed.

respectively in: Margaret Hastings, *The Court of Common Pleas in Fifteenth Century England* (Ithaca, 1947), 27; Marjorie Blatcher, "The Working of the Court of King's Bench in the Fifteenth Century" (Ph.D. thesis, University of London, 1936), 190–220.

The earliest records for the Exchequer of Pleas have been meticulously examined by Hilary Jenkinson and Beryl E. R. Formoy, who provide the best introduction to medieval Exchequer legal procedure. The Jenkinson-Formoy analysis of the early Exchequer of Pleas included a tabulation of the court's activity for 27–28 Edward I (1299–1300). The authors divided that litigation into three basic categories: actions touching the king's revenues (76), Exchequer officials (43), and local officials (such as sheriffs, bailiffs) who account to the king (87). The total number of actions was 213; 7 of these, labeled "abnormal," did not fit the categories because they were initiated on special royal favor.[11] Such actions do not appear in the later plea roll. By Henry VII's reign, the first category of legal actions touching royal revenues appeared only on the king's remembrancer's memoranda roll, not on the plea roll. Thus in comparing the two plea rolls, Edward I to Henry VII, we must subtract those 76 actions from the earlier total because, as a matter of record keeping, they are not Exchequer of Pleas actions. We can also remove the 7 "abnormals," giving a real total for 1299–1300 of 130 actions. Even this total of actions involving Exchequer and local officials is much larger than the 85 total for Exchequer of Pleas litigation two centuries later.

By 1300 circumstances had urged protection and privilege for Exchequer officials. Querulous subjects could systematically tie them into knots of litigation, suing in any or every secular and ecclesiastical court of the land, hoping for revenge, intimidation, or remedy. The crown had to protect its Exchequer officials; therefore the Exchequer of Pleas existed so that they could sue and only be sued within their own court. The definition of "Exchequer official" already extended to servants and dependents of actual officers. They could prosecute their own debtors and trespassers before the barons, even if a baron. In 1299–1300 Exchequer officials appeared as plaintiffs or

11. C. Hilary Jenkinson and Beryl E. R. Formoy (eds.), *Select Cases in the Exchequer of Pleas*, Selden Society, XLVIII (London, 1932), cxiii–cxiv (n. 7). The plea roll for 27–28 Edward I is E13/23. All tabulations made for the Exchequer of Pleas from this plea roll come from the data supplied by Jenkinson and Formoy.

defendants in 43 of the remaining 130 actions (*i.e.*, 33 percent). Two centuries later in 1506–1507, 18 of the 85 total actions (*i.e.*, 20 percent) involved Exchequer officials, all but two as plaintiffs. Who were the other litigants? Again, by 1300 the definition of "Exchequer official" had also expanded to the point where a different category of actions appeared. Jenkinson-Formoy called these litigants local officials, meaning anyone owing accounts into the Exchequer by virtue of office (*e.g.*, sheriff, customer, tax collector, royal baliff).[12] In 1299–1300 they constituted 87 of the remaining 130 actions (*i.e.*, 67 percent), and they were involved in 66 of the 85 total actions in 1506–1507 (*i.e.*, 78 percent). So after two centuries the Exchequer of Pleas had become somewhat more involved with local officials than with its own privileged officers. And the king remained absent from both parties in any action. The early Tudor Exchequer of Pleas was a common-law court exclusively for Exchequer and local officials, but one in which they could be defendants more often than plaintiffs.

Who exactly were the litigants? A breakdown for the 22 Henry VII plea roll provides the following scheme:

(Defendants)

		Exchequer Officials	Local Officials	Private Subjects	
	Exchequer Officials	0	7	9	= 16
	Local Officials	0	4	11	= 15
(Plaintiffs)					
	Private Subjects	2	44	7	= 53
	Pro rege	0	0	1	= 1
		2	55	28	= 85

Obviously the court's litigation was no longer for officialdom (31 actions) but against it (53 actions). And the quarrel was with local officials, especially former sheriffs (34 of the 55 defendants, or 62 percent). Those complaining of wrongdoing were

---

12. Several early statutes limited Exchequer of Pleas jurisdiction (e.g., 12 Edward I, and 28 Edward I, c. 4) but 5 Edward II, c. 25, established jurisdiction as described here, for and against Exchequer and local officials. Alexander Luders and others (eds.), *The Statutes of the Realm* (London, 1810–28), I, 70, 138, 163.

mainly private subjects (46 actions), of varying status and influence: Lady Margaret Beaufort, the king's mother (a private subject?), successfully sued Sir John Savage, knight, and sheriff of Worcestershire, for 116s. due on the annual fee farm of the vill of Wiche. John James asked £10 damages from the former bailiffs of Great Yarmouth (Norfolk), allegedly for seizing £1 from him. John Aleyn, 4th baron of the Exchequer, successfully sued John Wryght, former sheriff of Canterbury, before his fellow Barons for a £10 debt due on assignment by Exchequer tally. John Langrake, London sherman, sued William Lynche, farmer of the ulnage in Wiltshire and Southampton, for the 66s. allegedly owed to his wife for dyeing three woolen cloths crimson (10s. each) and rowing and shearing nine white woolen cloths. In one action brought *pro rege*, a husbandman named John Hosteler helped Laurence Taillour escape from the Huntingdon gaol. When Taillour did not come before the barons as ordered, Hosteler was singled out from his seven colleagues to make fine with the King for the gaolbreak. It is enrolled here because the original suit against Taillour began in the Exchequer of Pleas; normally this sort of process would be enrolled on the king's remembrancer's memoranda roll. Exchequer officials were defendants in only 2 actions. In 1300 they were plaintiffs in 13 percent of all actions enrolled, and in 1506–1507 they sued 19 percent (16 of 85 actions). The fact remains that by Henry VII's reign, the Exchequer of Pleas was essentially a court where private subjects sued local, royally appointed, officials.

The major complaint was for debt (54 actions of 85 total, or 63.5 percent). Next came trespass *vi et armis* (14), usually alleging a taking of goods where probably a replevin was wanted (10) or charging false imprisonment (4). Local officials were accused of allowing the escape or rescue of prisoners who owed answers to the plaintiffs' suits (4). Some officials supposedly failed to execute writs delivered to them by plaintiffs (6). And three former sheriffs allegedly violated 3 Edward I (Statute Westminster I), c. 19, by failing to record acquittances in the

Exchequer on royal debts paid by the plaintiffs. One action each complained of contempt, covenant, maintenance, and illegal export of currency. All of these actions were at common law, claiming civil damages. If the plaintiff wanted penalty and punishment, prescribed by parliamentary statute, then the monarch became party to the complaint, and the action would be enrolled on the king's remembrancer's memoranda roll. What distinguished Exchequer of Pleas actions is the claim for damages, as opposed to penalty. Even when a penal statute was cited, as in the three actions against sheriffs, the plaintiff requested damages rather than the penalty prescribed. If we look back to the activity in 1299–1300, we find far fewer actions of debt. Of the 130 actions in Edward I's court, 39 involved prosecutions against sheriffs by private subjects for improperly executing writs and 42 charged other local officials with trespasses against private subjects. Official actions were then under greater popular scrutiny, at least at the common law.

The actions for debt in 1506–1507 predominated (63.5 percent) and involved defaults mainly by local officials. In one-third of these, the plaintiff produced the original written obligation before the barons. Debts alleged ranged between 40s. and 400 marks, while damages claimed ran between 4 marks and £100. Thomas Stokys, an Exchequer attorney for the Duchy of Lancaster, sued a writ of account against his rent gatherer, Thomas Barley, for £12 18s. 3½d., one pound of pepper, and three capons. Henry VII's bowyer at the Tower, Henry Southeworth, successfully sued Godard Oxenbrigge, sheriff of Surrey and Sussex, for his £9 2s. 6d. assigned fee of office. Richard Sydnor (*clerico*) had sued Thomas Boterell for £4 at the Counter in Bredstreet Ward before Roger Grove, London sheriff in 1505–1506. David Went, the sheriff's servant, had seized Boterell, imprisoned him in the Counter and the sheriff then accepted the guilty plea, awarding Sydnor £4 plus 2s. 8d. damages. But three weeks later, Boterell finagled his freedom without paying a farthing on the £4 2s. 8d. judgment. Sydnor came into the Exchequer asking the Barons to award the

£4 2*s*.8*d*. to him against Sheriff Grove, plus 5 marks damages. Grove denied the escape, asked for a jury trial, then two weeks later acknowledged *quod ipsi non possunt dedicere accionem*. The barons ordered Grove to pay the debt and damages that he had originally awarded against Boterell as well as additional damages of 23*s*.4*d*. That peculiar precedent in responsibility should have haunted many early Tudor local officials.

Local officials were most vulnerable in the Exchequer of Pleas because the Barons considered them present in the court by virtue of their official accounts. Of the sixty-nine enrolled actions, forty-two (or 61 percent) recorded the defendant present through his Exchequer accounts (as sheriff, customer, tax collector, royal bailiff). This gave the edge to the plaintiff because once a defendant was present in a common-law court he must either obtain official delays or forfeit his plea by absence. In other words, the defendant could not play the usual games: ignore the writs, or avoid the sheriff's men as well as the plaintiff, or rely on his friendships or his purse. Little wonder then that many of these actions were resolved in less than a year. The next best way to secure appearance was by either of two mesne writs: *corpus cum causa* (3) or *capias ad respondendum* (5). If properly executed, the defendant landed in the Fleet Prison pending the plaintiff's complaint, as happened in eight cases. The defendant might send an attorney (9) or appear in person (3); two actions did not record the manner of appearance, and in five actions the executor or administrator of a deceased official had to answer the complaint. The Exchequer of Pleas, therefore, was exceptional in its ability to secure the defendant's appearance, even if through the attorney who had handled the defendant's accounts.

Attorneys represented forty-seven of the sixty-nine plaintiffs in the enrolled actions; eighteen appeared in person and four plaintiffs' appearances were not specified. Obviously in most actions Exchequer attorneys monopolized appearances; only 15 percent of all litigants appeared in person. Most attorneys were clerks to the clerk of the pleas, the one person responsible for making process and plea enrollments in Exchequer litigation; the rest worked for other Exchequer officials. The clerks had a strong closed shop. In 1506–1507, Robert Castelton, Thomas Broke, Thomas Petytt and Thomas Andrewe handled 87 percent of all attorney work in addition to their regular Exchequer duties. So whenever a plaintiff filed his complaint in the Exchequer one of the clerks ordinarily thenceforth represented him throughout the litigation. Most litigants might never set foot in the Exchequer. No mention was made of legal counsel, although lawyers probably appeared before the barons in everyone of these actions. Exchequer officials completely dominated proceedings and appearances, but never the actual pleadings at bar.

Actions began by written bill, in English, stating the plaintiff's facts, formal accusation and request for remedy and damages. Of the sixty-nine enrolled actions in 1506–1507, forty-five (65 percent) began by bill. Eleven more opened with an original writ issued from the Exchequer: of debt (six), trespass (four), and account (one). The remainder originated prior to Michaelmas term, 1506. Judicial process had been issued, and, probably after court-granted delays in appearance and difficulties in executing writs, the actions finally could proceed. Thirteen enrolled actions began by noting that the sheriff *preceptum fuit;* the order might have been a writ of *capias ad respondendum* (nine actions) ordering seizure of the defendant, of *scire facias* (three) to secure the defendant's appearance when execution for a debt judgment was requested, or of *fieri facias* (one) when the sheriff was ordered to collect a specific debt award made earlier by the barons.

Exchequer litigation during the four terms knew no special days of the week. One could initiate actions any time, and the dates for the 1506–1507 actions revealed this: Sundays (three), Mondays (twelve), Tuesdays (six), Wednesdays (eleven), Thursdays (eleven), Fridays (fifteen), and Saturdays (eleven). The barons usually sat on all of these days, hearing accounts and actions, excepting only major holy days. All mesne process was returnable on regular return days in each term. And as one might expect, over two-thirds of the enrolled actions (forty-five of sixty-nine total) originated in London and Middlesex, where Exchequer accounts were taken. Beyond that a sprinkling of twenty-four suits dotted England's map from York to Southampton, Hereford to Norfolk, with one-third concentrated in the home counties around London.

So far we have not gone beyond the first step in the actual judicial procedure, the point where the barons recorded receipt of the complaints. We have not heard from the defendants. We do not know what truth, if any, existed in the plaintiff's retelling of events. The above data came directly from the recorded bill or returned writ. What we do know is that Henry VII's Exchequer of Pleas in 1506–1507 mainly operated for private subjects in and around London suing their local officials (*i.e.*, Exchequer accountants) for debts and damages. The results of these accusations must be studied in detail.

One measure of a law court's effectiveness and popular confidence is the speed with which actions are brought before it after the alleged offenses. In the sixty-nine enrolled actions, only twenty-one came within six months of the offense (*e.g.*, due date on a debt). Nineteen injuries were at least one year old before the action was initiated, and another nineteen were two or more years old. In ten actions, the date of the offense or injury could not be determined. Even if these last ten were added to the first twenty-one, less than half of the actions were based on recent events. The preponderance of actions for debt would justify some delays, while nonlitigious attempts at collection or compromise occurred. And actions were as slow coming before the barons as they were in moving toward judicial resolution.

Because most defendants were *de jure* present at the initiation of the action, by way of their accounts, there was good reason to expect early pleadings. But in twenty-three actions (33 percent of sixty-nine enrolled) the defendant made no plea, simply asked for and received respite, and the plea roll stopped with eternal silence there. Perhaps these actions were settled out of court. In that way the court had played the important role of bringing the parties together. Of course we have no evidence that these twenty-three actions were ever settled, within or without the Exchequer.

For the remaining two-thirds of the enrolled actions, twenty-three ended with a full award (debt plus damages) to plaintiff. In nine of these the defendant either pleaded guilty (three) or defaulted appearance (six). Ten others pleaded *nichil dicit in barram et exclusionem* against the accusation, so the barons made full awards to the plaintiffs. And in four actions trial juries gave verdicts, all for the plaintiffs. In addition to these twenty-three, seven more actions effectively ended for the plaintiffs. The barons ordered writs of *cerciorari* to localities for damage assessments in three actions, two upon pleas of *nichil dicit* and one when the barons rejected a plea of *non est culpabilis*. And in four other actions, defendants pleaded *nichil dicit*, the plaintiffs requested judgment, but the record ended without the barons' award. Finally, Sheriff Sir John Savage of Worcestershire defaulted appearance to Lady Margaret's suit against him, and the barons immediately amerced him for 20s. on grounds of an insufficient writ return. So in at least thirty-one actions (*i.e.* 45 percent) the plaintiff won.

Defendants entered pleas in the remaining fifteen actions enrolled, but the Exchequer record ended variously. In seven instances (on five pleas of not guilty and two of *non est culpabilis*, *i.e.*, a not guilty plea to a trespass accusation) juries were called by the barons but never came, and the actions ended unresolved in the court. In four other actions the defendant entered a plea of not guilty (three) or *non est culpabilis* (one), asked for and received respite, and the record promptly ended. The one action of account, *Stokys* v. *Barley* (cited earlier), ended with the barons' order for Exchequer audit.

Finally, three separate defendants entered not-guilty pleas

in actions of debt, but each demanded trial by wager-of-law.[13] Normally when plaintiff accused and defendant denied, the issue of fact (what happened?) was joined in a deadlock that the trial jury would break through its verdict. But particularly in actions of debt, defendants could wage law instead of standing before a trial jury. To wage law in the Exchequer the defendant had to come *cum lege sua* before the barons with *duodecima manu ad proficiendum legem suam*. These three actions in 1506–1507 ended with plaintiffs' defaulting appearances and abandoning their complaints. Each defendant's twelve companions, therefore, did not need to swear oaths to his credibility and honest character; that would have been as legally sufficient as a trial jury's verdict of innocent. So it was only in these three instances that a defendant clearly won, as opposed to the thirty-one won by plaintiffs out of the sixty-nine actions enrolled for 1506–1507. Lay participation in judicial activity, therefore, only occurred with the four juries that rendered a verdict. Potentially it would have happened in the three wager-of-law actions and with the seven juries called but never in appearance. Laity had little personal involvement amongst the Exchequer professionals.

Finally, one surprising result of this quantitative analysis is that only six plaintiffs in the Exchequer used the *quo minus* process. From its earliest recorded activity the Exchequer allowed plaintiffs owing money to the king to sue actions of debt against third parties in its common-law jurisdiction. By collecting from the third party, the plaintiff would be able to repay the king. The medieval formula varied considerably, but the form by the Tudor period was simply called *quo minus*. The plaintiff's motive in suing the defendant was to obtain money enabling payment of his own debt to the king; if he could not sue in this manner, he might be "less able" to repay the king. Actions of *quo minus* appeared with such infrequency through the fifteenth century that we can reasonably expect

13. One defendant did plead guilty to part of the complaint and the barons ordered an award for that part only. He was allowed to wage his law for the remainder of the alleged debt.

that the assertion of an extant royal debt was truthful. In all six *quo minus* actions in 1506–1507, one or both litigants was an Exchequer official or royal accountant. More remarkable is that two of the *quo minus* actions were not for debt but for trespass and contempt, and none of the *quo minus* actions were resolved before the barons but probably settled out of court.

Quo minus and wager of law were historically associated with the Exchequer jurisdiction for actions of debt and, as we see here from the number of times employed, exaggeratedly so for the fifteenth and early sixteenth centuries. Professor Milsom, working from the Year Books, has noted that "it is asserted in 1496 and again in 1535 that it was common practice to sue executors" by *quo minus* in the Exchequer, although Justice Antony Fitzherbert denied this in 1535.[14] And in recent articles on late medieval contract law, Professor William McGovern, Jr., comments further that "paucity of evidence . . . suggests that it was not common to resort to the Exchequer to collect ordinary simple debts after the debtor's death"[15] or, for that matter, before death, by *quo minus*. Obviously ignorance or doubt surrounded *quo minus*, probably because the early Tudor barons strictly construed the necessity for plaintiff's royal debt and did not allow fictional claims. The analysis of this plea roll substantiates McGovern's argument from the Year Books and Reports. He carefully traced the growing competition to debt from those actions, particularly assumpsit, that developed out of trespass. Such actions did not permit wager of law by the defendant. Actions of debt could be maintained without producing written and sealed proof of the obligation; when

14. S. F. C. Milsom, "Sale of Goods in the Fifteenth Century," *Law Quarterly Review*, LXXVII (1961), 265. His random sampling of plea rolls for the court of Common Pleas between 1358 and 1549 indicated a shift from wager-of-law to trial by jury during the period in actions of debt.

15. William M. McGovern, Jr., "Contract in Medieval England: Wager of Law and the Effect of Death," *Iowa Law Review*, LIV (1968), 44. See also his "Contract in Medieval England: The Necessity for *Quid Pro Quo* and a Sum Certain," *The American Journal of Legal History*, XIII (1969), 173–201; "The Enforcement of Oral Covenants Prior to Assumpsit," *Northwestern University Law Review*, LXV (1970), 576–614; and, "The Enforcement of Informal Contracts in the Later Middle Ages," *California Law Review*, LIX (1971), 1145–193.

this happened, the defendant could use wager of law to avoid jury trial. The Exchequer of Pleas by 1506–1507 sat trapped in a world relying more and more on written, formal obligations for debt (*i.e.*, a specialty) and on trial by jury. Indeed, one-third of the plaintiffs for debt in 1506–1507 produced the original obligations, thus precluding wager of law by the defendant and virtually assuring full judgment to the plaintiff. Actions without written obligations produced before the barons usually remained unresolved on the plea roll, probably indicating compromise between the parties out of court.

In fact, *quo minus* was used only six times, and wager of law three times, during the entire Exchequer year studied. Both had little relevance for litigants able to recover their debts by the newer actions related to trespass or by producing the written obligation before the barons. And the barons' apparent reluctance to encourage *quo minus* actions based on a fictional debt to the king aided the Exchequer's decline in litigious significance. Much later, by the mid–seventeenth century, *quo minus* regularly rested on the fiction and such actions helped rebuild Exchequer business in competition with the court of Common Pleas.[16] For the early Tudor period, however, the Exchequer of Pleas depended for its major business on an increasingly narrower market in actions of debt. While Common Pleas continued to handle thousands of new and old actions for debt and trespass each term, the Exchequer languished.

If the Exchequer of Pleas was losing its special advantage in actions of debt, what about its special ability to attract litigation against officials regarding abuses of office? Where did Henry VII's subjects make complaints against officials for abuses or mistakes of office? In the Exchequer of Pleas there was an obvious dearth of accusations for peculation, harassment, extor-

---

16. Jenkinson and Formoy, *Exchequer of Pleas*, c–cii, found an earlier version of *quo minus* and that the alleged royal debt was also probably true. Harold Wurzel, "The Origin and Development of *Quo Minus*," *The Yale Law Journal*, XLIX (1939), 39–64, relies on Year Books and law reports exclusively to show that the fiction arose sometime in the century before 1660. Like many legal historians, he manages to treat the history of a law court or an action without consulting the plea rolls.

tion, false imprisonment, contempts, or unjust distraints. Such trespasses made up a majority of complaints in Edward I's court. And in 1506–1507 occasionally such charges appeared on the king's remembrancer's memoranda roll or in king's Bench, where the plaintiff might work his vengeance by obtaining fine and imprisonment, but not damages. He could also turn to Common Pleas for damages, to the conciliar courts, or to the equity side of Chancery. Still, the Exchequer was where local officials made accounts, even after Henry VII removed all land revenue accounting into the Chamber. Thus officials remained sitting ducks in the Exchequer for potential plaintiffs, but precious few tried to knock them down. And the Chamber-Exchequer competition probably had little impact on the members of Exchequer, and especially local, officials. The latter continued to provide points of most immediate popular contact for royal administration, and Henry VII did not replace sheriffs, escheators, customers, tax collectors, or bailiffs with Chamber and conciliar minions. It is possible that during the century preceding 1506–1507, Englishmen lost the habit of prosecuting their local official's transgressions, at least in common-law courts.

The Chancery and the newer conciliar courts provided the only alternatives in royal justice to common-law courts. Henry VII's councillors, sitting in Star Chamber and at Requests, apparently gave little encouragement to popular actions against officials. The Court of Requests, at least to 1547, almost exclusively attracted civil pleas for debt (here in direct competition with the Exchequer of Pleas), land recovery, and disputed bonds, while Henry VII's Star Chamber concentrated attention on forcible entry with riot, assaults, and disputed property.[17] The Exchequer of Pleas continued to sink as a jurisdiction

17. Stanford E. Lehmberg, "Star Chamber: 1485–1509," *The Huntington Library Quarterly*, XXIV (May, 1961), 189–214; C. G. Bayne (ed.), *Select Cases in the Council of Henry VII*, Selden Society, LXXV (London, 1958); and, the review of Bayne by G. R. Elton, *English Historical Review*, LXXIV (1959), 686–90. Lehmberg found only 128 cases after Bayne had uncovered 194 separate proceedings in the Star Chamber. I have here tabulated the types of actions using the PRO portfolios for-Star Chamber and Requests.

in which officials could be called to popular account, but this was not complemented by any rising conciliar moon in the Star Chamber.

Rather it was the equity side of Chancery that had taken up the Exchequer of Pleas' slackness here. The fifteenth-century Chancery filled with complaints against officialdom.[18] Like a church litany, petitions piled up before the lord chancellor detailing false arrests and imprisonments, extortions, officially condoned or conducted tumults, replevins refused, failures to acknowledge receipts of rents or fines, illegal distraints, brutal assaults. The lord chancellor, as the king's prime legal officer, had assumed responsibility for what C. G. Bayne called "offenses against public justice." By Henry VII's reign these actions accounted for a significant proportion of Chancery business; and a brief tabulation indicates that such proceedings expanded quantitatively under the Lords Cardinals Morton, Warham, and Wolsey. Procedures were simpler, and probably less expensive, relative to the common law courts, with litigants confronting each other through bills, answers, and depositions taken by commissioners wherever and whenever necessary. Also, like the newer conciliar courts, most Chancery litigation originated outside London and environs.[19] Paradoxically, then, the equity court of Chancery was more commonly administering royal justice throughout the realm than at least one common-law court.

Exchequer of Pleas litigation in 1506–1507 would indicate that the court was a backwater to a swelling sea of litigation in other common-law courts, Chancery, and the newer conciliar

18. *Lists of Early Chancery Proceedings Preserved in the Public Record Office, 1386–1515,* PRO Lists and Indexes XII, XVI, XX, and XXIX (London, 1901–1908). William Paley Baildon (ed.), *Select Cases in Chancery A. D. 1364 to 1471,* Selden Society, X (London, 1896), is a disappointment because of its sketchy, descriptive introduction and its poor selection of documents. The pre-Elizabethan Chancery awaits its historian(s), particularly for a quantitative analysis of its litigation.

19. I have not tabulated Chancery proceedings from the originals in the PRO but only from the lists cited above. Margaret E. Avery, "An Evaluation of the Effectiveness of the Court of Chancery under the Lancastrian Kings," *Law Quarterly Review,* LXXXVI (1970), 84–97, provides an excellent sketch of procedure but no systematic study of the actual cases, and so the title promises more than the article produces.

courts. For decades before and after, people were not suing less; they simply were not coming into the Exchequer of Pleas. In volume of business it recorded less than one percent of the civil pleadings in common-law courts each year. Its jurisdiction rested on the privilege of Exchequer officials and accountants to sue and be sued in their own court, but by 1506–1507 the Exchequer of Pleas had become mainly a debtors' court for London-Middlesex individuals suing officials, notably former sheriffs. The *quo minus* procedure was not exploited until much later. When individuals had complaints against officials they more than likely took them into the Chancery where process was more direct, there were fewer delays, lay involvement existed through depositions of witnesses (akin to wager-of-law), fewer fees were required, no corruptible jury trials, and the issue was one of fact and not mainly one of law. Like all common-law courts, and as this analysis has indicated, the Exchequer of Pleas interposed attorneys, lawyers, juries, writs, sheriffs, bailiffs, and clerks between the plaintiff and his many days in court. Once before the barons, the conflict would be resolved within one year, for the plaintiff, and by court professionals.

In its limited area of actions for debt, the Exchequer of Pleas appeared to be effective but standing still while royal justice expanded into new areas of law, especially in contract, the prerogative courts of Star Chamber and Requests boomed with business and popularity, and a reforming royal bureaucracy, at least for the moment, acted at the Exchequer's expense. In 1542, parliamentary statute (33 Henry VIII, c. 39) recognized an equity jurisdiction within the Exchequer to complement the Exchequer of Pleas. Further study might indicate that by the seventeenth century the two jurisdictions had expanded to accommodate new developments in the law and new needs of royal subjects. Here we must conclude that, having defined litigious activity for 1506–1507, the early Tudor Exchequer of Pleas had then a very minor and narrow role in royal justice. Building upon Professor Richardson's description of the

Exchequer's general loss of power in fiscal matters, it is obvious that its plea jurisdiction also suffered in isolation. In such circumstances, fees would not flow and litigants need not queue to sue in the Exchequer of Pleas.

W. J. Jones

the exchequer of chester in the last years of elizabeth i[1]

A modern writer can doubt if Cheshire has any great individual-
ity, and indeed the traveler going south or west towards the
Welsh massif will find the same kind of agricultural setting.
Elsewhere, however, natural boundaries invite memory of
exclusive characteristics which have now passed away. To the
east, hills announce the advent of Derbyshire and Staffordshire,
and to the north and northwest there flow the Dee and Mersey,
their estuaries parted by the Wirral peninsula. Between the
upper reaches of the Mersey and the Thamé, a thin arm of
the county reaches up to Yorkshire. These features once meant
something, and Tudor inhabitants of Cheshire spoke of going
into the "country of England." They were aware of Wales, but
old disputes were remembered more for pride than militancy,
and Chester was accustomed to Montgomeryshire girls serving

1. Throughout this piece, reference to the Exchequer is to the palatine institution
under consideration. The national institution is described as the Exchequer at Westminster.

as maids. This city was discovering that the silting of the Dee meant ruin—in 1594–95 it was ranked only twelfth out of eighteen outports—but it remained the artery of a "port" which extended from Barmouth to north Lancashire. Its cathedral was the center of a diocese which extended into several counties, and it has been well described as "the only town in the northwest with the dignity and stature of a true city." [2]

Chester was the county town, but it was also the capital of the county palatine of Chester and Flint. Hence the castle, headquarters of the county palatine, was legally outside the city, and the two authorities were periodically in conflict. Dissension of this kind could be found elsewhere. The Elizabethan structure of institutions was complex, and not too much should be made of the occasional outburst. A man living in Cheshire, for example, would be aware that there was a lord lieutenant, a vice-admiral, a sheriff, and a commission of the peace. There would be musters, a county court, quarter and petty sessions. There were manorial and leet courts, constables, and royal foresters. Borough and hundred courts enjoyed an active existence, and the city of Chester embraced Crownmote, Pentice, Portmote, and quarter sessions. Other towns also had their privilege: citizens of Congleton were exempted by charter from appearing in outside courts. The authority of the chamberlain of the county palatine, based most clearly upon the Exchequer court, was expressed through a host of officials. The justices of Chester, palatine officials, were also responsible for the Chester circuit of the Great Sessions of Wales. The bishop of Chester looked down upon another hierarchy—chancellor, archdeacons, churchwardens—and he was probably unique in having two consistory courts. The parish was also a unit of lay government. The archbishop of York had a real authority, the bishop of Durham had claims, and there was a slate of ecclesiastical com-

2. T.W. Freeman, H. B. Rodgers, R. H. Kinvig, *Lancashire, Cheshire, and the Isle of Man* (London, 1966), 45, 159, 180; G. Dyfnallt Owen, *Elizabethan Wales: The Social Scene* (Cardiff, 1962), 69; D. M. Woodward, *The Trade of Elizabethan Chester* (Hull, 1970), 1; J. Beck, *Tudor Cheshire* (Chester, 1969), 3, 9, 84.

missioners. The Duchy of Lancaster existed in Cheshire, and, though repelled, the Council in the Marches of Wales, of which the chief justice of Chester was sometimes virtual vice-president, peered over the border. Within the county, a multitude of ad hoc commissions were always being appointed to handle particular tasks. From afar, the Privy Council and great officers of state sent out a stream of directives. Despite limitations, Cheshire men sued or were sued at Westminster, and the intervention of national courts might be necessary in affairs which touched upon the competence of government. In 1568, after disputes over the conduct of quarter sessions, Lord Keeper Nicholas Bacon and Chief Justice Dyer ordered the matter from the Chancery bench at Westminster. Rarely has the organization of a society been so complex, suggestive of an interlocking and overlapping jigsaw of diverse pieces. Our conception of English government and the structure of courts will be dangerously unbalanced if we always begin at the center and ignore the fringes. The county palatine of Chester, halfway between these extremes, provides an illustration of Dr. Williams' observation that "throughout England and Wales the Tudors developed a hierarchy of courts to supervise and control national life."[3]

Government means authority and rule, management and organization. The success, however limited, of any system implies a degree of acceptance and participation. The Tudor world implicitly acknowledged Aristotle's maxim that governors and governed are woven of the same kind of cloth and yet are inherently different. The web of institutions and the intricacy of authority and responsibility were, in both action and theory, bound together by the Tudor crown, and the great chain of being was as true of instiutions as it was supposed to be true of moral, political, and social behavior. A great minister might have high thoughts on government, but he knew

3. R. A. Marchant, *The Church under the Law, 1560–1640* (Cambridge, 1969), 14; Public Records Office, Chancery Entry Books of Orders and Decrees, C.33/37, ff. 398–99 hereinafter cited PRO; P. Williams, "The Welsh Borderland under Queen Elizabeth," *Welsh History Review* (1960), 30.

how much depended on justices of the peace and others. Latitude was essential, but command might have to be supplemented with reprimand, perhaps in the Star Chamber at Westminster or in the Exchequer at Chester. Private persons also fought their litigious battles, but in so far as the courts were able to exercise control they were supervising the peace and organization of the country. From this point of view, it is misleading to think in terms of central and local government or to write of Elizabethan society as though administrative and legal history are separate entities. The justices of Great Sessions have been described as "key men in Welsh administration" [4] and the same could be said about all judges, just as a moment's reflection should tell us that most great men who are instinctively labeled administrators were also judges. In both law and politics, appreciation of the centralization of authority was a characteristic of the Tudor state. Other things were also happening. Emphasis on Parliament pointed towards London and Westminster, as did the massive and striking early Tudor reorganization of financial administration. Yet there were some indications in the opposite direction, and perhaps we would be more aware of the Henrician attempt to restructure society on the basis of provincial forms if the Council of the West had survived. Centralization of authority was indeed a major characteristic, and in this, revenue was vital. Compromise had to be allowed, however, since authority must be translated into effective power. Hence the decentralization of much bureaucracy was accepted. But both compromise and decentralization were rotting at the roots, although it was the Stuarts who had to discover this.

Elizabethans believed that Chester was the most ancient county palatine and that it existed by prescription. This, as Barraclough has shown, was a theory formulated in the sixteenth century "by persons interested in the maintenance of the county palatine and its courts." It is the earldom of Chester which can be traced back to the reign of William I and then only to 1071. In the twelfth century, royal legal innovation

4. Williams, "The Welsh Borderland," 22.

was imitated, procedure by writ developed, the status of the justiciar was enhanced, and the earl's secretariat acquired a new efficiency thus deserving the name of "chancery." This, together with his *camera*, developed into what would later be known as the Exchequer of Chester. After Henry III had annexed the earldom to the crown, local organization was further adapted and expanded in line with current trends. Royal officials moved in, but this did not mean conformity with some kind of national pattern. "It is after 1237 that emphasis on Cheshire custom as an inalienable right, different at most points from the law of England, becomes articulate, providing a popular foundation for the new conception of the county as a palatinate with a distinctive place in English government." The real history of Cheshire as a palatine, in the sense that it represented "royal powers in devolution," stretched from the mid-thirteenth to the mid-sixteenth century. Flint was added after Wales had been conquered and divided into shires. Vicissitudes included elevation into a principality, ordained by Richard II but quashed by Henry IV.[5]

The reign of Henry VIII was crucial in binding the area into a conformity with the rest of England. Henry VII had made *quo warranto* inquiries, but the real change came in 1536 when the lord chancellor was authorized to appoint justices of the peace for Cheshire. In 1542 the system of avowries was abolished, and in the following year came representation in Parliament. The justice of Chester commenced his career as head of a Welsh circuit. Most financial administration was transferred to the Court of Augmentations, and when this was dissolved its system of declaring accounts and granting leases was continued by the Exchequer at Westminster. Customs receipts for leather, iron, and wine were handled at Chester until the end of Mary's reign when William Glaseor, vice-chamberlain

5. E. Coke, *The Fourth Part of the Institutes of the Laws of England* (London, ed. of 1669), 211; *HMC Hatfield*, IV, 446; W. S. Holdsworth, *A History of English Law* (London, 1922–52), I, 117, 119; G. Barraclough, "The Earldom and County Palatine of Chester," *Trans. Hist. Soc. Lancs. and Ches.*, CIII (1953), 24, 34, 35, 37, 40, 43–45; R. Somerville, *History of the Duchy of Lancaster* (London, 1953), I, 41.

of the county palatine, became collector of customs, subsidies, and tunnage and poundage. He was required to render account into the Exchequer at Westminster, and this meant that Chester was now firmly part of the national customs system. The local Exchequer was henceforth only an accounting department for profits and fees of the seal and takings from legal proceedings.[6]

"The existence of the palatine courts no longer spelt immunity from, but simply an alternative form of application of the law common to the whole country." This assessment by Barraclough is fair, and it is also right to stress that a confirmation of judicial privilege in 1569 underlined the fact that national conformity had replaced provincial eccentricity. Even more apparent is the mid-Tudor collapse of financial responsibility. Dr. K. P. Wilson, noting the termination of the chamberlain's account rolls which extend from 1301, remarks that the independent Exchequer at Chester was "virtually dismantled." It is at this point that we must be careful not to write off the institution. As a court of law it began to look increasingly impressive, and in the first two decades of Elizabeth's reign it won jurisdictional battles against the Council in the Marches of Wales and the city of Chester. New clerical and procedural regulations were attempted, and the court was certainly influential in supervising other courts within the area of its jurisdiction. The physical appearance of its home was improved when the Parliament House within Chester Castle was rebuilt. Rules of jurisdiction enforced by great courts at Westminster would represent a creeping confinement, but a commentator writing at the beginning of James I's reign could applaud early Elizabethan developments: "The court of Exchequer began to flourish, being restored to the fairest flower in her garland, and her plume furnished again with the feathers she had lost." After a relatively insignificant chamberlain, Sir Rees Mansell, three noblemen

---

6. Barraclough, 45; R. Stewart-Brown, "The Exchequer of Chester," *EHR*, LVII (1942), 296; *Records of the Court of Augmentations relating to Wales and Monmouthshire*, ed. E. A. Lewis and J. Conway Davies (Cardiff, 1954), lix; *Chester Customs Accounts, 1301–1566*, ed. K. P. Wilson, (Lancs, and Ches. Rec. Soc. CXI, 1969), 6–7; Woodward, 75.

were appointed: Robert, earl of Leicester, flanked by two earls of Derby. In 1594 the Queen appointed Thomas Egerton, a commoner who was outstanding among her lawyers. His vice-chamberlain was Peter Warburton, a future justice of the Common Pleas, and so the Exchequer had an extremely capable bench. When Egerton became lord keeper, the power of appointing justices of the peace was once again in the hands of the man who was chamberlain. It is clear that the Exchequer at Chester had not been dismantled, but the emphasis of its functions was altered.[7]

Leicester, chamberlain from 1565 until his death, supported his deputy, Glaseor, against the Welsh Council and the city of Chester, but he was most worried by the internal organization of the Exchequer. In May, 1574, after consultation with Sir William Cordell, master of the rolls, and Thomas Bromley, solicitor general and future lord chancellor, the earl issued a set of orders dealing with the proper making of original writs, the sealing of process, and the custody of the seal when both the chamberlain and the vice-chamberlain were away. There were to be new books for noting grants and process which passed the seal. Major officials were in the future to attend the court regularly, and the pursuivant of the county palatine or his deputy was to be available at suitable times. Irregular proliferation of officials was denounced, and henceforth there were to be no more than four or six attorneys. Pleadings concerned with matters worth more than £5 were no longer to be accepted without the signature of counsel. Times for hearing causes, each covering about three weeks, were fixed for the four law terms, and it was stipulated that difficult legal points were to be composed into cases and submitted to the justice of Chester. Leicester was particularly insistent that the court must provide genuine equitable relief while not offending against principles of law. This was beyond the current capacity of the bench, and so a slate of qualified assistants was named,

7. Barraclough, 45; *Chester Customs Accounts*, 18; "The Rights and Jurisdiction of the County Palatine of Chester," ed. J. B. Yates, *Chetham Misc.* (1856), 24.

headed by Justice Harpur of the Common Pleas. An assistant was always to sit for the hearing of any case that was not entirely trivial.[8]

Leicester had made an important initiative, but his orders were too loose and depended unduly upon voluntary cooperation. His wishes were flouted, and in 1578, after consulting Cordell and Bromley, he issued further instructions. The baron and the attorneys were again required to attend the court, and unauthorized persons were forbidden to sit there, remove records, or otherwise engage in official business.[9]

Leicester's orders suggest that faction was threatening to tear the court apart. Glaseor, the vice-chamberlain, was locked in a struggle with William Tatton and John Yerworth, joint holders of the office of baron or clerk, and Alexander Cotes, the deputy baron. The baron was supposed to be the key official of the court, and in 1542 Lord Keeper Wriothesley had attempted to clarify the situation. The baron was to have free access to the court and to possess his own key. He was to make and write all process, writings, and grants under the seal. He was also to write all copies, decrees, orders, and rolls, and to engross records appertaining to his office. In return he was to present quarterly accounts to the chamberlain, and a division of the profits was stipulated. Unfortunately this settlement did not anticipate the development of a deputy who would control most of the work, and it said nothing about the right to appoint clerical assistants. It was around these matters, notably the division of profits, that trouble flared during the 1570's.[10]

Leicester, finding that his remonstrations were ignored, urged George Bromley, chief justice of Chester, and Thomas Egerton, appointed solicitor general in 1581, to sit in the Exchequer whenever possible. Entreating the latter "both to discharge me and to help your country," the earl wrote of his obligations as chamberlain. He acknowledged that he had a deputy but stated that the place was too much for one man.

8. PRO, Chester Entry Books, Chester 14/3, pp. 517–19.
9. PRO, Chester 14/3, p. 520.   10. PRO, Chester 14/3, pp. 510–11.

Leicester knew that decisions of the Exchequer had been challenged, and he was beginning to have serious doubts about Glaseor. In August, 1581, pointing out that the presence of expert assistants would be beneficial, he directly commanded Glaseor to obey his wishes. By 1583 Egerton was assisting at Chester whenever possible, and one plaintiff specifically requested that he be on the bench when the case was to be heard. In 1584 a new list of assistants included the earl of Derby, the bishop of Chester, Henry Townshend, second justice at Chester, Egerton, and Warburton.[11]

The dispute over the baron's office, in the meantime, had plumbed fresh depths of absurdity as the combatants and their clerks withheld documents from each other, so threatening to bring the court to a disreputable halt. Cotes was accused of embezzling documents and wrongful appropriation of fees. He was suspended, but there was an old agreement of 1575 that disputes between himself and Yerworth should be submitted to the arbitration of Egerton. Leicester now asked both Egerton and Serjeant John Puckering, a future lord keeper, to help. Independent auditors were employed, and a decision was reached in the spring of 1584. Cotes was severely criticized, but he was reinstated because he was not the sole culprit. Leicester acknowledged that he had been misinformed.[12]

Leicester's difficulties illustrate the problems of a big man who had accepted a sinecure but still felt responsible even though practical authority had been assigned to a deputy. Glaseor, entrenched behind his patent, could disrupt the chamberlain's attempt to impose his authority upon warring factions within the Exchequer. Leicester, however, was determined to obtain internal harmony and to see the court acting as an effective "Chancery" for the county palatine. If the Exchequer was to be a real court of equity there must be a proper order of doing things, and this meant capable lawyers on the bench. In 1584, after naming the new assistants and trying to settle

11. PRO, Chester 14/3, pp. 454, 458, 459, 520–21, 534, 538, 560.
12. PRO, Chester 14/3, pp. 494–509.

internal disputes, he issued another set of orders. Unless an assistant learned in the law was present, the vice-chamberlain was barred from hearing most cases, from granting injunctions and prohibitions and from mitigating fines, forfeitures, or penalties. Quashing his previous ineffective orders, Leicester directed the court to sit for hearings twice a year, beginning at the time of the assizes and continuing for a week thereafter. Any order set down by one of the assistants learned in the law must be entered in the book and executed. If the vice-chamberlain transgressed these orders, every other official had a duty to inform the Earl. It was a shattering reproof to Glaseor, and henceforth the assistants would make all the important decisions. Decrees were entered as made with their advice, and their signatures were appended.[13]

Leicester's efforts had provided Egerton with his first opportunity to act as a judge on something approaching a regular basis. However, he was busy as solicitor general, and it followed that Peter Warburton was probably the most active assistant at Chester. A contemporary of Egerton, he was born in 1540 and called to the bar at Lincoln's Inn in 1572. Sheriff of Cheshire in 1583, he was admitted a freeman of the city in 1584 and served as member of Parliament in 1586 and 1589. The earl of Derby, Leicester's successor, made him attorney general of the palatine in 1592. After Thomas Morte had replaced Glaseor for a few months in 1593, Warburton was appointed vice-chamberlain. He assumed the order of the coif, but his prospects were cast into a shade when Derby died in September.[14]

Both the new earl, Ferdinando, and Egerton, who had established a residence in the city of Chester, wanted the chamberlainship. The earl implied that the appointment of a commoner would be improper, and he instanced the great peers who had been chamberlains of Chester. Burghley, worried by this line of attack, informed Egerton in December, 1593, that there might be difficulties, and he requested information. Eger-

13. PRO, Chester 14/3, pp. 523–24.   14. D. K. Rep., XXXIX, App., 60.

ton, who had been attorney general since 1592, responded swiftly with a general description. He stressed that though Elizabeth had appointed noblemen "yet in ancient time men of much meaner sort for the most part had the place." In February, 1594, Warburton told Robert Cecil that Derby had promised him the office of vice-chamberlain but that he had few hopes since it seemed that Egerton would be appointed. He described the attorney general, whom he had known since birth, as a man of great learning and integrity. Warburton would not pursue a hopeless quest, but he would be glad to serve should Egerton want him. He professed to assume that Egerton would exercise the office in person, and it is impossible to know whether this was innocence or naïveté on his part. Many people knew already that Egerton would be the next master of the rolls. In any case, on March 2 Egerton was appointed chamberlain, and ten days later the queen permitted Warburton's continuance as vice-chamberlain. This was formally ratified on March 14. On April 10 Egerton also became master of the rolls. A few days later Derby died in mysterious circumstances. Rumors that he had been bewitched or poisoned were current, and Egerton took a leading part in subsequent inquiries.[15]

Egerton, born illegitimate, had enjoyed a slow but sure elevation in county, profession, and state. The bastard had defeated the earl. Years later he would take the earl's widow—a less satisfactory bargain—and his son would marry one of the coheiresses. Already chamberlain of Chester and master of the rolls, he acquired the stewardship of Denbigh and in 1596 became lord keeper. His personal estate grew, and in 1598, by devise on the death of Richard Brereton of Tatton, who had married Egerton's legitimate half-sister, he inherited Brereton estates. It was one of the most staggering success stories of later Elizabethan England.

As chamberlain of Chester, Egerton never relinquished

15. *HMC Hatfield*, IV, 376, 378, 392, 437, 446, 508, 515, 517; Huntington Library, Bridgewater and Ellesmere MSS, 18, 31, 1402, 1748; *CSP Dom.* 1591–94, pp. 438, 525.

supreme authority, but the practical running of the court
devolved upon his deputy. Warburton's dual position was not
sensible, and in 1595 he was replaced as attorney general by
Hugh Hughes. The official baron was William Tatton, but he
was forced out in 1595 in favor of Egerton's son and heir,
Thomas, who appointed Cotes and William Powell as his
deputies. After the younger Thomas Egerton died in Ireland,
his brother John assumed the office. Throughout these years
old disputes still festered. There was constant litigation between
Cotes and Tatton, and William Sutton joined the fray in suing
Cotes over profits. Among other officials, note should be taken
of the comptroller, Hugh Beeston, who was also receiver-
general of North Wales and the county palatine. The seal keeper
was important, as was the prothonotary and clerk of the crown
for Cheshire and Flintshire, an office held since 1507 by suc-
ceeding members of the Birkenhed family. Officials particularly associated with the daily life of the court were the
examiner—who at the beginning of James's reign had a
deputy—and the attorneys or clerks. Leicester's attempt at
restriction had failed: there were nine attorneys in 1603. There
was a carpenter, a mason, a surveyor, and a keeper of the
castle gaol. The offices of crier and messenger, technically
separate, were held by the same person in Egerton's time. The
Exchequer's bailiff itinerant, pursuivant for the county palatine,
worked through a deputy. His functions included the making
of warrants upon attachments, but some litigants tried to escape
fees by executing attachments directly. This was forbidden by
Egerton. The common-law judges, despite early Elizabethan
difficulties, must also be included in any description of the
Exchequer, and they provided increasingly valuable assistance
on the bench. Initially there had been only one justice, but
in 1578 he was restyled "chief justice" and a second or puisne
justice was added. Sir Richard Shuttleworth was chief justice
from 1589 until his death in 1599, being replaced by Sir Richard
Lewknor. Sir Henry Townshend held the second position from
its inauguration until his death in 1621. These justices, who

heard crown and common pleas, were responsible for the counties of Chester, Flint, Denbigh, and Montgomery—the last two had been added in 1542—and made circuit twice a year, sitting in each county town for six days. The county palatine also had its own list of serjeants-at-law, numbering between four and eight.[16]

Egerton, as chamberlain, had an interest in maintaining his rights but he appears to have made little effort to regulate officials or to improve recordkeeping and clerical methods. The system of records remained diffuse and disorganized. Pleadings and the machinery of evidence did not develop that kind of standard which was being set by Chancery, Exchequer, and Star Chamber at Westminster. It is these contrasts, not the general similarity of procedural outline, which must be noticed.

Bills of complaint, addressed to the chamberlain, contained brief statements of the alleged wrong. A *subpena* would be solicited but often this process had been obtained beforehand.[17] The plaintiff would conclude with an appeal for equity and conscience, "and this for God's love." The defendant's answer, exhibited on oath, would also embody a simple statement. There are few examples of disclaimer or demurrer: most objections to jurisdiction were apparently handled orally in court on motion of the defense attorney. Replication and rejoinder were often dispensed with and even when used were usually simple statements which reaffirmed the bill and answer, respectively. The defendant might put in a crossbill, and this was sometimes required by the court. Defendants were supposed to appear in person, but they could be licensed to appear through attorney for special reasons such as attendance on the queen's business, age, infirmity, and immediate residence outside the county palatine. The jurisdictional area was not large, and therefore few requests based upon distance or weather alone were likely to be successful. Even so, a number of commissions of *dedimus*

16. *D. K. Rep.*, XXXIX, App., 58–62; PRO, Chester 14/5, pp. 52, 271; PRO, Chester 14/6, f. 95v.; "Rights and Jurisdiction of Chester", 28; P. Williams, *The Council in the Marches of Wales under Elizabeth I* (Cardiff, 1958), 25–26, 137–38; 32 H8 cap. 43.

17. W. J. Jones, *The Elizabethan Court of Chancery* (Oxford, 1967), 191–92.

potestatem to take answer were granted, and in most instances a single commissioner, probably a local gentleman of standing, was named. In any case, defendants had to give surety for their attendance, and two sureties would be needed if the plaintiff deposed that his adversary was "insufficient" to answer the claim in the bill, or if an attachment had been necessary. Sureties were also taken to ensure compliance with court orders. Poor defendants could be admitted *in forma pauperis,* but there is little evidence of precautionary inquiries about their presumed financial inability.[18]

Issue was joined after pleadings had been completed, and often this meant no more than bill and answer. Hence examination of witnesses "to prove the issues" and publication commonly followed the joining of issue, although there are instances of issue being joined simultaneously with an order for publication. Formal examination on both sides through written interrogatories and depositions was normal, but publication might be ordered on one side only, with the stipulation that opposition witnesses were to be examined later. At other times, publication was granted on the understanding that remaining witnesses were to be examined *viva voce* at the hearing. The plaintiff himself could give evidence *viva voce* at the hearing, and it would seem that much evidence considered by the court was contained in oral depositions delivered by the parties before the bench.[19]

Commissions of *dedimus potestatem* to take examinations were restricted to the same kind of circumstances already noted with respect to answers. If it was a joint commission, the plaintiff had to give the defendant written notice—usually seven to ten days—of the time and place, and costs would be shared. If the opponent refused to join, the commission would only be empowered to examine on one side of the case. Commissioners

18. PRO, Chester Rule Book, Chester 14/59, ff. 56, 121v., 142v., 159; PRO, Chester 14/5, pp. 13, 115, 134, 156, 211, 264, 467, 518; PRO, Papers in Causes, Chester 9/2, Pt. 1.

19. PRO, Chester 14/5, pp. 1, 29, 31–32, 75, 401; PRO, Chester 14/59, ff. 15, 74v., 91.

were normally residents of the county palatine since the court had no power in other places, and it was sometimes necessary to enforce return of the commission. None the less some commissions were appointed to examine in the capital. This was made more feasible by Egerton's position, and a Chancery official could be appointed or a person like William Ravenscroft of Lincoln's Inn, one of the palatine serjeants-at-law, who was Egerton's relative by marriage and a personal legal adviser.[20]

Examination of witnesses in perpetual memory, as in the Chancery, was both a procedure and a segment of the court's business. The applicant would have to exhibit a special bill claiming that it was necessary to preserve evidence about boundaries or that the depositions of aged and sick persons might subsequently be needed. If a joint commission was granted, both sides would submit names, and each attorney would choose four from the opposing list. The plaintiff would be responsible for giving written notice—again usually a week or ten days—of the time and place of examination. The defendant did not always agree to join, a circumstance for which the Chancery had developed complex regulations. There do not appear to have been comparable safeguards at Chester, but it would be unwise to assume that none existed. In any case, all examinations of this type could only be exemplified after a special order.[21]

In handling suits the court, like others of its general type, favored referees and arbitrators. Officials of the court, the royal forester, merchants, and local gentlemen were employed. Advice was sought from the justices and, in 1599, with respect to an enclosure dispute, Attorney General Coke advised that verbal consent without consideration did not in law or equity extinguish title. Rejecting a supposed agreement, he said that the lands must be reopened so that all tenants could enter. This certificate was entered as an order of the court. As for arbitration, friends were often called upon, as when it was sus-

20. PRO Chester 14/5, pp. 123, 126, 143, 150, 232, 318, 335, 374, 471.
21. PRO, Chester 14/5, pp. 151, 201, 229, 945; PRO, Chester 14/6, f. 170v.; PRO, Chester 14/59, f, 7v.

pected that there were "causes of dislike" other than those revealed in the pleadings. Arbitrators could be empowered to examine witnesses, and their report—whether or not an accord had been achieved—might be confirmed and decreed by the court.[22]

Many suits, and this is again typical of courts of this kind, did not reach a formal hearing, perhaps because the parties were satisfied with an order. Dismissions on grounds of vexation were frequent, as when a bill was exhibited without the supposed plaintiff's knowledge or when defendants appeared, but there was no bill at all. Some plaintiffs failed to show cause. If a formal hearing was achieved, either party might secure issue of a *subpena ad audiendum judicium,* and if the adversary failed to appear judgment might be given in default. When both parties were present, they were expected to append their names to the decision and thus indicate assent. The format varied: reference to a "final hearing" was common as was the phrase "it is finally ordered and decreed." Furthermore, attempts to reverse decrees were often successful. It was necessary to obtain permission through a petition. A favorite argument was that witnesses had been absent or unknown, a fairly easy claim to make in view of the lax regulations covering examination. It was likewise possible to reopen matters which had been dismissed before a formal hearing but after issue had been joined.[23]

The court's initial powers of coercion represent a familiar pattern: attachment, attachment with proclamation, and commission of rebellion. If a defendant still failed to appear and answer, the case in most circumstances would be ordered against him. If breach of a decree was involved, proclamation would be made at the dwelling house of the offender and at the nearest parish church during divine service, the curate or minister reading it from the pulpit. If apprehended, the party might

22. PRO, Chester 14/5, pp. 46–49, 106, 197, 367, 540, 890–91; PRO, Chester 14/6, ff. 13v.–14; PRO, Chester 14/59, ff. 40v., 80.

23. PRO, Chester 14/5, pp. 1v., 9, 31–32, 51, 52–54, 69, 124, 145, 162–63, 478, 545, 660, 772–74; PRO, Chester 14/59, ff. 30, 117v.

find himself in gaol. Others ignored authority, individuals were stabbed, and commissioners of rebellion were threatened and assaulted. It is a familiar picture, but the Exchequer had its particular difficulties. Some pursued persons popped back and forth across the boundary as commissions expired or were renewed. The limitations of jurisdictional geography were always apparent, and even the threat of fines, £500 and over, might be little more than a gesture. More than one recalcitrant was in and out of prison several times. One man was always offering to enter into bonds and to compound, but he was equally willing to surrender himself into prison. His eventual petition to seek reversal of the decree against him was allowed, but in the meantime his lands, tenements, and profits were sequestered into the hands of the court. Sequestration could be ordered at any stage of a suit, and commissions were normally employed. If payment of a debt had been decreed, the commission might pay part of rents and profits to the debtor for his maintenance and part to the creditor until his claim was satisfied.[24]

English bill proceedings were at different stages of evolution in different courts, Chancery and Star Chamber being at the highest level. The Exchequer of Chester looked thoroughly disorganized by comparison. On the other hand, over-rigid rules may not have been appropriate to a local court. Requirements of pleading and evidence were probably conditioned by the proximity of the time allotted for hearings and by the fact that parties and even witnesses would then appear. Interested persons jostled before the bench, and hearings were rapid. Warburton was critized by Cotes for the offensive manner in which he disposed of cases, and he once heard twelve cases in a single day. It was the informal nature of hearings, the sense of contact between bench and litigant, which occasioned objection about Warburton's sharp tongue.[25]

24. PRO, Chester 14/5, pp. 7, 94, 128, 150, 166, 295–97, 302–303, 399, 411–13, 464, 948.
25. Huntington Library, Ellesmere MS, 30; PRO, Chester 14/6, ff. 78v.–83.

It is impossible to hazard a guess at the number of bills exhibited or the number of suits which made headway. The order book for 1594—this is not the only possible record—contains 104 entries, some dealing with the same case. However, it is possible to conclude that the court was kept busy—hence the increasing number of attorneys—and that most suits were quickly ordered if not ended. Two terms might be enough if the parties descended to issue after bill and answer, and perhaps three to four terms, or twelve months, represents the average time consumed by seriously contested suits. Naturally some disputes went on for a long time—one case was dismissed eight years after issue was joined. Single suits did not of necessity embrace all the proceedings aroused by the conflict between parties.[26]

The Exchequer was financially attractive. Accounts were made before an attorney, and if a case was dismissed with costs, it was customary to state that payment must be made within twenty days after sight of a true copy of the decree. The amounts involved were not large. Although they were not representative of all the money expended, a plaintiff who had lost suits in both the Exchequer and the Pentice was required to pay total costs of £1 4s. 0d. We have a plaintiff's accounts for a suit of 1593 which lasted three terms and in which the pleadings went to replication and rejoinder. The total came to £4 16s. 8d. In the Exchequer, counsel received 10s. for drawing a pleading and a similar sum for appearance at a hearing. The fee for an attorney was 20d. a term. The cost of examining four witnesses came to 4s. 8d. A *subpena* of any kind cost 2s. 6d. The court's eventual order cost 6s. 8d. for drawing, 2s. for entering, and 5s. for a copy—13s. 8d. in all. Outlay of this kind was reasonable in comparison with costs at Westminster, but swift and cheap proceedings would cease to attract if they did not have the desired authority.[27]

26. PRO, Chester 14/5, p. 507.
27. PRO, Chester 14/5, pp. 69, 73, 232, 243; PRO, Transcripts of Decrees and Orders, Chester 13/3, *Spencer* v. *Crosse* 1593; PRO, Seal Book, Chester 6/1.

Cheshire and Flintshire formed a reasonably prosperous agricultural region. Production of mutton and wool, with the development of a market in the cloth industries of northern England, increased in the sixteenth century. It was, of course, a proud dairy district, and there was already some specialization in its celebrated cheese. Bacon and salt beef, so pleasing to London customers in later decades, were already developing as products of note. Industry was firstly represented by salt, and Nantwich, in spite of a terrible fire, had no rival in this production. As a port, however, Chester was clearly decaying. The Dee had become its despair, its Spanish trade had been wrecked, and Shrewsbury had held on to the staple for Welsh cloth. None the less, war in Ireland made Chester a major staging post for troops and supplies. These factors are important to an understanding of the substance of litigation. The Exchequer served local people. The odd name may attract the romantic eye—Arabella Stuart was locked in litigation with Edward Egerton—and leading local families used the court in order to fight their battles or to achieve accord. However, most bills were presented by lesser folk who were concerned with mundane things. The court found its life in seized cows and other livestock, obstruction of pathways, rent charges, closes, recovery of valuables, and conflicts over customs and charters.[28]

Plaintiffs always claimed a point of equity and conscience, in effect advancing a difficulty which prevented them from obtaining their rights at law. Claims for the discovery or recovery of documents and evidences were common. The assertion might be fictitious, but at other times the plaintiff put it forward because he was genuinely seeking security, because it was intrinsic to the case which he intended to develop, or because he was concerned with litigation taking place or anticipated in another court. The defendant in his answer was supposed to reveal all things in his knowledge, and the court could compel produc-

28. C. Stella Davies, *The Agricultural History of Cheshire, 1750–1850*, (Chetham Soc. 3rd. ser. x, 1960), 7, 12; Freeman, Rodgers, and Kinvig, 53; Beck, 54; *Chester Customs Accounts*, 5; PRO, Chester 14/6, f. 131; *CSP Dom.* 1603–10, 153.

tion of documents—bonds, court rolls, leases, rentals—through issue of a *subpena duces tecum*. If recovery was requested, the evidences could be held in court pending a decision. A defendant who swore that there was nothing else in his possession was discharged: "his costs to be considered upon the hearing of the cause, if any cause be." [29]

Many bills requested protection of possession, and orders to this effect usually stated that the ruling would stand until further order or until the other party recovered at law. Forcible entry would be treated as a contempt, and the plaintiff's right to receive rents and enjoy quiet possession might be supported by an injunction. One order was made conditional upon the plaintiff prosecuting his suit with effect. This was because many plaintiffs, successful at this stage, had no wish to proceed further. The court, however, was always conscious of the distinction between possession and title. Since there was no pretension of jurisdiction over title, careful wording was needed when plaintiffs sought possession "according to the custom of the county palatine time out of man's memory had and used" or for the "right and title" of three pieces of land. Bills dealing solely with title would be dismissed to law with costs coupled with an order protecting the defendant's possession. This was done when the defendants and those from whom they claimed professed possession for forty years "by and under the title of their answer pleaded." [30]

The court often acted upon standard principles of conscience. A plaintiff was ordered not to proceed at law because his suit was fraudulent. A suit between father and son over living expenses was deemed unnatural, and a commission was appointed to determine this and future controversies. Another defendant, described as "very hard and unconscionable," was urged to accept a financial compromise although he had a legal case. However, the essence of the Exchequer's existence as a

29. PRO, Chester 14/5, pp. 117, 146, 310, 408; PRO, Chester 14/59, f. 10.
30. PRO, Chester 14/5, pp. 18, 30, 129–32, 177, 266, 381, 447; PRO, Chester 14/59, ff. 68, 109.

court of equity and conscience is to be found in its handling of debts and penalties.[31]

It is probable that the largest number of bills concerned debt in some form: simple debts, debts founded on bonds claimed to have been lost, debts resulting from sales when goods had been transferred but not paid for or when payment had been made without the goods being received, debts claimed by executors and administrators or claimed from them. A claim could be "proved" on the basis of the allegation and a deposition in open court by the plaintiff, but the defendant had an equal chance through denial in his sworn answer and deposition. In addition, the period is significant because of the evolution of common bills.[32]

The essential principle was that debts must be paid but that debtors might properly be relieved from penalties. This was one of the most fundamental and debatable themes of conscience: even if debtors had entered into some kind of penalty agreement with open eyes, the bad conscience of creditors who sought more than reimbursement must be cleansed. This meant that the Exchequer constantly came into contact with other courts. Many plaintiffs were debtors who had only partially satisfied, and so execution on a bond or other proceedings were started at law. The Exchequer might stay the proceedings, remove the record, and order payment only of the outstanding portion of the debt. Sometimes there was dispute over whether all or part had been paid, the debtor—plaintiff in the Exchequer—claiming that an acquittance had been lost. If the court was satisfied about the truth of this, the case would be dismissed to law on condition that advantage of the lost acquittance was not taken. Even a debtor whose behavior aroused distrust and whose bill was dismissed with costs received some help. He had sought assistance only after judgment in the Pentice, and he had compounded his neglect by an improper request

31. PRO, Chester 14/5, pp. 306–307, 452–53, 458–59.
32. PRO, Chester 14/5, pp. 11, 162–63, 554, 597. For common bills, see below, pp. 145–46.

for an injunction when neither Egerton nor Warburton were present. Even so, costs were to be withheld from those creditors who intended to take execution at law. Such intent, it was declared, would be contrary to equity and conscience.[33]

When debtors, although afforded relief, defaulted, they forfeited protection, and in consequence costs might be awarded or a *procedendo* permitting continuation of proceedings at law. Furthermore, the court usually required sureties when it granted relief; it used these on other occasions, and so it was not interested in helping these persons. This attitude might bring creditors to the Exchequer. One plaintiff had obtained judgment and execution in Macclesfield against a surety who refused to pay because the original debtor had saved him harmless. The Exchequer upheld the decision of the lesser court.[34]

Accounts are intrinsic to debt. The simplest procedure was for the debtor to submit a sworn list of his obligations to a commission, usually made up of two persons. These, if satisfied, would certify the account to the court; but if they were dubious, the respective attorneys had to reexamine everything. Whenever possible, trade accounts were referred to commercial men. Settlement did not always follow. A cluster of suits, removed from the Pentice, were referred to a commission of aldermen, but they found the matter "too intricate and uncertain." The Exchequer discovered that the dispute was not "meet" to be heard before it, and a *procedendo* was issued. This was the kind of vacillation which made some wonder what it was that provincial courts of this type thought they were doing.[35]

Creditors were often plaintiffs. Sometimes an action at law might have been brought, but it was claimed that bonds, notes, and other documents concerning a debt had been lost, that other evidence necessary to support the facts was insufficient, or that the precise sum could not be remembered. The defendant could deny all or part of the bill, the matter could reach

33. PRO, Chester 14/5, pp. 9, 31–32, 155, 349–56, 570, 810.
34. PRO, Chester 14/5, pp. 319, 539.
35. PRO, Chester 14/5, pp. 327, 331; PRO, Chester 14/59, ff. 25v., 118.

a formal hearing, and occasionally the lost bonds were discovered. If so, they would remain in court to be cancelled when the debts had been paid. If the defendant confessed that the bonds had been made, the court would direct payment.[36]

The Exchequer of Chester was often described as a "mixed court" of equity and common law, similar to Chancery. This description, adopted by Coke, is rather misleading, but it can be understood in the sense that Chancery's common-law jurisdiction was based upon its rolls, and the Exchequer had its own recognizance rolls. Even so, there was little that was equivalent to Chancery common law or Petty Bag proceedings. It is possible that the idea of a "common-law" jurisdiction owed much to the simple procedure of handling real or pretended disputes over debt.[37]

The procedure of common bill and confession, which can look like a transposition out of English bill proceedings, was speedy. Hence it accorded mutual satisfaction to creditors and debtors, the latter being possibly anxious to secure adequate record that they had satisfied a debt. From the early 1560's, a series of entry books noted orders and decrees upon confessions.[38] Most entries in the book for 1587–1601 concern simple debts—the kind that were often based upon notes and non-recorded bonds, or bills as they are best described—and depositions made by plaintiffs when defendants had failed to observe a court directive to pay.[39] There was always fear about collusion and the possibility that some confessions might only indirectly be related to debt. A confession might result from dispute over the sale of an animal or some other article—but did the plaintiff have the right to sell?—or it might concern property. After one confession, the plaintiff's right to a rectory, parsonage, and tithes was affirmed.[40] Reasonable defendants in the Chan-

---

36. PRO, Chester 14/5, pp. 85, 101, 447, 478.
37. Coke, 211; The point is that the court could be accused of exercising a wrong jurisdiction by a wrong procedure.
38. PRO, Chester 14/35–50.
39. PRO, Chester 14/36.
40. PRO, Chester 14/5, pp. 777–78.

cery at Westminster could confess that claims against them were just, and there was nothing intrinsically wrong with the idea of confession. The trouble was that so many defendants at Chester appeared "reasonable" that a separate book was needed in which to record their confessions.

The procedure was legitimate, but there was a growing disbelief in such equitable claims as loss of documents, and it was natural to worry about the interests of third parties. It is worth noting a prohibition granted by the Common Pleas against proceedings at York. There were differences in procedure, but the essential point was that the archbishop had exhibited a bill on an obligation which, he claimed, was in the nature of an action of debt brought at common law. Coke, however, insisted that the matter was determinable at common law and in accordance with common-law procedures. The king, he said, was being deprived of his due percentage on a judgment for debt, and no writ of error lay under the supposed procedure being adopted. Whatever the significance of this episode, common bills continued to be popular at Chester. A later pamphleteer, instancing the courts of Wales, the Council in the North, the Duchy of Lancaster, and the Exchequer of Chester, said that provincial courts of equity had dispensed with common law, invaded "the right of property," and "laid about them as if they had no bounds or limitations." The intent of that act which is best known for abolishing Star Chamber was, he said, that the right of trial by jury and due course of law should not be dispensed with. Certainly, the procedure of common bill and confession remained a burning issue at Chester during the late seventeenth and early eighteenth centuries. It was convenient, but it introduced "a method of determining property in an arbitrary manner and without the interpretation of a jury." Robert Fenwick, an eighteenth-century vice-chamberlain, would have liked to abolish the procedure, but he discovered that the remaining business of the court was "so small that probably no attorney of reputation would attend." [41]

41. J. P. Kenyon, *The Stuart Constitution* (Cambridge, 1966), 96–97; R. Acherley,

Disputes over money formed the mainstay of business, but the Exchequer had no wish to be inundated with every quarrel of this kind. Indeed, the Exchequer, even when it removed a suit from another court, often hoped to rid itself of the proceedings as soon as possible. Sometimes this wish was thwarted by earnest suitors. Proceedings for execution of a bond, arising out of a dispute over delivery of wheat, were stayed in the Pentice and removed into the Exchequer. The court had intended to return the suit, reserving consideration of equity, but the debtor requested determination and this was agreeable to the defendant. The plaintiff was ordered to pay costs and to deliver two bushels of "good, sweet and marketable wheat of the measure used within the city of Chester," or the monetary equivalent at current market prices. This was not an earthshaking dispute, but it is interesting because the Exchequer was being asked to supervise a practical commercial issue.[42]

The chamberlain was the greatest official in the region, and therefore it was expected that he would oversee local performance. When a group of merchants engaging in the illegal export of corn were apprehended, the pursuivant was ordered to impound the corn and sell it, turning the proceeds over to the merchants after deducting fees and expenses. General activity ranged from the common enough task of binding persons to keep the peace to determination of claims for exemption from taxation. In October, 1594, arrangements for the repair of Frodsham bridge, important because it was near to the mouth of the Weaver, were completed. The Exchequer's decision was made with the advice of the justices and with the assent of the justices of the peace and gentlemen of the county "in this court assembled." An order of 1579 was reactivated, and taxation of one thousand marks was levied upon the county. Two justices of the peace were to act as collectors in every hundred, and in townships a similar task was to be performed by consta-

The Jurisdiction of the Chancery as a Court of Equity Researched (London, 1733), 27, 29; Cheshire Record Office, DDX 15, Umfreville MSS, No. 19, "A Short Essay on the Exchequer at Chester or an Attempt to Explain the Practice of that Court," 151, 152.

42. PRO, Chester 14/5, p. 243.

bles. A commission was subsequently appointed to determine responsibility for building and repairing bridges, a task of increasing significance as military traffic bound for Ireland grew. The chamberlain, aided by national legislation, could assume the necessary consent for taxation, but his intervention had little effect, and road facilities remained poor in this part of England.[43]

Right of way was a frequent subject of litigation. This entailed the taking of inquisitions which the sheriff returned into the Exchequer, examination of witnesses, appointment of commissions, and direction of trial in local courts, perhaps with an Exchequer attorney acting as steward. After some or all of these steps, the eventual conclusion might be formulated as a decree. Equally prominent were cases concerning local custom. With respect to salt manufacture in Middlewich, ancient customs governing "walling" and the "occupation of walling" were upheld. It was decided that custom at Northwich gave possession for a year to the person who was in possession when the bell rang for walling. To cite a different kind of problem, the Exchequer intervened in a violent faction fight at Macclesfield. The mayor had been deprived of his seat in the parish church during the Christmas holidays. A piper who played in his honor was assaulted by supporters of a rival "mayor" who, it was alleged, spoke of marshaling the local women to stone him.[44]

Incidents like that noted above bring us to the so-called Star Chamber jurisdiction, an inflated title. The palatine attorney general, whose general duty was to look after crown interests, was responsible for most informations, but these were also exhibited by private persons and by officials. The queen's forester prosecuted several people for killing deer, an offense which could result in six months imprisonment.[45]

Defendants to informations could submit joint or separate

43. PRO, Chester 14/5, pp. 114, 200–201, 209–11, 309, 415–16; Beck, 58–59.
44. PRO, Chester 14/5, pp. 244, 431–32, 555, 577, 861–63, 972.
45. PRO, Chester 14/59, f. 130; PRO, Chester 14/5, pp. 182, 223, 1050.

answers, and they were examined on oath through written interrogatories. A number of accusations were occasioned by abuse
of the court's procedures. A man who used "school paper"
to forge an attachment was sent to prison. A defendant was
accused of helping to frustrate the bailiff's attempt to serve
an attachment. Affrays, riots, and other misdemeanors were
alleged, and punishments included imprisonment, fines, and
compulsory payment into the poor man's box. One convicted
defendant had in open court used "uncomely and undecent"
words against Robert Whitby, an attorney, whom he later
stabbed and knocked into a ditch. More interesting are those
informations which charged officials with default. Two constables were imprisoned and other defendants punished because
ditches along the highway had been "unscoured, uncleansed
and not diked" to the inconvenience of the subject and of forces
traveling to Ireland. In another case, a justice of the peace
and two constables who had misappropriated funds were
imprisoned, fined, and compelled to disgorge their illgotten
gains.[46]

The Exchequer of Chester, like other Elizabethan institutions, lived in a climate of overlapping jurisdictions and multiple
litigation. A surety, who was defendant in the Exchequer at
Westminster, exhibited a bill at Chester in which he sought
to be saved harmless by the debtor. The latter, who denied
that his surety would be greatly damaged, commenced proceedings against him in the Pentice. This was quashed, the palatine
court having priority of jurisdiction, and the debtor was ordered
to save his surety harmless in respect of costs and payments
which might be sustained at Westminster. In support of this
order, the debtor was required to produce two sureties. Three
courts, each at a different level, had been involved.[47]

Apart from treason and error, foreign plea and foreign
voucher, inhabitants of the counties of Chester and Flint were

46. PRO, Chester 14/5, pp. 166, 811–12, 894, 909–10, 935, 937, 956; PRO, Chester
14/6, f. 73.
47. PRO, Chester 14/5, pp. 483–84.

to sue and be impleaded in the county palatine. Early in Elizabeth's reign, the greatest outside threat was posed by the Council in the Marches of Wales, but Glaseor seemed determined to restore eroded rights. Matters came to a head when the Welsh Council ordered the release of a man imprisoned by the Exchequer. In 1569 a committee of judges, headed by Chief Justice Dyer, decided in favor of the county palatine, and their certificate was enrolled in Chancery. Shortly after, there was a tremendous row between Glaseor and Sir John Throckmorton, justice of Chester, who thought of himself primarily as a member of the Welsh Council and who accused the vice-chamberlain of meddling and dishonesty. This episode, however, served only to buttress the newly affirmed rights of the county palatine.[48]

The Exchequer's jurisdiction was legitimate if both the matter in dispute and the residence of all the parties was within the county palatine. After the 1569 opinion, courts such as Chancery and Requests did dismiss a number of suits to Chester, but it gradually became clear that a tighter definition of jurisdiction could be attempted. If a bill had been exhibited in Chancery, then that court had priority of jurisdiction, and the objector had to appear at Westminster in order to plead his privilege. If even one of several parties was not an inhabitant of the county palatine, the Exchequer did not have jurisdiction. When Egerton became chamberlain, it meant that the Exchequer was ruled by a lawyer who was essentially a Chancery man. A bill seeking stay of common-law proceedings in the Exchequer at Westminster was dismissed because the defendants were inhabitants of London. Actually, the palatine court had no power to intervene, but it was pointed out that the plaintiff could appear through attorney in the Westminster court. Another suit was dismissed with costs because all the parties lived in Manchester. It was still possible for a compliant defendant who lived elsewhere to appear, but local plaintiffs might be

---

48. *HMC Hatfield*, IV, 446; Williams, *Council in the Marches*, 198–200.

suspicious. One Londoner appeared initially, but the plaintiff refused a composition and requested dismissal since there could not be a hearing without the defendant's presence, and this could not be enforced.[49]

Even if the jurisdiction of the palatine appeared valid, other considerations might have weight. Local jurisdictions were always challenged on the ground that great local men had an advantage. Specified hardships and the fear of unfair trial were cited in support of Chancery decisions to reject claims of privilege in the midperiod of Elizabeth's reign. A dispute between inhabitants over a matter within the palatine might become proper for another court. One resident, recognizing that he could not sue outside in his own name, requested a letter of attorney from the dean and chapter of Christ Church, Oxford, allowing him to sue for tithes in whatever court his counsel advised.[50]

The most obvious limitation upon the Exchequer was its inability to direct process beyond its borders or to enforce orders against nonresidents. The common injunction, for example, could not be used against nonresidents, but it could be issued to inhabitants who had commenced proceedings outside the county palatine. However, national courts were not willing to tolerate such behavior, and the Chancery certainly felt that the proper procedure was a demurrer to jurisdiction or a motion. Westminster courts were agreeable to dismissing suits to provincial courts, but the possibility of these lesser courts issuing restraining process, even if directed only to litigants, was an impertinence. Cheshire men impleaded at Westminster found that they could only expect indirect support from the Exchequer. On the other hand, much might be done through influence. In 1592, Derby asked Dr. Aubrey, master of requests, to permit transfer of a case to the Exchequer. Egerton must have been influential in this kind of communication. One set of Chancery proceedings was terminated because of an arbitra-

49. Jones, 370–71; PRO, Chester 14/5, pp. 167–71, 374, 462, 915.
50. CSP Dom.Add., 1580–1625, 332.

tion agreement which the plaintiff subsequently sought to enforce at Chester. In another instance, after a suit at Chester was dismissed to law, the plaintiff began proceedings in Star Chamber. After a fresh hearing at Chester, he agreed to drop the Star Chamber bill in return for a more specific direction to commence suit at common law and an order that he was to have possession if the verdict was in his favor. It would be unsafe to assume that all problems were ironed out, but there does seen to be a suggestion that communication and compromise could have effect.[51]

On the other side of the picture, Westminster courts could not directly issue process effective in the county palatine. The distinction was one between seals. As Dyer's certificate of 1569 made clear, the Queen's writ must run under the palatine seal. Hence, process under the great seal was issued from Westminster and directed to the chamberlain. He was expected to issue similar process under the palatine seal, and it was assumed that he would take action if nonobservance or contempt resulted. When Common Pleas directed a *capias utlagatum* to Egerton, a similar writ was directed under the palatine seal to the sheriffs of Chester and made returnable to Common Pleas. The offender was captured, but he escaped, and the sheriffs neglected to make a return. They were fined in the Exchequer after an information had been brought by the palatine attorney general. The chamberlain was really a judicial cipher in this respect, but Egerton had the stature to disrupt the simple two-stage procedure. When it was argued that a bill in Chancery was vexatious, it was ordered that a Chancery attachment, if issued, would "not be made further under the seal of this court" until Egerton or Warburton had discussed the affair with Lord Keeper Puckering. When Egerton assumed the office of lord keeper, this kind of cooperation presumably became even more possible.[52]

51. PRO, Chester 14/3, p. 310; PRO, Chester 14/5, pp. 51, 205, 873–74; PRO, Chester 14/59, ff. 80, 118v., 141v., 157. *CSP Dom.* 1591–94, 269.
52. British Museum, Harleian MSS, 227, f. 299; Barraclough, 45; PRO, Chester

Some suits involved Westminster courts indirectly. Satisfied that an absolute promise had been made, the Exchequer ordered one of several defendants to contribute his share of costs in Star Chamber. In another case, the plaintiff hoped to escape from proceedings upon a bond in Common Pleas, but his opponents promised to exhibit their own bill at Chester to prove fraud and collusion. Difficult problems were unavoidable, but they were sorted out with ease or difficulty according to the mood of the parties involved.[53]

A good example of sensible relations is provided by wardship. The Exchequer was an ancient depository. An inquisition from the reign of Edward III was produced from its files to establish that the manor of Marbury was held from the queen by knight's service as of the earldom of Chester. In the reign of Mary, commissioners of the Court of Wards had been directed to make a calendar of all records in the Exchequer at Chester pertaining to lands held by knight's service. In 1572 another search was made, this time by palatine officials, and it was found that some documents were in London. The work of making an inventory was disrupted by a rather typical episode, the feodary taking advantage of Glaseor's absence to seize papers on the grounds that they belonged to his office. There was still disquiet that the crown was losing some of its rights, and a statute of 1576 laid down that process and commissions for finding offices must be issued from the Exchequer and then transcription made into the Court of Wards, just as inquisitions received by the Chancery were passed on to the Wards by the Petty Bag. Thereafter, arrangements appear to have been reasonably satisfactory. Certainly there is no sense of conflict. A suit brought by tenants of a royal ward was flatly dismissed because the Wards was the only proper place. A dispute over wardship was referred to Thomas Hesketh, attorney

---

14/5, p. 714; PRO, Chester 14/60, entry of September 30, 1594 (this Rule Book is in poor condition and the section is not foliated). It should be noted that there was a special rule governing proclamations upon *exigent*, I Edward VI, c.10.

53. PRO, Chester 14/5, pp. 280–81, 446–47.

of the Wards, who was to return his certificate to the Exchequer. In the reverse direction, Burghley, as master of the Wards, ordered a bill to be exhibited at Chester. The case was then to be referred to Warburton for determination and settlement. In this instance, the Wards was supervising the course of proceedings in the provincial court.[54]

One serious problem was posed by Duchy of Lancaster lands at Halton and Congleton. There was trouble in the 1580's, but in 1587 Egerton, acting as solicitor general and as an assistant at Chester, reached an interim agreement with John Brograve, attorney of the Duchy. The authority of the palatine was recognized for the "meantime," and Exchequer process was to be executed in these areas. Special arrangements, however, were made for immediate disputes which involved the deputy steward of Halton and the mayor of Congleton.[55]

If relations with outside courts were reasonably stable during the last part of Elizabeth's reign, the Exchequer's communication with the mosaic of courts within the county palatine was more complex. Indeed, in many ways and for its own area, the Exchequer's responsibilities can be compared with Chancery's national role. It removed or stayed suits in lesser courts; it also supervised, supported, and used these tribunals. They were particularly valuable as agencies to settle little disputes, but their inferiority was underlined. Only the city of Chester, despite early Elizabethan defeats, threatened resistance.

The common injunction was the most significant weapon. Leicester had confined its issue to times when a legal assistant was present. Under the different circumstances of Egerton's time, it could only be issued by the chamberlain or vice-chamberlain. This restriction did not apply to writs of *certiorari*. They appear to have been more numerous, and here perhaps there was a greater possibility of abuse, but the applicant had

54. PRO, State Papers Domestic, Supplementary, S.P. 46/126, f. 229; H. E. Bell, *The Court of Wards and Liveries* (Cambridge, 1953), 50; *HMC Hatfield,* II, 36; 18 Elizabeth I, c. 13; PRO, Chester 14/5, pp. 302–303, 399, 1100–101.

55. Cheshire Record Office, Cholmondeley of Cholmondeley MSS, Box "E," Nos., 111, 112; PRO, Chester 14/3, p. 522.

to prove his case within a week or eight days. Otherwise a *procedendo* would issue with costs—these amounted in one case to £3 6s. 8d.[56]

The Exchequer stayed a range of suits in Chester, Macclesfield and other places. Technicalities of law and equity were cited, as were claims of partiality and assertions that debts had been satisfied but no quittance given. Privilege of litigants already proceeding in the Exchequer was a particular concern. Restraint or proceedings in another court were reprehensible. When a plaintiff was arrested in the city of Chester for a different matter of debt—one which he professed to be willing to pay—a *corpus cum causa* was issued requiring the city sheriffs and the keeper of Northgate prison to bring him into the Exchequer.[57]

The Exchequer, perhaps through a temporary stay of suit, was constantly supervising proceedings in other courts. Impartial stewards were appointed for manorial trials. Litigants were ordered to join in demurrer at common law. Even so, there was an intrinsic possibility that the dispute would return to the Exchequer. One plaintiff, alleged to be a man of straw, was encumbered with careful directions as to the empanelment of a jury and sent to law. If he obtained the verdict, he was to stand to the further order in equity of the Exchequer. The plaintiff in a suit over possession of land was ordered to bring an action on the case at the next assizes. The defendant was ordered to appear, declare, and answer, and both sides were to plead to issue at the same assizes. If the verdict was for the defendant, or if the plaintiff failed to bring an action or became *non suit,* the defendant's position was to be sustained. On the other hand, if the plaintiff gained the verdict, he was not to take judgment, but further order would be made by the Exchequer. One more case may be mentioned. Robert Brerewood, alderman of Chester, turned to the Exchequer when his right and title to a messuage and garden in the city

56. PRO, Chester 14/5, pp. 8, 152, 349–56; PRO, Chester 14/59, ff. 8, 63.
57. PRO, Chester 14/5, pp. 8, 158–59, 285; PRO, Chester, 14/59, ff. 83, 159, 159v.

was denied. It was said that the original vendor, Sir Edward Fitton, had not had the right to sell. Brerewood was ordered to pay costs, charges, and arrears of rent since the supposed purchase, but within fourteen days he was to put some goods on the disputed property, and his adversary was to distrain on the basis that he had a claim prior to Brerewood's purchase. Brerewood was then to sue a *replevin* in the city of Chester, it was to be avoided on the ground that rent was behind, and this was to be the issue.[58]

The Exchequer could arrange the course of proceedings, but it was capable of providing support in other circumstances. It ordered observance of verdicts gained in the county court before the sheriff, and a successful plaintiff in two actions at Nantwich obtained an enforcement order with additional costs. However, principles of equity were maintained. A verdict for payment of £12, gained before a jury in the fee of Halver, resulted in the debtor being released from imprisonment in Halver Castle, but five years passed without satisfaction. The debtor apparently relied upon the Exchequer doctrine that penalties were unconscionable. Proceedings had not in fact been commenced in that court, and the episode may reflect how such doctrines could occasion irritation. Eventually a bill was exhibited, and the debtor only had to pay the principal—£6 13s. od.—plus costs.[59]

Whenever possible, the Exchequer referred or dismissed suits of little value to a lesser court, sometimes announcing that it would either decree the verdict or reassume responsibility if there were grounds of equity. A dispute over barley, beans, and peas for which a certain value could not be stated, was referred to trial before the steward or his deputy of St. Thomas court in Chester city. If verdict was found for the defendant, the Exchequer was "mindeth" to decree the matter and order costs. A number of cases were dismissed, apparently because they were trivial. Examples range from *detinue* of small things

58. PRO, Chester 14/59, f. 152v.; PRO, Chester 14/5, pp. 43, 361, 499–500.
59. PRO, Chester 14/5, pp. 10, 31–32, 311.

to a debt of 10s. Dismissal might be interpreted as a hint that the plaintiff would be well advised to give up his quest. His right, however, was not denied, and it cannot be assumed that direction to seek remedy in lesser courts was an empty formula. Manorial and other jurisdictions still had an equitable pretension. The only body capable of resisting this paternal supervision was the city of Chester.[60]

The mayor and corporation of Chester had authority over the city, her suburbs, and some lands beyond the walls. Areas exempt from their jurisdiction included the cathedral precincts and the castle with its verge, an area known as Gloverstone. The status of this enclave occasioned dispute, as did fugitives who fled there and nonfreemen who traded there. The city authorities sometimes tried to collect taxes. In other respects they were always sensitive about their courts and customs.[61]

The most significant city courts were the Portmote, held before the mayor, and the Pentice, held before the sheriffs. Other courts were the Crownmote, the Passage court which specialized in debts, and quarter sessions. The corporation claimed cognizance over pleas—real, personal, and mixed—of lands and tenements, and over debts, compositions, trespasses, covenants, bargains, and so on. At the very least, the city frowned upon aldermen and freemen who sued each other outside, and from the fifteenth century there was an attempt to prevent such suits in the Exchequer unless a license had been obtained from the mayor. The city initially based its claims upon its charter of 1506, a patent of 1560, and a confirmation in 1564. The old charter was withdrawn and replaced in 1574. The city was wracked with plague, but the great issue of that year was a head-on clash with the Exchequer.[62]

60. PRO, Chester 14/5, pp. 202, 384, 499.
61. *Calendar of Chester City Council Minutes, 1603–1642*, ed. M. J. Groombridge (Lancs. and Ches. Rec. Soc. cvi., 1956), ii–iii.
62. M. J. Groombridge, "Introduction to the Records of the City of Chester," *The Cheshire Historian*, II (1952), 34–40; *The Political History of the City of Chester* (1814), 28–44; *Calendar of Chester City Council Minutes*, xiv.; M. Weinbaum, *British Borough Charters, 1307–1660* (Cambridge, 1943), 11; *CPR* 1560–63, 471–73.

In all the disputes that arose, the city was weakened by dissension—in 1569 the sheriffs were imprisoned after breaking their wands over each others heads. The Aldersey family, which itself provided mayors, was prominent in the two big Elizabethan explosions. In 1562 Fulk Aldersey was disfranchised because he had sued an alderman in the Exchequer. Eventually a decision in favor of the palatine was given by Lord Treasurer Winchester in the Exchequer at Westminster. The biggest quarrel burst out in 1572 when trouble over the election of aldermen and common council resulted in a bill being exhibited in the Exchequer. In consequence the mayor, Ralph Dutton, disfranchised not only the plaintiffs, including William Aldersey, but also Glaseor, the vice-chamberlain and a former mayor. Aldersey's shop was shut down because he no longer had the rights of a citizen. He appealed directly to Leicester, pointing out that quite apart from any rights of jurisdiction which the city might or might not have, his principal adversary, the mayor, was the chief officer of the courts there. Feelings were running high, and Dutton was described as a former coiner, "a man notoriously suspected of sundry crimes and misdemeanors from his youth upwards. . . ." Dutton had already been attached by the Exchequer, and so he commenced an action of false imprisonment against the vice-chamberlain at the assizes. This was an extremely explosive situation. There was a conflict of jurisdiction between the Exchequer and the city, and it was threatening to cause trouble between the Exchequer and the palatine common-law jurisdiction; the possibly genuine question of jurisdictional rights was really only a weapon being wielded by rival factions in the city. A Privy Council committee was struck, its members including Cordell, Thomas Bromley, Sir Walter Mildmay, the chancellor of the Exchequer, and Sir Francis Walsingham, the secretary of state. It was evidently these deliberations which resulted in Leicester seeking the advice of Cordell and Bromley about other aspects of the Exchequer court.[63] In the immediate dispute, the city relied upon its patent

63. Cf above, 129.

of 1560. This was an interesting document because, in recognizing that the city could not provide adequate relief in equity,
it had specified the Welsh Council and the Chancery but
refrained from reference to the Exchequer of Chester. By 1574,
however, the claims of Ludlow had been defeated. On April
9 the committee declared that the patent had been influenced
by fraud, and hard things were said about the corporation.
The document was to be surrendered into the Chancery and
cancelled, the jurisdiction of the Exchequer was upheld, and
those who had been victimized were to be refranchised. The
irregular closing of a city gate which had seriously inconve-
nienced Exchequer officials was also regulated. After this,
restraint seems to have marked relations between the city and
the chamberlain. The corporation realized that the help of great
men could be of assistance in trade disputes, and the chamberlains eyed Chester as a possible area of patronage. Thus Warburton, who must be regarded as representing a palatine interest,
sat in Parliament for the city on three occasions. However, his
first attempt to secure election in 1584 was fruitless in spite
of Leicester's sponsorship—instead he found a seat at Newcastle-
under-Lyme—and later the fourth earl of Derby failed in his
bid to get Peter Proby appointed as clerk of the Pentice.[64]

Although the city's pretensions had been crushed, the new
charter of 1574 contained some valuable additions, and certainly
the spark of resistance remained alive. In 1590 the city sheriffs
tried to ignore an Exchequer order requiring them to arrest
a defendant. On the other hand, the palatine court really had
no desire to deny civic competence, and it often dismissed suits
to city courts. However, it was the obvious tribunal when city
groups were in conflict or when the corporation was challenged
by outsiders. Both these elements surrounded the Mystery of

64. *A Concise History of the County and City of Chester* (Chester, 1791), 111, 112; R.
H. Morris, *Chester in the Plantagenet and Tudor Reigns* (Chester, 1893), 185n., 191–92,
198, 241; British Museum, Harleian MSS, 2016, ff. 37–45, 48–53v.; G. L. Fenwicke,
A History of the Ancient City of Chester (Chester, 1896), 174; *Political History of Chester*,
4–5; *CPR* 1560–63, 471–73; *CSP Dom.* 1547–80, 476–77; *CSP Dom. Add.* 1566–79,
460–61.

Bakers who had exceptional privileges with respect to the purchase of corn and a monopoly over the sale of bread. The condition was that the bakers must accept prices set by the mayor, but sometimes they wanted the best of both worlds. In 1557–58 they went on strike but were forced to submit. There was another angry passage in the late 1580's which ended after the mayor threw open the right to sell bread. The bakers were afraid of interlopers and were always plagued by free-traders selling bread in the verge of Chester Castle. The most persistent challenge came from the inhabitants of the queen's manor and lordship of Handbridge who claimed the right to sell bread in Chester at the two weekly market days. The Exchequer, on the advice of Attorney General Popham, refused to allow this claim in the 1580's. The matter was again before the court in 1595. This time the monopoly of the bakers was decreed until such time as it should be decided otherwise either in the same court or in the Exchequer at Westminster.[65]

The city was damaged by inadequacy in its arrangements. There was a tendency to regard the Pentice as a place which relieved the Portmote from pressure, but there were complaints, in particular about the haphazard attendance of the sheriffs. The Exchequer often stayed suit in the Pentice and removed the record, only to grant a *procedendo* with the addition that proceedings were to be in the Portmote where, as it was once said, the case "shall receive better examination." In the latter instance, the Exchequer attorneys were to pick the jury, and if the plaintiff was successful, he was to refrain from procuring judgment or execution until further order in the palatine court.[66]

The most persistent embarrassment to the city was still provided by officials who sought resource in the Exchequer. In and around 1600 there was a complicated dispute over the

65. PRO, Chester 14/5, pp. 172, 193–95, 386–89; PRO, Chester 14/59, f. 73v.; Morris, 416–21, 423; J. H. Thomas, *Town Government in the Sixteenth Century* (London, 1933), 69–70, 72–73.
66. PRO, Chester 14/5, pp. 95, 413, 509, 597; Groombridge, "Introd. to Records," 38.

position of clerk of the Pentice. The Exchequer ruled that he was properly elected by the mayor, aldermen, and councillors "representing the whole estate and body of the said city." Ellis Williams, named clerk by the mayor in 1599, was expelled by the recorder, Richard Birkenhed, who claimed that by custom the city courts were kept by two of his clerks. The recorder was defeated and was then sued by his former fellow defendant, Peter Starkey, who had already paid over money for the clerk-ship and now wanted to be reimbursed especially since he was in difficulties with a London wine merchant. Birkenhed said that he had returned £70 leaving only £10 outstanding, but after his death Starkey sued the executor. Williams also died and the next clerk, Robert Whitby, appointed in 1602, was a follower of Egerton and one of the Exchequer attorneys. He was challenged several times, and there was a serious erup-tion in 1608 when he tried to obtain a freshly worded grant more clearly associating him with his son. Egerton, now Lord Chancellor Ellesmere, came to his aid with a letter affirming that the original grant had been to each of the two Whitbys for life or to the survivor, and that their appointment as clerk of the Pentice was also for the clerkships of Crownmote, Port-mote, sessions, and county courts in the city. Opponents argued that the clerkships of Pentice and Portmote were separate, and for a time the Whitbys were turned out, but in 1611 there appears to have been a settlement.[67]

The above dispute reveals weaknesses in the city; it also makes it clear that decrees of the Exchequer might have only a limited effect. In 1605 the city again attempted to discipline freemen who sued in the palatine court without license. It was stated that a writ to remove proceedings from the Portmote must be brought in person. Matters reached a head when an official representing the palatine receiver general tried to attach plate and goods belonging to the mayor and city. The mayor,

67. PRO, Chester 14/5, pp. 1062–63; PRO, Chester 14/6, ff. 11–12, 55, 83, 205v.; Morris, 204–206; *Calendar of Chester City Council Minutes*, 36–37; British Museum, Har-leian MSS, 2091, ff. 15, 138v.–39, 202, 202v.

who restrained him, was in turn attached by the Exchequer for contempt. In 1611 the city begged the chamberlain not to issue further writs of *corpus cum causa* which, they said, subverted their authority. Yet nothing could stop litigants from starting suits for the same matter in both the Exchequer and the city, and in 1612 yet another fine was imposed because a bill against a freeman had been exhibited in the Exchequer.[68]

A distinct element within the county palatine was provided by the ecclesiastical courts. The dean and chapter were often litigants in the Exchequer. Egerton, with his sons, was joint steward of their manors. The Exchequer issued a number of prohibitions, tithes being the most common source of difficulty. The Exchequer did not claim jurisdiction, but it might, for example, be necessary to protect tenants from hindrance in harvesting corn when the plaintiff claimed tithes against their landlord. One bill was based upon an agreement arranged by the 4th Earl of Derby which allowed the plaintiff to proceed either in the Exchequer or in an action of trespass. Egerton took the opportunity to clarify the rules: "The right of tithes . . . is not a matter determinable in this court, but the connusance thereof doth appertain to the ecclesiastical court and to be determined by the sentence of that court." The case was dismissed so that it might "be determined in the ecclesiastical court or tried in a prohibition as the parties think good, or otherwise in an action of trespass." The proper evidence is lacking, but it may be that Egerton disapproved of the former agreement. In 1596 it was ruled that a plaintiff might prosecute at law for the taking away and subtracting of tithes for corn, and an injunction was awarded when he went to the ecclesiastical court. The spiritual judge refused to take notice, and this was quite proper since an injunction only applied to parties and advisers. A prohibition was therefore issued in 1597, and since the bishopric of Chester was vacant, it was directed to the com-

68. *Calendar of Chester City Council Minutes,* 18, 36, 49 n. 1, 51 n. 2, 57.

missary of the archbishop of York who had jurisdiction in these circumstances.[69]

In the first three decades of Elizabeth's reign, the Exchequer of Chester, albeit deprived of financial significance, had reasserted its position against the Council in the Marches of Wales and the city of Chester. An accomodation had been arranged with the Duchy of Lancaster. There had been an attempt to regulate the conduct of officials and some aspects of proceedings. Egerton might have been expected to build on this situation but in fact he did very little. One obvious explanation for this can be found in his duties at Westminster. Initially, he was at Chester quite regularly, and even when in London he heard one Exchequer case at the Rolls. However, after his appointment as lord keeper in 1596, he was no longer able to make regular visits. All this meant that immediate responsibility rested upon the shoulders of Warburton. He was a good deputy, but he was hampered by his own irascibility and by the nature of some disputes.[70]

The Egerton family in all its branches was as united, divided and litigious as any other. Egerton himself, if only indirectly, was sometimes involved with suits before the court. In 1601 Hughes, the attorney general, brought an information with respect to affrays and misdemeanors arising out of a dispute over toll corn which Egerton had leased to one of his servants. Other members of the various Egerton family lines appeared before the court, notably Sir John Egerton and his son John and Sir Ralph Egerton and his son Edward. A chain of litigation surrounded Lady Mary Egerton, her former servant, Thomas Chambers, and his executors. Quite apart from his two sons, who successively held the office of baron, Cotes, Powell, and Whitby were clients of the lord keeper. Families notable in

69. Huntington Library, Cal. Bridgewater and Ellesmere MSS, 518; PRO, Chester 14/5, pp. 30, 198, 220, 537.
70. PRO, Chester 14/5, pp. 41–62, 64, 65, 95, 96, 133, 148–49.

the region who were associated with the Egertons throng the records—Brerewoods, Fittons, Ravenscrofts, Stanleys, Traffords, Venables, and so on. The danger was that faction and personal rivalry, or the suspicion of such, would affect the reputation of the bench and the conduct of the court.[71]

One of the most persistent litigants was Alexander Cotes, the deputy baron, who as a privileged official had the right to sue and be sued in the Exchequer in so far as that court had jurisdiction. This meant that he obtained free process, and so when he successfully rebutted a claim for debt, the defeated plaintiff did not have to pay costs. Cotes had interests all over the place, and in the 1570's, quite apart from his involvement with internal Exchequer troubles, his conduct as comptroller of the port of Chester had aroused Burghley's ire. In 1581, he had been admitted a freeman of Chester without payment on condition that he gave his best advice and counsel to the mayor. His property included lands once held by Sir Christopher Hatton, and for years he engaged in acrimonious dispute with the parishioners of St. John Baptist in Chester city. Cotes was fee farmer of the church, and the Exchequer and commissions appointed by it had to decide running disputes over upkeep, ownership of the body of the church, the right to appoint the vicar, and fees. However, his greatest battle was that with William Tatton over the profits and records of the baron's office, which still festered despite attempts at settlement in the 1580's.[72]

Egerton could not but be involved in this poisonous affair since with respect to other past disputes, Tatton evidently regarded him as an enemy. In a dispute over lands with Egerton's ally, Roger Puleston, it is probable that Tatton had reached the conclusion that Egerton, while acting legitimately and ostensibly as solicitor general in the interests of the crown, had in fact used his position to give advice, introduce complications,

71. PRO, Chester 14/6, f. 73.
72. PRO, Chester 14/3, p. 560; PRO, Chester 14/5, pp. 386–89, 393–94, 460, 1100 –101; *A Calendar of Lancashire and Cheshire Exchequer Depositions by Commission, from 1558–1702*, ed. C. Fishwick (Lancs., and Ches., Rec. Soc. xi., 1885), 106; PRO, S.P. 46/31, ff. 176, 335; PRO, S.P. 46/32, ff. 1, 3, 7, 7d, 103; *CSP Dom.* 1581–90, 335.

and aid his own friends and relatives. From Tatton's point of view, he was outclassed by the solicitor general's relationship with Puleston, Egerton's "ever loving friend," not to mention the adverse attitude adopted by Chief Baron Manwood, whose general conduct would soon be called in question. Faced by a series of reverses, Tatton had approached Egerton directly in November, 1590. His letter, formally courteous, was pointed. He sought Egerton's "lawful friendship therein (hoping you will not go about seeking the overthrow of any of your lordship's countrymen) a thing, trust me, as yet I never heard you worthy the touch of, and must be very sorry if it should be my good luck to receive the first hard measure at your hands. Let me therefore, I beseech you, depend of your goodness so far as by law and conscience the equity of my cause desireth. In so doing, I shall not only think myself greatly bounden to you ever, but the same lands proving, as I trust in God they will, my own, yourself may have the refusal of them before another." After Egerton became chamberlain, the office of baron was sequestered, and although this was suspended for a time, Tatton's arrest was ordered in early 1595. In the summer, he was committed to John Jones, an attorney, on the grounds that he had continually ignored orders and evaded process. In September he surrendered the office of baron, which incidentally had already been granted to Egerton's son. However, this did nothing to end the old quarrel over profits. Tatton was in and out of prison, his seizure was again ordered in 1597, and the whole issue was hopelessly complicated by disputes between himself and Cotes which had nothing to do with the Exchequer office. Tatton in turn harried Cotes through cross bills and counter actions. He seemed to be making some ground in the spring of 1598 when Cotes was ill. Tatton won an order for examination of witnesses in London. Shortly thereafter he gained a real triumph.[73]

Cotes and his wife, Ursula, had exhibited a bill against

73. National Library of Wales, Additional MSS, 251 D; PRO, Chester 14/60, entries of December 23, 1594, and January 11, February 26, 1595; PRO, Chester 14/5, pp. 175, 183, 334–35, 567, 753, 786; *CSP Dom.* 1598–1601, 50.

Tatton and Ralph Hurleston alleging riots and misdemeanors arising out of a dispute over tithes and timber. After publication, the plaintiffs announced that they would go no further. The defendants, however, demanded a hearing, and Warburton ordered the attorney general to report. Hughes decided that the charges of riot and misdemeanor were without foundation, and the case was dismissed with costs. The bill was declared to be slanderous, and defamatory words about Hurleston were to be defaced.[74]

Cotes, who, it must be remembered, had previously criticized Warburton, complained to Egerton with the result that the decree was suspended and Cotes permitted to examine witnesses to prove his charges of riot and misdemeanor. Yet Warburton had acted after publication and with the advice of Hughes. It seemed that the good sense of both the vice-chamberlain and the attorney general was now thoroughly in question. Egerton himself appears to have questioned witnesses but the picture was not changed. In October, 1599, it was decreed that Cotes was to pay the original costs plus the further costs sustained. All this, of course, had provided background to the still continuing dispute over the baron's office. Warburton had lost his wife, and in April, 1599, he and Egerton asked Henry Townshend, the second justice, to take Exchequer cases at the assizes save for the dispute over the baron's office, which, if it came up, was to be put over to the summer. It was another distinction which infuriated Cotes even though the stipulation was that the case must be heard by Chief Justice Shuttleworth and Townshend as well as by Warburton. There was a clear deterioration of goodwill within the court, and even though Warburton had been vindicated it could not escape notice that debate over a slanderous bill, although dismissed by him, had been allowed to drag on for a year. Furthermore, Cotes had openly accused him of "hard courses" in his and other suits. This may have had reference to Christopher Thimelthorpe, a litigant, who was aggrieved by Warburton's order in a major

74. PRO, Chester 14/5, pp. 845–46, 908.

case which involved the earls of Derby and Oxford, Robert Cecil, and the Egerton family. Thimelthorpe petitioned the queen claiming that Warburton "had done him wrong." Elizabeth referred the matter to Chief Justice Anderson and Justices Glanville and Walmsley, who, in the presence of parties and counsel, dissected the complaint at Serjeant's Inn in Fleet Street. Their decision of February 3, 1599, was that Warburton's order had been made "upon good cause" and that Thimelthorpe's petition was "very slanderous and untrue." [75]

That it had been a difficult time is apparent from the entry book. Between September, 1598, and the end of April, 1599, it had not been made up apart from a few November entries. Items for May, 1599, were followed by those for the months of December to March, and so the arrears were caught up. For a time, orders had been made and signed by Townshend with lesser matters being handled by Cotes and Powell, the deputy barons. By July, 1599, Warburton's name reappeared and the crisis was over. None the less, the vice-chamberlain's local reputation may have been hurt. Our anonymous early Jacobean author, who was so enthusiastic in the cause of the county palatine, urged the appointment of a good vice-chamberlain who could run the Exchequer effectively while pleasing "the country." He should not be a common lawyer, "such being men more fit to be employed in courts of learning than in cases of conscience, for if those shall be corrupted with affection (as all men of flesh and blood may be) they have a far greater scope to do amiss than other men . . . ." Such men would incline with the law "to serve their turn" or with conscience because of "favor and partiality." The piece can read as a devastating criticism of the unnamed Warburton, and the author, perhaps, saw the late Elizabethan Exchequer of Chester as Cotes had seen it. [76]

Warburton became a Common Pleas justice in November,

75. PRO, Chester 14/5, pp. 532–34, 535–36, 561–62, 586–87, 626, 645, 648, 719, 722, 765, 852, 867, 869–70, 908, 909, 1031; Cheshire Record Office, Cholmondeley of Cholmondeley MSS, Box "B," No. 427; CSP Dom. 1598–1601, 519.

76. PRO, Chester 14/5, pp. 871–95; "Rights and Jurisdiction of Chester," 25.

1600, and henceforth he, too, had responsibilities outside Chester. In August, 1603, the new king informed Egerton that Derby would become chamberlain. The old regime continued in effective charge for a short time, Derby assuming real control in January, 1604. Warburton was knighted, and his future tasks included serving as a commissioner to hear Chancery cases in 1611 and appointment to the Council in the Marches of Wales in 1617. Outliving Egerton—with whom he had in common three marriages—he died in 1621.[77]

The subsequent history of the Exchequer falls into two phases, divided by the civil wars and interregnum. When Star Chamber was abolished "the like" jurisdiction at Chester was also erased. Yet this aspect of jurisdiction was not very important. The palatine was abolished by the Long Parliament in 1646 but this had no legal relevance at the Restoration, and the Exchequer continued into the nineteenth century. In its survival it can best be described as a small debts court, whereas in Elizabethan times it had been a muscular tribunal, active in many areas of litigation. The traumatic effect of events in the 1640's cannot be ignored, but even so it must be asked whether there were not also other reasons which help to explain why the worn-out institution of Restoration and subsequent times looks so different.

In the 1590's Egerton acquired simultaneous charge of Chancery, Star Chamber and the Exchequer of Chester. He was unique among modern chamberlains, but he did not produce unique results for the Exchequer. Cotes could assert in 1596 that the court was "in good sort reduced to its ancient jurisdiction," but in fact the summit of achievement had passed. In 1600 it could be noted that despite gestures, nothing had really been done to restore the duties, privileges,·and profits of the baron's office, that held by Egerton's son. This was again the opinion of Cotes, but it need not be discounted. Procedure and recordkeeping remained formless and disorganized. The so-called privilege of the palatine might have stood in the future

77. *CSP Dom.* 1603–10, 27; PRO, Chester 14/7, ff. 30v., 38.

as a defense for the court, but it was a court which increasingly could not match, for example, the Chancery at Westminister in terms of effectiveness, in the authority of its decrees, in the reach of its powers of coercion. The Exchequer lacked the necessary sinew which would have enabled it to play a sustained role in future decades. This does not mean that it would not be busy in early Stuart times, but it does suggest that we may reach a conclusion similar to that of Dr. Williams on the Council in the Marches of Wales: "this volume of business was probably as great as any court could tackle efficiently; it may well have been greater." For the Exchequer would be busy, but its inadequacies and supervision from Westminster would henceforth represent dominant themes. After Egerton's departure, the shadow of Westminster became suddenly apparent. Sir Henry Townshend assumed the role of effective judge, a heavy load for the second justice to carry since he still exercised his responsibilities at the assizes. In October, 1605, he pointed out that royal commissions to levy *mises* had been appointed under the great seal whereas this should only be done under the palatine seal. It was, he said, "a course against the prerogative." His general complaint was telling: "I determined fourscore causes at hearing, besides the rules at the bar, where I find great encroachments offered to that jurisdiction by the courts in Westminster Hall; and now, which was never seen or heard of in Cheshire, prohibitions come down to the chamberlain of Chester out of the Common Pleas. . . ." In 1608, there were complaints about suits decreed at Chester being called into other courts.[78]

Egerton had been the prisoner of conflicting interests. He headed the Chancery, one of those great courts which was imposing a suffocating straitjacket of supervision upon lesser and provincial courts, and yet he was also responsible for one of the most compact provincial jurisdictions in the country.

78. Huntington Library, Bridgewater and Ellesmere MSS, 30, 89; P. Williams, "The Activity of the Council in the Marches under the Early Stuarts," *Welsh History Review* (1961), 139; *HMC Hatfield*, XVII, 466; XX, 17–18.

His devotion to Chancery and to great affairs of state meant that he could not be in real control at Chester. Even so, he could not divorce himself from personal and factional considerations. Even before his appointment as chamberlain, he was regarded as a foe by Tatton, but he could not lead a united party since Cotes had little regard for Warburton. Perhaps it was impossible for a leading local man to be effective in such circumstances. However that may be, the failure of Egerton and his generation of palatine administrators was underlined by later reformers who wanted local courts. The Exchequer and other tribunals existed, but they were incapable of providing the required service.

Jay P. Anglin

Che Essex Puritan Movement anò Che "Bawòy" Courts, 1577 - 1594

The unique information contained in the Minutes of the Dedham Conference and the stimulus they have given to additional studies have provided us more knowledge of the presbyterian movement in Elizabethan Essex than for any other English county.[1] Just recently Patrick Collinson shed considerable new light on the identification and role of the leading figures in the Essex movement in his *The Elizabethan Puritan Movement,* itself a beneficiary of the Minutes, and cast into proper perspective the aims of the Essex conference and its relations with the national movement.[2] As a consequence of that study we are now more acutely aware of the frustrations and the limited success which accompanied the attempts of Whitgift and Aylmer to secure clerical conformity in Essex, the lay and clerical politico-legal obstacles which tempered their

1. *The Presbyterian Movement in the Reign of Queen Elizabeth as Illustrated by the Minute Book of the Dedham Classis, 1582–1589,* ed. Roland G. Usher (Royal Historical Society, 3rd ser. VIII, 1905), cited as Usher.
2. Berkeley and Los Angeles, 1967, cited as Collinson.

program, and especially the overwhelming problems which
Aylmer met in implementing Whitgift's program within the
sprawling diocese of London. Thanks to the labors of church
and nonconformist historians, who have drawn heavily from
contemporary puritan documents, episcopal sources, and the
discoveries of amateur historians, we now possess fairly accurate
accounts of the effects of Aylmer's labors, the identities of the
persecuted, and the action taken against them.[3]

Yet we still lack a study of the Essex puritan movement
from the perspective of the inferior jurisdictions, the so-called
"bawdy" courts, which maintained a practically autonomous
jurisdiction over the puritans except in the brief interludes of
the primary and triennial episcopal visitations. These courts
played a crucial role in Aylmer's program, for it was in the
hands of the subordinate judges that the success or failure of
Aylmer's program ultimately rested. This study is an analysis
of the activities of the inferior judges as reflected in the surviving
court records for the Essex jurisdictions and episcopal and puritan sources.[4]

Regrettably the records of the inferior jurisdictions furnish
no new information on the activities of the puritans within
the conference movement. No new groupings of the clergy
are apparent, and Usher's suggestion of conferences other than
those of Dedham and Braintree must still be kept in the realm
of historical speculation. The secrecy and peripatetic nature
of the meetings, the scrupulous care taken by the clerical partici-
pants to keep within the confines of canon and ecclesiastical
law and hence beyond the jurisdiction of the ecclesiastical courts,

3. Most valuable are *The Second Part of a Register,* ed. Albert Peel (2 vols.; Cambridge,
1915), cited as Peel; Daniel Neal, *The History of the Puritans* (2 vols.; New York, 1844),
cited as Neal; T. W. Davids, *Annals of Evangelical Nonconformity in the County of Essex*
(London, 1863), cited as Davids.

4. The following abbreviations will apply to manuscript references *Essex Record Office
Ms* (ERO)—D/ACA—court *acta* of .the Archdeacon of Colchester; D/ACV—visitation
acta of the Archdeacon of Colchester; D/AEA—court *acta* of the Archdeacon of Essex;
D/AEC—court causes of the Archdeacon of Essex; D/AEM—book of inductions for
the archdeaconry of Essex; D/AEV—visitation *acta* of the Archdeacon of Essex;
Q/SR—quarter sessions rolls; *Guildhall Library Ms* (GL); and *Greater London Record Office,
London Division, Ms* (GLRO).

the intentional ignoring of local and diocesan boundaries, and the state of ignorance which was so characteristic of the inferior courts kept the movement outside the cognizance and competency of the inferior judges. But as subjects of these inferior officers the puritans were liable to corrective measures for their nonconformists practices, and it was as judge that the archdeacons and commissaries joined with the bishop in the role of protector of church interests against them. That the local magistrates failed in their tasks will become apparent in this study. As we shall see the hesitation of the inferior judges to take Aylmer's initiative seriously limited the aspirations of metropolitan leaders to achieve clerical conformity; as a consequence, the puritans in Essex were able to enjoy a large measure of freedom in their pursuit of "further reform."

We will limit our attention to the relationship which existed between the inferior courts in Essex and the sixty Essex clerics and two schoolmasters whom Usher has identified within, or on the fringes of, the puritan classical movement in Essex during the eighties. Since historians have not properly identified many of these obscure clerics (especially the curates and lecturers), we will attempt to trace their activities and provide biographical information as feasible.[5]

I

Although the Essex conference movement was not formalized until 1582, its composition goes back to the sixties when the puritans Robert Moncke, Thomas Upcher, John Wilton, William Seredge, Oliver Pigge, and Edmund Barker joined the Cambridge Marian exile and rector of Fifield, Robert Ed-

5. Usher, xxxv–xlviii, where they are listed alphabetically among members of other classes. An almost complete list based on the 1584 membership is found in Harold Smith's *The Ecclesiastical History of Essex* (Colchester, 1931), 13 (Smith omits the curates Andrews, Bird, Bishop, Reynolds, and Wingfield and includes Forth and Waltham who are not members). Generally biographical information is provided when the puritan is first mentioned. Unless specifically stated the dates and references for beneficed clerics and curates in donatives come from Richard Newcourt, *Repertorium Ecclesiasticum Parochiale Londinense* (2 vols.; London, 1710), II.

munds.[6] During the course of the episcopate of Sandys (1571–77) this small puritan group engaged in proselytizing at Chelmsford, Colchester, Horndon-on-the-Hill, Maldon, Rochford, and South Weald (Brentwood). They had the blessings of the three puritan archdeacons, John Calfhill, Thomas Cole, and Thomas Watts and recruited thirteen new members, most of whom had gained nominations to Essex benefices following their graduation from Cambridge. Among these new men were Bartimaeus Andrews, Thomas Farrar, Robert Lewis, Laurence Newman, and William Tay—all future members of the Dedham Conference—Richard Rogers, lecturer at Wethersfield for forty-six years and a leader of the Braintree Conference, Robert Searle, and Roger Carr.[7]

The Essex puritan movement experienced its greatest growth following the official ban on proselytizing in 1576. It grew rapidly during the first five years of the episcopate of John Aylmer and especially in 1582 and 1583 when twenty-two clerics and two lay schoolmasters assumed positions within the county. By the time of Whitgift's enthronement at Canterbury on October 22, 1583, the membership of the Essex coterie was practically complete, although two of the earlier members, Andrews and Pigge, had departed to neighboring Suffolk and Hertfordshire. Elsewhere Richard Allison and William Bird

6. *Moncke:* rector Woodham Ferrers (1561–1601); rector Wakes Colne (1565–1601); will proved in Consistory December 11, 1601; GLRO DL/C/336, fol. 36v. *Upcher:* rector Fordham (1561–96); rector St. Leonard's, Colchester (before 1577–82); ordained by Grindal June 4, 1560; licensed to preach by Archbishop Grindal on January 19, 1577; ERO D/ACA 7, fol. 132; D/ACA 14, fol. 281v; D/ACA 17, fol. 11v. *Wilton:* rector Widford (1561–63); rector Aldham (1563–99); rector Little Bentley (1587–89); Davids, 110. *Seredge:* rector East Hanningfield (1566–1600); licensed to preach May 1, 1581; GLRO DL/C/333, fol. 256. *Pigge:* rector All Saints, Colchester (1569–71); vicar St. Peter's, Colchester (1569–79); rector Abberton (1570–78); Davids, 69. *Barker:* vicar Prittlewell (1569–93); ordained priest in Ely on August 24, 1566; died in 1593; John Venn, *Alumni Cantabrigiensis* (4 vols.; Cambridge, 1922–27), I, 85, cited as Venn; GLRO DL/C/335, fol. 127v. *Edmunds:* rector Fifield (1560–62); vicar Maryland (1562–86); rector East Mersea (1586–1602); licensed to preach October 20, 1581 by Aylmer; GL 9537/3, fol. 98; GL 9537/4, fol. 38v; ERO D/ACA 14, fol. 281v; H. C. Porter, *Reformation and Reaction in Tudor Cambridge* (Cambridge, 1958), 91, cited as Porter.

7. *Andrews:* curate Rochford (1575); curate Fordham (1577); vicar Braintree (1579–80); vicar Wenham, Suffolk (1584–85); town preacher Yarmouth (1585–86);

were completing degrees at Cambridge, Issac Morley, and William Cook were experiencing difficulties with Suffolk authorities for their nonconformist practices, and William Negus was tuning the pulpit as town lecturer at Ipswich.[8] Within the manufacturing towns and ports located in the north and northeastern part of Essex, forty-three of the puritans eventually acquired benefices and nine accepted cures. The majority of the beneficed puritans owed their nominations to short-term patrons, and only twenty found favor from active puritan sympathizers.[9] Of the unbeneficed, Arthur Gale and Thomas Tye, who were unordained, assumed teaching positions at Dedham and Thorrington respectively, although they did try their hands as clandestine preachers on various occasions.[10]

curate Rochford (1603–1608); moved to Clophill, Beds., 1610; GL 9537/3, fol. 92; ERO D/AEV 3, fols. 179, 182v; D/AEV 4, fols. 13, 39v, 56, 91v, 96, 125v; Collinson, 229–30; Venn, I, 29. *Farrar:* vicar Boxted (1572–73); vicar Langham (1573–1607); ordained by Grindal January 25, 1559; licensed to preach by Sandys June 13, 1577. He is not to be confused with another puritan of the same name who served as curate at St. Botolph's, Colchester (1588–1607) and as rector of St. James, Colchester (1591–1610); ERO D/ACA 14, fols. 217v, 281v; GLRO DL/C/334, fol. 247. *Lewis:* rector Markeshall (1572–82); vicar St. Peter's, Colchester (1579–89); curate St. Runwald, Colchester (1586–88); he removed to Bury St. Edmunds on January 13, 1589; ERO D/AEV 1, fols. 5v, 32v, 41; Usher, 73; Davids, 113. *Newman:* vicar Coggeshall (1575–1600); "M.A. licensed by Matthew, late Archbishop of Canterbury"; ERO D/ACA 16, fol. 79v. He died in March, 1600. ERO D/ACV 1, fol. 89. *Rogers:* see Davids, 108; M. M. Knappen, Tudor Puritanism (Chicago, 1939), 387; Porter, 230. *Carr:* rector of Rayne (1572–1611); DNB, III, 1086. *Searle:* rector of Lexden (1576–87); ordained by Edmund, bishop of Sarum March 3, 1573; licensed to preach by Ep. London July 19, 1577; ERO D/ACA 14, fols. 218, 281v.

   8. Collinson, 229; William Urwick, *Nonconformity in Herts* (London, 1884), 603; Venn, I, 22, 156; Peel, I, 243. *Allison* served as curate at Purleigh but resigned in 1584. He became curate at Burnham (1588–89) and vicar of St. Leonard, Shoreditch (1596–1613); ERO D/AEV 2, fols. 92, 99v; GLRO DL/C 334, fol. 207. *Morley:* minister at Walsham-in-the-Willows (Suffolk); lecturer Ridgewell (1582–84); rector High Roothing (1601–1607); died 1616; Venn, III, 240; Davids, 116; S. B. Babbage, *Puritanism and William Bancroft* (London, 1962), 160.

   9. After 1570, puritans exclusively occupied only six benefices in Essex: Sir Richard Franck's Maldon, Walter and Sir Humfrey Mildmay's Woodham Ferrers, and Lord Robert Rich's Coggeshall, Leigh, South Shoebury, and Prittlewell. Historians have traditionally exaggerated the role of Lord Rich as patron of Essex puritans. Although Richard and Robert Rich held advowsons in twenty-three Essex parishes, conformable priests occupied sixteen of them at the height of the classis movement.

   10. *Gayle*, licensed by Stanhope on July 25, 1589, to teach grammar to boys, entered the school at Dedham on March 3, 1589. He was still there on April 27, 1593. Usher, 73; ERO D/ACA 19, fol. 227v; D/ACA 21, fol. 31. *Tye,* who was licensed by Thomas

The remainder preferred to become endowed lecturers, positions which afforded considerable independence as local and episcopal judges possessed a minimal control over them. While several of these lectureships had been established by puritan laymen to provide temporary substitute preachers for non-preaching incumbents, others received long-term endowments from town corporations or private individuals. These provided long tenures for such important Essex puritans as Richard Rogers at Wethersfield from 1572 to 1618, Edmund Chapman at Dedham from 1578 to 1601, George Northey at Colchester from 1580 to 1593, and George Gifford at Maldon from 1585 to 1620.[11]

Several members of the group also combined itinerant preaching with their assigned duties, but only three seem to have assumed the function of domestic chaplain. Robert Wright, the Calvinist chaplain to Lord Rich in 1582, upset both his puritan colleagues and the crown with his disturbing sermons at Rochford Hall and suffered by consequence an extended stay in Fleet prison following his appearance before the high commissioners. Nicholas Colepotts served Sir Thomas Bromley, the lord chancellor. Activities elsewhere forced William Tay to give up his chaplaincy for a "Mr. Ford at Butley" in 1587 to the Suffolk puritan, Anthony Morse.[12]

The puritan contingent made fewer positional changes than the conformist clergy since their university connections and high educational qualities allowed them to secure the more profitable benefices. Most changes derived from the policy

Taylor, Commissary of Essex and Hertfordshire (1587–91), had ceased to teach by June 1, 1598. ERO D/ACA 21, fols. 97, 125. For their preaching activities see Collinson, 226.

11. Davids, 106–108, 117, 123–24; Porter, 92, 230.

12. John Strype, *Annals of the Reformation* (4 vols.; Oxford, 1820–40), III, i, 179–80; Usher, 13, 65; C. H. and T. Cooper, *Athenae Cantabrigienses* (2 vols.; Cambridge, 1858–61), II, 161. *Wright* subsequently served as lecturer at Fryerning (1583), town preacher at Ipswich (Suffolk) (1585–89), and rector of Woodford (1589–1610). D/AEA 12, fol. 101v; Collinson, 342, 403. *Colepotts* also served as vicar of South Weald (1576–93) and rector of Dunton (1585–93).

Aylmer introduced in his triennial visitation of 1583 to force the puritans into conformity. Although the severity of Aylmer's measures affected the entire group of beneficed puritans, the majority of whom suffered suspensions and threats of deprivation, his prosecution was, in the final analysis, more a display of authority than a persecution; only Gifford, Culverwell, and Whiting were deprived.[13] The rest of the beneficed puritans remained firmly placed in their livings and held them until their deaths. The reaction did induce three puritans who lacked sympathetic patrons to seek security elsewhere. Thomas Howell obtained the rectory of Great Stambridge on the nomination of Peter Wentworth and became a pluralist, and Geoffrey Josselin and Thomas Lorkin resigned their livings at Shellow Bowells and Little Waltham respectively for the security of Lord Robert Rich's benefices at Goodeaster and Ashingdon.[14] Several of the curates gained additional security with nominations to benefices within the county. Arthur Dent, the curate at Danbury from 1577 to 1580, became rector of South Shoebury in 1580 on the presentation of Lord Rich.[15] Three years later John Reynolds, curate at Lambourne from 1572 to 1582 and at that time preacher at West Waltham, assumed the vicariate at Walthamstow.[16] John Knight, temporarily forced by the bishop

13. Peel, I, 160–64; Davids, 72–126, provides a synthesis with accompanying documents of Aylmer's activities. The *acta* for the episcopal visitations of 1583, 1586, and 1589 contain few details. Gifford, Culverwell, and Whiting served as vicar of All Saints, Maldon (1582–85), vicar of Felsted (1583–90) and rector of Panfield (1582–87) respectively.

14. *Howell:* rector Paglesham (1578–99); rector Great Stambridge (1588–99); *Josselin:* vicar Goodeaster (ca. 1586–1635); Lorkin: rector Little Waltham (1572–85); rector Ashingdon (1586–96). DNB XII, 139–40 incorrectly confuses the Essex Lorkin (Luckyn, Larkin) with the Cambridge professor of physic by that name. The Essex Lorkin (d. 1596), a grammarian, was licensed to preach on September 10, 1577. GLRO DL/C/333, fol. 85v; GLRO DL/C/336, fols. 115, 120v.

15. GL 9537/4, fols. 44v, 104v; ERO D/AEV 2, fol. 10v. He also served as preacher at Leigh in 1583 and died in 1602 with probate on March 11, 1603 at London. GL 9537/5, fol. 79; GLRO DL/C/338, fols. 92v, 100; *cf* DNB, V, 826–27.

16. ERO D/AEM 4, fol. 14; GL 9537/5, fol. 101v. For references to his tenure at Danbury see my "The Court of the Archdeacon of Essex, 1571–1609" (Ph.D. dissertation, University of California, Los Angeles, 1965), 387, cited as Anglin. This Essex puritan is not the prominent John Reynolds (d. 1607) of Corpus Christi.

to leave the diocese and his cure at Hempstead in 1583, returned as rector of Goldhanger on November 5, 1586.[17] In the same year William Cook left St. James for the cure at St. Giles, a Colchester donative, on the appointment of the puritan sympathizer, John Lucas.[18] William Bird, the schoolmaster at Cockfield, Suffolk, in 1585, assumed the cure at the donative of Theydon Bois in 1592, but resigned in 1597 to become rector in the more valuable benefice of Holy Trinity, Colchester.[19] Two other puritans awaited the calmer days near the end of the reign to acquire benefices. Ralph Hawdon, curate at Fryerning and Margaretting, became the pluralist holder of the rectory of Rayleigh and the vicarage of All Saints, Maldon in 1600,[20] and Thomas Stoughton left his Suffolk lecture post at East Bergholt to assume the cure at Lord Rich's parish of Great Burstead in 1594. In 1600 he resigned to become vicar of the puritan parish of Coggeshall, a position he held until his deprivation in 1606.[21]

The most immediate effects of Aylmer's policy were felt by the clandestine lecturers and especially by the suspended puritan curates. Eleven eventually emigrated to less hostile territory. Suspensions in 1584 forced four of them to leave Essex. William Dyke, preacher at the market town of Coggeshall, a Rich stronghold, transferred to the parish of St. Michael's in the city of St. Albans, where as a preaching curate from 1584

17. ERO D/ACA 16, fols. 79v, 80; Davids, 122; Neal, I, 167. From Roydon, Norfolk, Knight received his orders of presbiter from the bishop of Rochester March 25, 1580 and was licensed to preach by Aylmer October 10, 1585. He died in office in 1606.

18. ERO D/ACA 10, fols. 156v, 167 for references to his cure at St. James. The first reference to his cure at St. Giles is ERO D/ACV 1, fol. 6. Cook (Cock), who received ordination from John, Bishop of Rochester, on September 29, 1579, and his license to preach from Aylmer on August 20, 1583, served at St. Giles until his death in 1625. ERO D/ACA 14, fols. 217, 281v; Davids, 114.

19. Usher, 47; ERO D/AEV 3, fols. 33, 117v; Newcourt, II, 583 (under "Bord"). He was licensed to preach by Stanhope on September 4, 1592. GL 9537/8, fol. 13v. Another by that name served as vicar at Great Chishall (1566–1605).

20. ERO D/AEV 2, fols. 165v, 180v; D/AEA 12, fol. 347; Essex Assize Files, I, file 3 1584/5–1593 (35/28/H), 242–43. Hawdon (Houghe, Halden, Haydon, Hawkden, Houghton) was licensed to preach by Aylmer on May 9, 1586. GL 9537/10, fol. 54v.

21. ERO D/AEV 3, fols. 51, 241v; Venn, IV, 172; Collinson, 225–26. His name is sometimes spelled "Stocton."

until 1589 he enjoyed the benevolent protection of Lady Anne Bacon. Continued pressure by Aylmer finally forced him to move to Hanbury in Staffordshire.[22] John Ward, father of four Jacobean puritan ministers, preacher in the peculiar of Writtle, 1583–84, and schoolmaster at Hatfield in 1584, returned to his old benefice of Haverhill, Suffolk, where he remained until his death.[23] John Paine, the lapsed Brownist curate of Tollesbury, departed for Hanbury in Staffordshire, from which place he was brought to London in 1590 as a defendent in the Star Chamber trial with Cartwright and six other puritans.[24] After having been silenced in the pulpit at Birch in 1583, George Tuke assumed the position as preacher at St. Germans in Cornwall in 1586 and later as preacher at Chesterfield (1594–95).[25]

Refusal to wear the surplice led to the suspension and departure of Thomas Carewe, Charles Chadwick, John Gardiner, and Mark Wiersdale in 1586. Carewe, the "elected" curate at Hatfield Peverel (1584–86) and the founder of a temporary presbytery there, moved to Ipswich, where he served puritan congregations in two donative curacies.[26] Chadwick, the curate at Danbury, 1582–85, left for Cambridge, but eventually returned to the county in 1602 to the rectory of Woodham Ferrers to which he was nominated by Sir Humphrey Mildmay.[27] After temporarily replacing George Gifford, who had

22. Strype, Aylmer, 104, 202; Urwick, 427; Davids, 72–73, 78.

23. GL 9537/5, fol. 1; ERO D/ACA 13, fol. 18; Peel, I, 260–61; Cooper, II, 310; Porter, 230–31.

24. Collinson, 325, 412. Another by this name served as schoolmaster at Beaumont in 1588 and as vicar of Greys Thurrock from March 10, 1589 to 1592. ERO D/ACA 17, fol. 22v; D/AEM 4, fol. 20; D/AEV 2, fols. 203v, 219v; D/AEV 3, fol. 3, 16v; GL 9537/8, fol. 9v.

25. He was licensed to preach in London diocese on February 12, 1582 and preached at Birch and Stebbing. Another by that name was curate of Stepney in 1607. GLRO DL/C/333, fol. 27v; ERO Q/SR 87–88, XI, 70; Peel, I, 262; Cooper, II, 24; GL 9537/10, fol. 89.

26. Collinson, 340–41; Davids, 119. For indirect references to his difficulties with Aylmer and the High Commissioners see ERO D/ACA 12, fol. 136v; D/ACA 13, fols. 92v, 187v. He claimed he was licensed to preach by the archbishop of Canterbury. ERO D/ACA 13, fol. 76v.

27. ERO D/AEV 2, fols. 53, 72, 90, 103v; 128v; Newcourt, II, 682; Davids, 122; Venn, I, 314; GLRO DL/C/338, fol. 43.

been deprived of the vicariate at All Saints', Maldon, in 1584, Wiersdale, the former curate at Brentwood, visited Cambridge in 1585 and eventually settled in Gaddesby, Leicestershire.[28] Gardiner, who was incarcerated at Newgate in 1586 for his nonconformist activities in the peculiar of Heybridge, left for Surrey, where he became associated with the Wandsworth Conference.[29] These Essex émigrés were probably joined by four other puritans whose subsequent activities still cannot be traced: Giles Whiting, a member of the Braintree Conference who was deprived of his rectory at Panfield in 1587,[30] and three curates, Samuel Cottesford of Doddinghurst, who lost his curacy on the resignation of the rector Roger Brown in 1584,[31] John Bishop, the curate at Stanford Rivers from 1580,[32] and Augustine Pigot, the curate at Tilty.[33]

II

The Essex segment of London diocese contained five inferior ecclesiastical jurisdictions headed by two commissaries and three archdeacons. The puritans came under the jurisdiction of four of these—the archdeacons of Colchester, Essex, and Middlesex and the commissary of Essex and Hertfordshire. Technically the commission of the commissary provided him concurrent jurisdiction over the three archdeaconries, but the archdeacons traditionally exercised an exclusive corrective jurisdiction over matters relating to those clerics who resided within their respective jurisidictions. Only a few of the puritans lay outside the

28. ERO D/AEM 4, fol. 16v; GLRO DL/C/334, fol. 61v; Venn, IV, 401; Davids, 126. Wiersdale was curate to the puritan Nicholas Colepotts in 1583–84 in which post he also preached without authority at Doddinghurst and Horndon-on-the-Hill. ERO D/AEV 2, fols. 63v, 106v; GL 9537/5, fol. 103.

29. Davids, 126; Usher, 19; Cooper, II, 10 incorrectly places Gardiner at Maldon.

30. Newcourt, II, 461; Cooper, II, 354; Davids, 109; GL 9537/5, fol. 2v. He became rector in 1582 and was in trouble the next year. GL 9537/5, fol. 2v.

31. ERO D/AEV 2, fols. 65, 84, 107v; Peel, I, 41. Cottesford assumed his cure in 1582 and was licensed to preach on July 16, 1583. GL 9537/5, fol. 95.

32. Bishop lacked a license to preach in the 1583 episcopal visitation. GL 9537/4, fol. 109; GL 9537/5, fol. 1.

33. GL 9537/5, fol. 2; Davids, 121.

competency of the archdeacons.[34] The exchange of benefices and the shifts by the curates eventually placed all but eight of them within the jurisdictional confines of the archdeacons of Essex and Colchester.[35] This development is fortunate, since the records of the courts of the archdeacon of Middlesex and the commissary of Essex and Hertfordshire for this period are now lost, but it does limit our examination to the two jurisdictions.

The constitution of the Elizabethan church maintained an extremely intimate relationship between the archdeacons and their clergy. The basis for the relationship rested on the oaths of office extracted by the bishop from the clergy. These oaths committed each cleric to a state of obedience to the bishop and his inferior officers exercising episcopal authority through grant or composition. This special relationship commenced at the local level upon induction or the acceptance of curiatal licenses. The assumption of office automatically subjected the cleric to the supervisory and corrective powers of the judge and committed him to perform a considerable number of obligatory duties both at court and within his parish. At the court he was obliged under the penalty of contumacy to attend annual synods and visitations and special ad hoc convocations.[36] At these meetings the archdeacon conducted an inquisition into the state of clerical affairs, assigned additional functions to the clergy such as taking charge of or participating in clerical exercises assigned to nonpreachers,[37] collected synodals and impor-

34. Those situated in the parishes of Aldham, Goodeaster, Mayland, and West Waltham were exclusively subject to the commissary; those in the peculiar parishes of Heybridge and Writtle were subjected to the ordinaries of the dean and chapter of St. Paul's and Oxford's New College respectively. Newcourt, II, 5, 233, 328, 411, 629, 687.

35. I.e., Carr, Gardiner, Huckle, Josselin, Morley, Pigoff, Rogers, and Whiting.

36. This applied to nonclerical schoolmasters, midwives, and medical doctors, thus affecting both Gayle and Tye. These officers and curates were generally licensed by the archdeacon.

37. At Colchester, Stephen Beaumont (rector of Easthorpe 1579–1609), Thomas Lowe (rector of St. Leonard, Colchester, 1582–1615 and rector of St. Mary Magdalene, Colchester 1586–97; 1603–1607) served with their fellow puritans Chapman, Edmunds,

tuned for charitable donations, and examined clerical orders and licenses. During the regular court the archdeacon or his assistant handled clerical violations of the canon and ecclesiastical laws, including the use of nonprescribed liturgical forms, failure to maintain the chancel and parsonage houses,[38] contempt of jurisdiction, and personal delicts requiring punishment *pro salute animae*.[39] The court also afforded the cleric an opportunity to protect his rights and dignity of office. There he frequently appeared as plaintiff in the tithe disputes,[40] defamation suits,[41] and *ex officio mero* suits against contemptuous parishioners.[42] The cleric frequently acted as proctor at the court for his parishioners and friends, provided required court certificates for them, and assumed the duties of executor of wills and the administrator of the personalty of intestates. Sometimes

---

Tay, and Wilton as supervisors over clerical exercises. Thomas Knevett, rector of Mile End (1584–after 1607) and Henry Cornwall, curate at Marks Tey (1582–1606) were the only puritans assigned clerical exercises. ERO D/ACA 14, fol. 282; D/ACA 15, fol. 79v; D/ACA 19, fol. 312.

38. Knevett, Beaumont, Seredge, Reynolds, Colepotts, and the puritan rector of Vange (1581–1609), Camille Rusticus, were ordered to make repairs. ERO D/ACA 14, fol. 63; D/ACA 18, fol. 173; D/AEA 7, fols. 180, 195; D/AEA 15, fol. 134; D/AEA 16, fol. 57v.

39. Cases of this type, excluding contentious quarrels, were rare. The serious charge of incontinency was made against four, but only two were tried. The charges against Robert Lewis of Colchester and William Wingfield, the curate of Wix (1585–1603) were dropped. D/ACA 14, fol. 189; D/ACA 19, fol. 326v. After a temporary halt to proceedings by an inhibition from the court of Arches, the ex officio action against Thomas Howell for incontinency with Alice Page was terminated by a successful compurgation, which included the compurgators Arthur Dente and William Negus. ERO D/AEA 15, fol. 160v; D/AEA 16, fols. 13, 36, 53v. The charge against Richard Parker (vicar of Dedham 1582–90) on December 5, 1589 for accepting "Robert Thorne's wife sundry times to have the carnal use of her body" was declared true by his inability to get compurgators. His public penance was changed to a semiprivate penance by Archdeacon Withers on November 24, 1590, and certification of its performance was made on January 22, 1591. ERO D/ACA 17, fols. 238, 267, 304v, 317; D/ACA 19, fol. 101v, 117. For additional details see Collinson, 438–39.

40. The Essex puritans seldom resorted to these in the archidiaconal courts. For actions by Robert Searle, rector of Lexdon (1576–ca.1587), and by Farrar, Knevett, Reynolds, and Howell see ERO D/ACA 9, fols. 89v, 192v; D/ACA 14, fol. 41; D/AEC 1, fols. 254v, 263v; D/AEC 3, fol. 127.

41. Most were treated as regular ex officio cases. For suits brought by John Reynolds and Arthur Dente see ERO D/AEC 1, fol. 234; D/AEC 3, fol. 81v.

42. See for example the suits of John Maiburn (vicar of Much Wakering 1577–87) and Thomas Howell. ERO D/AEA 12, fol. 311; D/AEC 1, fol. 203.

a fellow cleric asked him to serve as a compurgator. At times the judge authorized him to act as a surrogate judge or as court excommunicator.[43]

In addition to his functions as priest the cleric at the parish level performed tasks for the court which made him an essential cog in its successful operation. He assisted convicted parishioners in the performance of court ordered penances, participated in their public confessions within the parish church, and provided them certificates that such had been completed. The cleric also gave notices of impending purgations in the court by his parishioners, and he exhorted the congregation to participate in the court proceedings should they feel the compurgators unworthy persons or the charges false. At services he read the names of excommunicate parishioners and exhorted the rest to avoid association with them. He also denounced obstinate excommunicates and furnished the court a certificate to that effect, so that the judge might commence proceedings to secure secular assistance. In the pulpit he disseminated news and other information forwarded from the judges and exhorted his listeners to donate to charitable causes. He acted as informer to the court and provided the judge a list of crimes overlooked by the churchwardens. It was also his task to assist the churchwardens in drawing up the quarterly presentments and other necessary papers required by the court, which he generally wrote and signed.[44]

By 1583 the Essex puritans had commenced to question and to criticize this traditional relationship. The Dedham Minutes afford us insight into both the reasons for the criticism of the inferior ecclesiastical courts and the changes the puritans proposed to make in that relationship. On May 6, 1583, at a conference meeting in Colchester the radical William Tay

<hr />

43. Chapman, Cottesford, Lewis, and Moncke served as surrogates in the Colchester court. ERO D/ACA 7, fol. 126; D/ACA 8, fol. 290v; D/ACA 9, fol. 88v; D/ACA 10, fol. 119. The Essex court commissioned Seredge and Colepotts. ERO D/AEA 7, fol. 151v; D/AEA 16, fol. 234.

44. Anglin, 56–57.

initiated an examination of the jurisdiction of the inferior courts by posing the question of "whether a man may goe into the courts of an Official being cited by the Somner." The congregation proposed that he "give in his reasons to some of the brethren to be answered." [45] From these beginnings they proceeded during the course of the following year to work out suggested constitutional changes in the existing court system, which they presented in the form of a petition to Archdeacon Withers in early September, 1584.[46] In their proposals the Dedham Congregation placed prominently at the beginning their key reform: "that he would free the godly learned ministers from his Courts, inasmuch as by the word of God they ought to be free from such bondages. . . ." But the Dedham Congregation pragmatically recognized a need for local ecclesiastical courts as disciplinary organs. While they desired as godly clerics to assume the initial task of correction, they were willing to concede the authority to correct and punish obstinate parishioners who refused to be controlled by their ministers to the more powerful archdeacons and secular authorities.[47] Discipline over ungodly or insufficient ministers, on the other hand, was properly the tasks of godly clerical superiors and the archdeacon, who should meet for that purpose in revived synodal congregations so designed that they might replace traditional visitations. In short the program sought to reverse the roles of the clergy and the inferior judges, to make the latter a handmaiden of the former, and to revive the ancient disused decanal synods. Since this program, which Usher has called "the most rational play under discussion for transforming episcopacy into modified presbytery," was impossible to effect, the puritans had no alternative but to resort to the assistance of the local courts for disciplinary measures against offensive parishioners. In fact they went so far as to support the traditional means of detection in the courts

---

45. Usher, 30.
46. *Ibid.*, 87–89. For a discussion of discipline in general see Collinson, 346–55.
47. The Minutes indicate that the Dedham members preferred the help of secular officials. Usher, 53, 67.

by agreeing that churchwardens should "keep their oaths" and make presentments against contemptuous parishioners even though the detection might indirectly hazard the ministry of a conference member.[48]

The puritans nevertheless continued to consider the interference of the inferior judge in their ministries through the frequent use of excommunication and suspension an abuse of office and concentrated on that specific grievance in their public criticisms of the inferior jurisdictions. In 1584 this subject served as one of the major themes in their petitions for redress to the councillors, who incorporated it in their own complaint to Aylmer and Whitgift of "irregularities committed against the godly ministers in Essex by the bishop's inferior officers, the chancellor, commissary, and archdeacons." [49] In effect the puritans charged that excommunications and suspensions pronounced against them by the commissary and the archidiaconal officials were illegal, since the inferior judges were "no judge" because they failed to meet statutory qualifications of office, especially the possession of a doctor of laws degree.[50] These charges only served to cloud the real issue of contention which centered on the clerical oaths of obedience: the right of the inferior judge to utilize existing disciplinary weapons to maintain the laws of the church and his authority as judge versus the scripturally accorded freedom of a "godly learned minister" from all hierarchical supervision. At stake for the puritan was his own urgent sense of duty "to bear up the scepter of His holy truth" for "the zeal of many decayeth and the spiritual slumber invadeth and possesseth many." [51] Beyond the obvious merits of the charges as propaganda, the puritans only managed to secure a perfunctory examination of the abuses from the

48. *Ibid.*, 60.
49. Collinson, 271. For the complaint of the councillors, see Davids, 80. It should be noted that none of the complaints levied by the members of the Dedham Conference against the ecclesiastical courts were specifically directed against the Essex courts. Usher, 37, 39, 51, 63–65, 69–70.
50. Usher, 252, states the disputed point in *37 Henry VIII c. 17* was resolved to the disadvantage of the puritans in *Pratt v Stocke.*
51. Letter from Chapman to Withers, September 17, 1584; Usher, 87.

ecclesiastical hierarchy.[52] At the local level the officials continued to pronounce these two disciplinary forms against the puritans mainly on three accounts: the correction and punishment of those guilty of nonconformist practices; violations of the strict requirement that only authorized clerics exercise a ministry in the church; and contempt of jurisdiction. In general the main difficulties encountered by the puritan clergy at the local level arose from the last two accounts. Owing to the existence of several factors within the inferior jurisdictions which permitted the tolerance of nonconformity, authorized Essex puritans suffered little serious interference in their nonconformists practices from the local judges.

It was the good fortune of the Essex puritans that the heyday of their movement coincided with the time when the inferior courts were achieving their peak of efficiency and activity. This state of affairs, which Marchant has also discovered in the courts of York diocese, was partially occasioned by the new responsibilities assigned the courts in the Elizabethan Settlement, the recusancy legislation, and a continuous stream of new directions from the church hierarchy. For the expanded administrative duties and a large increase in the number of ex officio and contentious actions forced the inferior judges to shift court priorities as local and national needs dictated. In the process they frequently ignored clerical nonconformity. Puritan clerics found temporary relief in the plight of the recusants, whose ex officio cases hid their own, and in the inadequate records system of the registrars, where their names and past crimes lay buried among those of the hundreds of itinerant curates and a large portion of the common populace.[53] Ironically the joint efforts of Aylmer and Whitgift to eliminate non-

52. GL 9531/12, fols. 365–66v. A list of those punished was required in 1586, but no real steps were taken to curb the abuses until the episcopacy of Fletcher. H. R. Wilton Hall, *Records of the Old Archdeaconry of St. Albans* (St. Albans, 1908), 51, 98–101.

53. R. A. Marchant, *The Church under the Law* (Cambridge, 1969); Anglin, 101–103, 273–74. Between 1570–1603 the Essex archdeaconry alone had 345 stipendiary curates, the majority of whom moved at least three times if they elected to remain within the jurisdiction.

conformity were beneficial to the puritans as they severely taxed the inferior judges by increasing their heavy administrative responsibilities. For the successful counterattack by the puritan polemicists forced the hierarchy to take positive action to improve the state of the clergy and to correct abuses within the court system. These responsibilities were shifted mainly to the local authorities.[54] As a consequence visitations, synods, and convocations ceased to be gatherings of the clergy devoted to the discovery of nonconformist practices; instead, they became instruments for the examination of licenses to preach, the establishment and management of programs to provide training to nonpreachers, the performance of a host of ad hoc administrative assignments on behalf of the archbishop, and the gathering and compilation of statistical information for the bishop so that he might reply to his puritan critics. In short, then, the success of the inferior jurisdictions provided the puritans a degree of autonomy and temporary respite from prosecution.

The movement also coincided with the time when the inferior jurisdictions were locked in an intensive competition for business. The dependence of the archdeacons and the commissaries upon lay civilians for the performance of their legal and administrative tasks had the harmful side effect of emphasizing the financial side of the court. As a consequence the more profitable contentious and testamentary causes received preferential treatment at the expense of ex officio corrective causes in all the courts, but was most pronounced in that of the commissary. The commissaries, who purchased their offices for profit, totally relied on civilian officials who treated their offices as remunerative interim posts to important assignments at the capital. By strictly interpreting their commissions the officials hoped to increase the profits they derived from the twenty-six Essex parishes over which they exercised exclusive jurisdiction by gaining exclusive jurisdictional rights over the profitable instance and probate business of

54. *Ibid.*, 105–106.

archidiaconal parishes proximate to their court centers of Chelmsford, Billericay, Braintree, Stortford, and Colchester. As the acquisition of the quarterly bills of presentments was imperative for the furtherance of business, especially since they contained the names of recent decedents, the churchwardens of the contested parishes became liable to summons before both courts. Disciplinary ex officio actions against both clergy and laity suffered and the punishment of offenders became difficult as the actions shifted back and forth between the jurisdictions. By the nineties the contest for business was near an end as the archdeacons and the commissary compromised by dividing the contested parishes. But the struggles had severely diminished the effectiveness of the corrective machinery over crimes in the contested parishes and engendered severe and legitimate criticism because of frequent duplication of effort owing to poor communications between the courts.[55]

Other advantages accrued from the inherent weaknesses in the structure of the ecclesiastical jurisdictions themselves. Of prime importance was the almost total dependence of the inferior judges upon the quarterly bills of presentments for their main source of information. When supplemented by the *comperta*, or discoveries uncovered in the ex officio suits against parishioners, and the occasional information the judges derived from the apparitors, this source was amazingly extensive and detailed. But it suffered from serious defects.[56] The articles of enquiry, a perfunctory set of questions modeled on the episcopal visitation articles, occasionally modified to incorporate topical matters, and generally weighted toward administrative matters determined the nature of the presentments. Their value as an instrument for maintaining clerical discipline was proportionate to the conscientiousness and personal capabilities of the churchwardens in the performance of their assigned duties.

55. *Ibid.*, 161–66 for fuller details and documentation.
56. *Ibid.*, 51, 58–59, 82, 272, for details and references on the churchwardens. One of the rare instances of spying occurred in 1589 when the apparitors in the Colchester archdeaconry were sent to observe whether the priests wore surplices. ERO D/ACA 17, fol. 276v.

Because the office of churchwarden required the performance of multifarious tasks, not the least being frequent appearance before the inferior courts, it was extremely unpopular. Consequently the more substantial members of the parish "elected" unwilling and mainly illiterate laborers—many of them puritans—to perform tasks they were ill prepared to undertake.[57] The inferior judges then faced the disadvantage of having for its eyes and ears at the local level this constantly changing and motley group of unwilling men whose only sense of loyalty to the court was that extracted by the mandatory oaths of office.

The negligible number of cases in the *acta* of the courts which indicate definite collusions between the churchwardens and their puritan clerics suggest that the puritan cause was better served by the churchwardens' ignorance of the law, their gullibility, their neglect of duty, and in the undue influence of the priest in drafting the responses to the articles of enquiry.[58] These shortcomings especially weakened the controls devised to restrict preaching and were extremely important in affording unlicensed and suspended puritans and "foreign" preachers an opportunity to preach within the county.[59] That the system of control broke down at the local level is reflected in the following reply of the churchwardens of Buttsbury in answer to a *comperta* that they had permitted the parson of Stock to preach without first having examined his license. After denying the charge they declared they had "first seen his license as they think for as they said [they] saw a thing in writing with a red seal on it which Pinder did tell them was a license."[60] Other churchwardens were less cautious, and the *comperta* suggest that

57. *Ibid.*, 272.
58. I can determine collusions only at Easthorpe and Peldon. For the indictment of the churchwardens at Easthorpe for inciting and abetting Stephen Beaumont "who used an unauthorized rite" see ERO Essex Assize Files, I, file 2 1573/4–1584 (35/25/T), 206; for Peldon, see ERO D/ACA 19, fol. 261.
59. For the regulations see Edward Cardwell, *Documentary Annals* (2 vols.; Oxford, 1839), I, 180, 291; Edward Cardwell, *Synodalia* (2 vols.; Oxford, 1842), I, 126, 274–75. For the slackness in the archidiaconal courts in dealing with intruders see Anglin, 262–63.
60. ERO D/ACA 14, fol. 289v.

the extent of clandestine preaching was considerable. The following examples drawn from these chance discoveries are illustrative of the problem. John Huckle of Goodeaster admitted
to Aylmer on July 18, 1583, that "he hath preached at
Chelmsford and at Roxwell, Maldon, Stebbing, Chignall Mary
and James, and at diverse other places in London diocese." [61]
In order to permit John Ward to preach without authority
Gilbert Peacock of Beauchamp Roothing and several others
broke into the locked church of Abbess Roothing.[62] Thomas
Carewe succeeded to preach at Great Sampford and Hatfield
Peverel while still suspended as did William Tunstall at Inworth;
Bartimaeus Andrews and Thomas Chaplain, both lacking
licenses, preached at Woodham Ferrers and Hempstead respectively.[63] The victory of the puritans over the restrictions was
doubly sweet when they lived in neighboring jurisdictions, for
local judges lacked jurisdiction over "foreign" preachers; all
the judges could do was to bring ex officio actions against the
resident cleric and the hapless churchwardens for failure to
do their duties.[64]

The frequent turnover in the composition of the
churchwardens and the inevitable factions within the parish
church prevented long-term collusions between the puritan
parish officers and their puritan priests, but sympathetic
churchwardens did abet and encourage nonconformist practices

61. GL 9537/5, fols. 2, 109v. Huckle, who is erroneously assigned a benefice at
Aythorpe Roothing served as preacher at Goodeaster (1583–84). *cf.*, Cooper, II, 23;
Collinson, 379.
62. ERO D/AEA 13, fol. 70v.
63. ERO D/ACA 13, fol. 187; D/ACA 16, fols. 110, 185. Tunstall served as curate
of Inworth (1589) and lecturer of St. Lawrence, Dengy, in 1592. He was also vicar
of Maryland (1593–98); vicar of Great Tottenham (1598–1608); and rector of
Goldhanger (1608–17). ERO D/ACA 18, fol. 277; GL 9537/8, fol. 25v; Newcourt,
II, 284, 412, 610. Chaplain, who was ordained by the bishop of Norwich on May
9, 1582, was curate at Hempstead from ca. 1583–88. He is also named as curate
of Radwinter in 1586. D/ACV 1, fols. 1, 53v, 57v; D/ACA 13, fol. 195v; D/ACA 15,
fol. 17; Davids, 121.
64. The foreign clergy enjoyed the same advantages when they held conventicles
and performed christenings, marriages, etc. in Essex churches. The case involving
Richard Dowe's performance of a marriage in Dedham church is typical of court
proceedings. ERO D/ACA 14, fols. 249, 262.

in strongly puritan parishes. This is indicated most clearly in the negligence of several to provide the incumbents with "comely and decent" surplices, which enabled the priests to administer communion without them and to justify their actions before the courts.[65] Thanks to sympathetic churchwardens Camille Rusticus was able to avoid wearing the surplice at Vange for more than seven years simply because the parish lacked one. The churchwardens, presented at the Colchester court on May 26, 1585, for lacking a Bible, the Book of Common Prayer, and the surplice, still lacked these essentials on May 2, 1592, even though Chancellor Edward Stanhope had intervened in the matter.[66] A slightly different situation existed at Dedham Parish, where the churchwardens eventually acquired a suitable surplice but the priest never used it. In an ex officio suit handled on May 26, 1587, the Colchester court learned that Richard Parker did not wear the surplice. For the next two years the *comperta* lay in abeyance, but the emphasis on the surplice in the episcopal visitation articles of 1589 revived the issue. On April 11, 1589, Stephen Helenett, one of the churchwardens, admitted the parish lacked a surplice. He was instructed to procure one and to reappear on June 20 to give certification that they tendered the surplice to Parker prior to the commencement of service. After seven contumacies the two churchwardens finally appeared on February 9, 1590, and reported that Parker and his wife had taken the new surplice from William Elmes, the late sexton, and had burned it.[67] A court citation to Parker had the desired effect in the return of the surplice to the churchwardens, but it lay unused for the remainder of his ministry at Dedham.[68]

65. For select cases see W. J. Pressy, "The Surplice in Essex," *Essex Review*, XLV (1937), 36–45.
66. ERO D/AEA 12, fol. 274v; D/AEA 13, fol. 157; D/AEA 16, fol. 22; GL 9537/6, fol. 156v; GL 9537/7, fol. 80v.
67. ERO D/ACA 14, fols. 144, 154; D/ACA 17, fols. 155v, 207, 293v. Parker's refusal to allow the wife of Thomas Barker to receive communion forced her to bring suit in the Court of High Commission ca. October, 1587. ERO D/ACA 14, fol. 233v.
68. ERO D/ACA 17, fol. 307. On May 30, 1589, Parker was dismissed on the charge of refusing to wear the surplice by alleging that Aylmer "hath given him liberty to

The inherent fairness which characterized the medieval canon law procedures used by the inferior courts provided the Essex puritans another advantage. The technicalities of the law made procedure slow and cumbersome, thus providing nonconformists considerable time to acquire advice and to continue the practice of their illegal activities.[69] After presentment an accused cleric enjoyed at least a minimum of three months' freedom in a contumacious state before he became liable to the penalty of excommunication. Attending the court session nearest his parish church at its three-week interval sessions, the accused puritan suffered excommunication at the third contumacy at the discretion of the judge.[70] Provided the ex officio action was in progress at the annual harvest break, the Christmas recess, or at the beginning of the episcopal visitation when all inferior jurisdictions were temporarily inhibited, he enjoyed even longer respite.[71] Appearance either in person or by proxy automatically ended the contumacy once the puritan paid the court fees. The defendant could then question the presentment or declare it insufficient, which if justified in the slightest sense required the judge not only to order the citation of the churchwardens for questioning but also to issue a new citation to the accused should the proceedings be continued. The accused could once again recommence his contumacious conduct and gain additional time. Denial of the charges by the accused forced the court to resort to compurgation, an antiquated method of proof subject to abuse, which permitted the cleric to bring his own compurgators. The advantage this offered to the equivocating puritan is self-evident.[72]

use his conscience in that respect until the next visitation." He resigned the vicarage in 1590. ERO D/ACA 17, fol. 191.

69. That they exploited the advantage is patently clear in the Dedham Minutes. Usher, 37, 39, 60, 64–65.

70. The court, for example, reserved the penalty of contempt against Tay twelve times. ERO D/ACA 19, fol. 40v.

71. Harvest breaks included the entire month of August and the early part of September; Aylmer's visitations were conducted in July (1592 excepted), but the courts were usually inhibited through September.

72. The ex officio case against William Seredge for conducting private conventicles in his house is a good example. Put to compurgation he chose Charles Chadwick,

More important to the puritans than these advantages, however, was the all but complete autonomy exercised by the inferior judges in the long interim between the triennial visitations. This provided the puritans respite from Aylmer, who alone in the diocese possessed the right to deprive, reduced likelihood of trials before the High Commissioners, and insured a considerable amount of liberty. For once the bishop shifted the responsibility for the implementation of his policy to his subordinates, it deteriorated before the forces of particularism. Each of the inferior ecclesiastical judges worked independently, his authority limited to those puritans immediately subject to his jurisdiction, and his "nettle" tempered by his private attitude to puritanism and by increased pressure from local sources. Aylmer was extremely unfortunate because he was forced to rely on subordinate judges picked by his predecessors. For the puritan and moderate Anglican archdeacons of Colchester and Essex provided the puritans with what might be conveniently termed "salutary neglect" throughout his episcopate. From 1570 to 1596 the archdeaconry of Colchester remained in the hands of George Withers, whose own moderate puritanism was a compromise between his earlier presbyterianism and his obligations to Anglicanism. While he was "himself conformable to the orders of the church," his sympathies lay decidedly with the puritans.[73] In the adjoining archdeaconry of Essex on July 10, 1571, the puritan canon of Norwich, Dr. John Walker, succeeded the presbyterian Thomas Cole, archdeacon since 1560. Walker sympathized with the cause of reform of rites and ceremonies. His frequent activities in the early eighties in London, where he maintained his residence, forced him to rely

---

Richard Blackwell, Thomas Lorkin—all puritans—and Derick Heldon, rector of Little Stambridge and possibly a puritan, who cleared him by narrowly defining the term *conventicle*. ERO D/AEA 12, fol. 123v. Blackwell, curate at Rayleigh from 1577–87, died in 1588. GL 9537/4, fol. 41; D/AEA 13, fol. 58.

73. Strype, *Ann.*, III, i, 263–64; Newcourt, I, 92; ERO D/ACA 23, fol. 86. In 1568 Withers gained notoriety as a defender of presbyterianism in a debate with Thomas Erastus and later took a significant role in implementing Calvinism in the Palatinate. His puritan leanings are especially reflected in his letter to Whitgift in 1584 which defends his clerics who refused to subscribe. Collinson, 81, 96, 223–34, 256.

heavily on his official.[74] William Tabor, a former Lady Margaret preacher at Cambridge University and a moderate Anglican studiously tolerant towards nonconformists, succeeded Walker on August 27, 1585.[75] In the face of pressure from Aylmer none of these inferior dignitaries elected to become a "hammer" of the puritans, thus catering to the decidedly puritan sympathies of the county, whose inhabitants, in Neal's words, "had a vast esteem for their [puritan] ministers; they could not part from them without tears; when they could not prevail with the bishop, they applied to the Parliament, and to the lords of the privy council." [76]

III

The surviving *acta* of the courts of Essex and Colchester provide demonstrable proof that the puritans enjoyed an era of "salutary neglect" at the archidiaconal level during Aylmer's episcopate. Prior to Aylmer's visitation in 1583 the inferior judges permitted the clergy complete freedom in matters of rites and ceremonies. It was only under Aylmer's steady pressure during the following decade that the judges commenced to prosecute nonconformists. But prosecution in the inferior courts was neither systematically pursued nor severely applied, and the judges reserved their highest penalty of suspension almost entirely for those puritans guilty of contempt of court, rather than of prayer book violations. As prosecutors of the nonconformists the inferior authorities assumed the role of admonitioner and placed the odious responsibility of forcing the puritans into line on Aylmer. For this reason the consequences of their prosecution were generally negative; the puritans continued their nonconformist practices, and the court was forced to take repeated actions against them. The initiative in local prosecution lay almost entirely with the officials, who acted under the stimulus of the

74. Newcourt, I, 72; Cooper, II, 37; DNB, XX, 529; John Le Neve, *Fasti Ecclesiae Anglicanae* (3 vols.; Oxford, 1854), II, 336, 412, 498. Walker lived at St. Botolph's, Billingsgate. ERO D/AEA 8, fol. 23v.
    75. Venn, IV, 197; Newcourt, I, 72.
    76. Neale, I, 168; Peel, I, 187–92; Smith, 13–14.

episcopal visitors, but even the conscientious officials failed to coordinate local prosecution with that of Aylmer. The role of the archdeacons throughout was negligible. In the absence of an official the archdeacon devoted his attention to the handling of profitable contentious and testamentary causes and generally ignored nonconformist practices. An examination of the court cases against nonconformists in the two archdeaconries will clarify these generalizations.

In specific the *acta* indicate that twenty of the thirty-four puritans subject to the jurisdiction of the Colchester archdeaconry escaped prosecution for nonconformist practices during the episcopate of Aylmer.[77] In the decade 1577–87 the Colchester court gave little concern to the matter of clerical nonconformity and few puritans were bothered. After the court in 1577 ordered Thomas Upcher, the pluralist rector of Fordham and St. Leonard's (Colchester), to denounce publicly before his two congregations his fault for not wearing the surplice and making the sign of the cross in baptism, the puritan clergy enjoyed five years of unrestrained freedom.[78] During most of that time the office of official was held by the puritan Ralph King, who as rector of Little Bromley was himself to appear before a more exacting official in 1587 and 1588 to answer for nonconformist activities.[79] The court recommenced prosecution of nonconformists just prior to Aylmer's controversial visitation in 1583 by convening Stephen Beaumont, rector of Easthorpe, and Henry Cornwall, curate of Marks Tey, on charges of surplice violations.[80] In the next thirty-five months the court summoned five more puritans. Of these Withers alone

77. Escaping prosecution were Andrews, Bird, Edmunds, Farrar, Lewis, Lowe, Moncke, Morse, Newman, Paine, Pigge, Searle, Tuke, Tunstall, and Wilton, all holders of benefices and cures; Chapman, Crick, Dikes, Tilney, and Stoughton were lecturers and Gayle and Tye, schoolmasters.

78. ERO D/ACA 7, fol. 132

79. ERO D/ACA 8, fol. 161v for his commission. King, who lacked a university degree, served from July 28, 1579, to October 2, 1581. He was also the pluralist rector of Little Bromley (1579–1611) and Lawford (1584–85). For charges against him see D/ACA 14, fols. 220v, 233v.

80. ERO D/ACA 10, fol. 44v.

demanded a subscription to the three articles from John Knight, curate of Great Sampford, but "for certain causes" relaxed the suspension he tendered when the puritan persistently refused.[81] The official examined puritans from Hatfield Peverel, Thomas Carewe, the curate, and John Ward, the schoolmaster, to see if they possessed valid licenses; and he also ordered William Cook, the curate of St. James's (Colchester), to instruct boys in the catechism, which the puritan had neglected for that "he doth make expositions of some part of the scriptures every Sunday as well in the forenoon as in the afternoon [in] his parsonage." Finally he examined the rector of Easthorpe, Stephen Beaumont, on an accusation by the churchwardens that he had refused to wear the surplice and had committed other prayer book violations.[82] In the year of the triennial visitation of 1586, when seventeen puritans within the jurisdiction suffered an episcopal suspension for refusal to wear the surplice, the court did not hail a single puritan cleric before it for nonconformist practices.

Thomas Taylor, who served as official under Withers from May 26, 1587, to January 22, 1591, undertook the only "serious" prosecution of the beneficed puritans.[83] He brought charges of prayer book violations against eight beneficed puritans, two curates, John Chaplain and William Wingfield, and George Northy, the town lecturer of Colchester and the only lecturer in either jurisdiction to be cited "for not fulfilling the bishop's injunctions in not saying divine service and for not ministering the sacraments with the surplice." [84] Most of these actions dealt

---

81. ERO D/ACA 13, fol. 73.

82. ERO D/ACA 10, fols. 156v, 167; D/ACA 12, fol. 128; D/ACA 13, fols. 18, 59v.

83. ERO D/ACA 14, fol. 151v; D/ACA 19, fol. 111.

84. The beneficed clerics consisted of King, Knevett, Knight, Lewis, Newman, Parker, Tay, and Tunstall. For proceedings against King see n. 79. For proceedings against the curates John Chaplain and William Wingfield and the above (except Tay) in chronological sequence see D/ACA 14, fols. 134v, 138v, 142v, 144, 152v, 154, 162v, 171, 177, 177v, 189, 192, 215v, 227, 242, 269, 278v, 286, 287, 290; D/ACA 16, fols. 105v, 135, 138v; D/ACA 17, fols. 4, 26, 83, D/ACA 18, fols. 18v, 25v, 27, 35, 39, 70, 78, 85v, 86v, 110, 167v; D/ACA 19, fols. 47, 60.

with surplice violations and commenced after the visitation of 1589. For the remainder of his office Taylor levied repeated charges of surplice violations against Chaplain Knevett, Knight, Parker, and Tay.[85] But prosecution immediately subsided following Taylor's resignation. In the visitation year of 1592 the court revived only Tay's old surplice case.[86] In the next year the court continued Tay's case and renewed the old charges against Knevett for surplice and other prayer book violations. It dropped its attempt to revive charges against Upcher when it learned the matter had been assumed by the commissary.[87]

Although most of the puritans within the archdeaconry suffered the penalty of lesser excommunication for contempt of court, only thirteen suffered the more serious penalty of suspension *ab ingressu ecclesiae* at the hands of the archdeacon and his officials during Aylmer's episcopate. Not a single puritan was silenced by the court for actions specifically involving prayer book violations. Of those suspended only the radical puritans John Knight and William Tay were forced to accept and support a court appointed cleric during their incapacity.[88] As the penalty of suspension was automatically lifted at the petition of the cleric or his proctor, its use as a deterrent was never a serious threat to the exercise of the puritan ministry. The most common cause for suspension was nonappearance at the regular synods and visitations which carried an automatic penalty. Henry Cornwall, Thomas Farrar, Arthur Gale, Robert Moncke, Richard Parker, William Tay, William Wingfield, and John Wilton all suffered for this reason, and Parker on four different occasions.[89] Failure to furnish the court with canonically required orders and licenses accounted for other suspensions.

85. ERO D/ACA 15, fols. 3v, 18, 41, 49, 70, 80v; D/ACA 17, fol. 26; D/ACA 19, fol. 257v.

86. ERO D/ACA 19, fol. 261.

87. *Ibid.*, fol. 432v; D/ACA 21, fol. 58v.

88. ERO D/ACA 16, fol. 105v; D/ACA 19, fols. 26, 36.

89. ERO D/ACA 10, fol. 133; D/ACA 14, fol. 293; D/ACA 16, fols. 24v, 79v; D/ACA 17, fols. 18v, 74, 239v; D/ACA 18, fol. 201; D/ACA 19, fols. 3v, 70, 160v, 435v; D/ACA 20, fol. 115v; D/ACA 21, fol. 116v.

Such was the fate of Thomas Knevett, who failed to provide his letters dimissory and mandate of induction for his rectorate at Milend, and of Thomas Carewe, Henry Cornwall, and William Tunstall who assumed cures within the jurisdiction.[90] Failure to exhibit his license to preach led to the suspension of John Knight, while the nonpreacher Knevett was suspended for failure to exhibit certification of his performance of assigned clerical exercises.[91] Suspension for contempt of court was rare, but continued obstinancy by Thomas Carewe and Robert Lewis, who refused to acknowledge court summonses, ultimately forced the judge to resort to that penalty.[92]

The proceedings taken against William Tay, rector of Peldon, perhaps best illustrate the lack of a sense of urgency which prevailed in the Colchester court. Tay, an original member of the Dedham Conference and "always the extremist in the group" had received institution ca. 1583 on the nomination of the widowed Constance Tay, a member of an "ancient" family in the county.[93] Tay had previously served as rector of Little Bentley, 1573–74, which he resigned, but his activities subsequent to his tenure at Peldon are uncertain. He apparently remained within the vicinity of Essex, for on February 12, 1577, he was involved in a subtraction of legacy suit at the Colchester court.[94] While at Peldon Tay also served as part-time lecturer at Layer-de-la-Hay, 1585–88. He moved there in 1587, settling in "Layer Hall," where he housed a series of puritan schoolmasters, commuting to Peldon for services.[95] He also temporarily served as household chaplain to "Mr. Ford at Butley" in 1587

90. ERO D/ACA 12, fol. 142v; D/ACA 14, fol. 283; D/ACA 16, fol. 116v; D/ACA 18, fol. 44v.

91. ERO D/ACA 16, fol. 140; D/ACA 17, fol. 179.

92. ERO D/ACA 12, fols. 142v, 150v; D/ACA 14, fol. 192.

93. Newcourt, II, 180, 467 incorrectly states Tay's institution at Peldon on May 6, 1596. Tay's institution occurred prior to May 6, 1583, when he is first mentioned in the Colchester *acta*. ERO D/ACA 10, fol. 133. At the archidiaconal synod of March 24, 1597, Tay's name is replaced by that of Hugo Branham. ERO D/ACV 2, fol. 11v; Collinson, 319.

94. ERO D/ACA 7, fol. 126v.

95. Usher, 52, 69, 82–83; ERO D/ACA 17, fol. 20v; D/ACA 19, fols. 380, 424v; D/ACA 21, fols. 28v, 71.

and appears after a bout of illness in 1593 to have engaged in preaching activities at Harwich, providing curates to serve in his parish at Peldon from time to time during his absence.[96] Although Aylmer suspended Tay in his visitations of 1583 and 1586, it was not until September 4, 1588, that the fiery puritan encountered difficulty at the local level. After a fifth contumacy Tay finally appeared before Thomas Taylor to answer charges that he had preached against the statutes of religion and the church magistrates.[97] Taylor dismissed him with a judicial warning.[98] In between the court citations and suspensions the fiery puritan regularly incurred for absences at the archidiaconal synods and visitations, Tay received summons on April 11, 1589, to account for his failure to observe the Book of Common Prayer, to wear the surplice, and to catechize the children as well as for the charge that he baptized "where he preacheth, the fount being not there." [99] Tay's persistent refusal to appear and respond to these charges forced the judge on July 16, 1590, to sequestrate temporarily his benefice and to appoint a curate and a temporary preacher, actions which induced Tay or one of his supporters to remove "My Lord's Injunctions and the Queen Majesty's Injunctions" as a contemptuous gesture.[100] The repeated citations of the ineffective official, William Rust, failed to secure Tay's appearance, and Nicholas Nevell, Wither's last official and Rust's successor, quietly dropped the charges. Tay persisted in his puritan practices until his death in 1596.

A situation similar to that in Colchester existed in the archdeaconry of Essex, whose judges instituted ex officio actions for clerical nonconformity against fourteen of the twenty-six puritans.[101] Here as at Colchester the ex officio actions mainly

96. Usher, 65; ERO D/ACA 21, fols. 28v, 71, 241v, 253.
97. Davids, 123; Peel, II, 261; ERO D/ACA 17, fol. 300v; D/ACA 16, fol. 104.
98. ERO D/ACA 16, fol. 131v.
99. ERO D/ACA 17, fol. 238.
100. ERO D/ACA 19, fols. 26, 36; D/ACA 17, fols. 250v, 251.
101. Allison, Barker, Bird, Bishop, Chadwick, Culverwell, Hawdon, Howell, Moncke, Paine, Stoughton, and Tunstall escaped prosecution.

centered on the disputed "indifferent" matters of the surplice, churching of women, the ring in marriage, and the cross in baptism. The court also handled cases involving prayer book omissions, the overly rigid restrictions against communicants, the neglect of holy days, and the holding of conventicles. As at Colchester the judges in the Essex archdeaconry practically ignored clerical nonconformist practices until 1583.[102] In 1584 and 1585 the official William Bingham conducted the only serious prosecution against the puritans for the entire period when he brought thirteen original actions against ten puritan clerics. Of these he revived an old surplice violation against John Reynolds, now vicar at Walthamstow, whom he dismissed with a judicial warning to obey the law.[103] He charged prayer book violations against Thomas Lorkin, the rector of Little Waltham who had just suffered Aylmer's suspension for refusal to subscribe.[104] He brought similar charges against Samuel Cottesford, Mark Wiersdale, William Seredge, and Arthur Dent, who earlier with Lorkin and twenty-two other puritans had petitioned the council for protection against the bishop's repressive measures.[105] Bingham also put to compurgation Thomas Reddrich, the vicar of Hutton (1576–88) who had denied participating in a conventicle, and made the vicar respond to charges that he had improperly received excommunicates at communion.[106] He found unjustified the presentments which charged that Gifford and Wright lacked proper licenses and dismissed them[107] Bingham also entertained the *ex officio mero* suit of Nicholas Colthurst, a layman, against John Maiburn, the vicar of Great Wakering who had refused to church the plaintiff's wife after childbirth, and he heard a counter suit brought by Maiburn against Colthurst.[108]

    102. For charges against Blackwell, Colepotts, Dente, and Reynolds see ERO D/AEA 10, fols. 33v, 46v, 108, 115v, 120; D/AEA 11, fol. 162. None were handled in 1579, 1581, and 1583.
    103. ERO D/AEA 11, fol. 162; D/AEA 12, fol. 281.
    104. ERO D/AEA 12, fol. 55; GL 9537/5, fol. 4v; Davids, 120.
    105. ERO D/AEA 12, fols. 59v, 106v, 117v, 123v, 129v; Davids, 178.
    106. ERO D/AEA 12, fols. 199, 215, 278; D/AEV 2, fol. 107v. Reddrich had previously served as vicar of Childerditch (1572–75).
    107. D/AEA 12, fols. 101v, 265v.
    108. *Ibid.*, fol. 311.

Following the resignation of Archdeacon Walker in 1585, the court of Archdeacon Tabor devoted its attention almost entirely to routine business and left the puritan problem to Aylmer. The tenure of Daniel Dunn, Tabor's first official and a man destined to become Whitgift's vicar general and a leading apologist for the oath ex officio, was especially remarkable in that he did not hear a single case against a puritan for nonconformist practices.[109] In 1587 Dunn's successor, William King, renewed the warning to John Reynolds that he wear the surplice. He belatedly tried Seredge on two old assize indictments for baptismal irregularities and introduced new charges that both he and William Negus had unjustifiably rejected communicants. Like his contemporary at the Colchester court, King resolved the pastor-parishioner conflicts by licensing rejected parishioners to receive elsewhere.[110] In 1590 King instructed Camille Rusticus, rector of Vange, and Nicholas Colepotts, rector of Southweald, to wear the surplice and to certify their compliance, but he suspended further proceedings against Rusticus when he discovered the consistory had commenced a similar action in 1589.[111] For the remainder of Aylmer's episcopate the puritans enjoyed respite from the official. In that time the court expressed willingness to consider Seredge's declaration "that he doeth not use the sign of the cross in baptism . . . that he doeth not utterly refuse to use it," [112] and accepted a certificate from Rusticus that he had "worn the surplice orderly according to the Book of Common Prayer." [113]

109. Venn, I, ii, 75; DNB, V, 1127. Dunn served from November 5, 1585, to October 19, 1586. For other biographical data and references on all the officials in the archdeaconry see Anglin, 35–38.

110. ERO D/AEA 13, fols. 80, 188; D/AEA 14, fols. 137, 266, 287v; D/AEA 16, fol. 52; Essex Assize Files, I, file 3 (1583/4–1593), 235–236. King served as official from November 5, 1585 to October 21, 1590.

111. ERO D/AEA 14, fols. 250, 253; D/AEA 15, fols. 10v, 27v; GL 9537/7, fols. 75, 80v.

112. ERO D/AEA 16, fol. 64. For additional details on his activities see Anglin, 264–69 and Collinson, 349–50, 379.

113. Rusticus, a non-graduate at Corpus Christi, Cambridge, continued to remain adamant in his refusal to wear the surplice and was deprived along with Negus and Culverwell by the High Commissioners in 1609. GL 9537/10, fol. 69v; GLRO DL/C 306, fol. 30v; DL/C 339, fol. 57. For additional references to Colepotts see Anglin, 434.

The Essex court was at no time overly rigorous in the application of its punitive powers against nonconformists. On rare occasions the court directed the puritan to acknowledge his faults either before his congregation or in private before the churchwardens.[114] But normally the official warned the offender to comply with the Book of Common Prayer or else to suffer the full penalty of the law, and he required certificate of compliance from the churchwardens.[115] Like their contemporaries at Colchester, the puritans in the Essex archdeaconry often lived in an excommunicated state, and a few were restricted in their ministry by suspensions incurred for contempt of court.[116] But only two suffered suspensions as a consequence of prayer book violations. On January 14, 1584, the Essex court placed Thomas Lorkin, rector of Little Waltham, on temporary suspension because he failed to wear the surplice and to make the sign of the cross in baptism—violations which would also lead to an indictment at the assizes.[117] On May 15, 1584, the court examined the licenses of Mark Wiersdale, the curate of Brentwood and occasional preacher at Doddinghurst and Horndon-on-the-Hill, and questioned him on a detection for violations of the Book of Common Prayer. In response to the detection, a duplicate of the charges made against him in Aylmer's visitation of 1583, Wiersdale declared that he did "neither wear the surplice nor minister the sacraments according to the book for that he gave the cup to [one] and that one delivered from one to another" and he omitted parts of the book "according to the brevity of the time." The court suspended him, reexamined him again on July 24, and then on September 8, 1584, sent him to see the archdeacon, apparently because he was only a deacon and did not possess a license to preach.[118]

114. ERO D/AEA 12, fols. 117v, 265v; D/AEA 14, fol. 266.
115. ERO D/AEA 10, fols. 33v, 93v, 108v, 120; D/AEA 12, fols. 258, 265; D/AEA 13, fol. 80; D/AEA 14, fols. 70, 250, 253, 282.
116. For suspensions against Seredge, Rusticus, and Howell see ERO D/AEA 12, fols. 53, 300v; D/AEA 13, fol. 71v; D/AEA 14, fol. 149v; D/AEA 16, fol. 13.
117. ERO D/AEA 12, fol. 55; Davids, 120.
118. ERO D/AEA 12, fols. 106v, 164v, 166; GL 9537/5, fols. 5v, 103. Wiersdale, originally of East Deeping, Linc., subsequently succeeded the deprived George Gifford

IV

Collectively the *acta* of these courts offer conclusive proof that the hesitation of the inferior judges seriously inhibited Aylmer's efforts to achieve clerical uniformity. They provide one more illustration of the difficulty faced by the Tudor state in the enforcement of its laws and serve as a reminder that the aspirations of Tudor government are less important historically than its particulated achievements. Restricted by an outdated and unreformed church constitution and by the lack of a systematic codification of the canon law; overwhelmed by a massive diocese which prevented effective personal supervision; forced to rely on unsympathetic inferiors who required continuous pressure to make them cooperate; faced with resistance from the council, the common-law courts, and Parliament without the direct support of his vascillating queen; and subjected to an intensive and effective propaganda campaign as well as overt local opposition—Aylmer was doomed at the onset to limited success.

He owed his achievements almost totally to his personal visitations, for it was through these cumbrous and awkward episcopal courts that he initiated the only positive corrective measures against the Essex puritans. By providing temporary unity to his splintered diocese visitations afforded Aylmer an opportunity to overcome the inherent weaknesses within the particularistic inferior jurisdictions which fostered diversity and permitted considerable freedom to the puritans. But the instrument of visitation could only inquire and correct; it could not prevent. Only firm, steady pressure from the inferior courts could force the nonconformists into line. This was lacking. Left to their own devices, the archdeacons shrouded their eyes to nonconformist practices by concentrating on administrative and judicial activities until the episcopal visitors forcibly directed

---

as vicar of All Saints, Maldon (with St. Peter's) on January 18, 1585, but resigned following his suspension by Aylmer in 1586. After a brief period at Cambridge he became minister at Gaddesby, Leics. (1588–90) and rector of Costock, Notts. (1595–1639). Venn, IV, 401; ERO D/AEM 4, fol. 16v; GLRO DL/C/334, fol. 61v; GL 9537/6, fol. 75v.

their attention to the problem of clerical nonconformity. It was only then that the officials acted, but with limited success. The admonitionary nature of their prosecution, tempered in part by the personal religious inclinations of the archdeacons and officials and by the puritan mood of the county, served as an irritant rather than a remedy and permitted nonconformity to flourish in the midst of persecution.

Essex puritans profited from these inherent weaknesses and enjoyed considerable freedom to do as they pleased, unless the dreaded Court of High Commission stepped in to fill the vacuum. Nevertheless they remained highly critical of the "bawdy" courts. This was occasioned not so much because they were subjects of sporadic prosecution but rather because the church constitution permitted ecclesiastical judges to interfere in the preaching of the word by administering sentences of excommunication and suspension. The puritans believed this interference to be scripturally unjustified, and in their attempt to end it they attacked the judges by questioning the legality of the sources of their power: the use and manner of excommunications, the application of oaths ex officio, the collection of fees, frequent court sessions, and the requirement of quarterly presentments, and the licensing system to control clerical movement. Much of the hardship which the godly incurred at the local level was self-perpetrated and owed not to the constitution but rather to the stubborn refusal of the puritan to abide by existing rules. For it was the puritan's contempt of court which kept him in trouble with the "bawdy" courts and made much of his criticism of the courts unjustified.

R. W. Heinze

Che ENFORCEMENT OF ROYAL PROCLAMATIONS UNDER THE PROVISIONS OF THE STATUTE OF PROCLAMATIONS, 1539 – 1547

Two sections of the Statute of Proclamations were devoted to defining the membership and procedure of a special conciliar court specifically established to enforce royal proclamations. Enforcement was clearly one of the principal concerns of the statute, and when it was altered in 1543 the revision dealt entirely with improving the effectiveness of this court.[1] Although a number of efforts have been made to explain the creation of this court and its relationship to the existing Court of Star Chamber, answers to some of the central questions are not at present clear, possibly because the study of the actual operation of the court has been for the most part neglected.[2]

1. 31 Henry VIII, c. 8; 34 & 35 Henry VIII, c. 23. The official title of the Statute of Proclamations was, "An Acte that Proclamations made by the King shall be obeyed." Six of the ten sections of the statute dealt with enforcement.

2. For previous comment on the court see Edward R. Adair, "The Statute of Proclamations," *English Historical Review*, XXXII (January, 1917), 42–43; I. S. Leadam, *Select Cases Before the King's Council in Star Chamber* (London, 1911), II, xix-xx; G. R. Elton, *The Tudor Revolution in Government* (Cambridge, 1953), 340–44; G. R. Elton, *Star Chamber Stories* (London, 1958), 94; G. R. Elton, "Henry VIII's Act of Proclamations," *English Historical Review*, LXXV (April, 1960), 212–13.

Unfortunately, as is so often the case in the study of the administrative history of the early Tudor period, the materials necessary for such a study are incomplete. The records most needed to determine the effectiveness of the court, its decree books, have not survived. Nevertheless, there are sufficient documents available to learn a good deal about the procedure of the court and its relationship to the Court of Star Chamber. It is also possible, by judicious use of the evidence, to isolate what may have been the major problems faced by the court and to judge the validity of the reasons given in the amending act of 1543 for the changes introduced by that statute. Finally by studying how the powers granted in the Statute of Proclamations were actually used, one has a better possibility of determining why this enforcement procedure was introduced and why the act was repealed in 1547.[3]

The theoretical structure of the court is described in the Statute of Proclamations. This act defined the membership, procedure, and powers of what seems to have been intended as a special conciliar court meeting in the Star Chamber, but separate from the Court of Star Chamber, set up specifically to deal with violations of royal proclamations. The court was to be composed of twenty-six judges including members of the Privy Council as well as lesser officials and heads of governmental departments. Thirteen members including at least two of the most important officers of the realm, the lord chancellor, the lord treasurer, the lord president of the Council, the lord privy seal, the lord chamberlain, the lord admiral, and the two chief justices, were necessary for a quorum. The court was to sit "in the Sterr Chamber at Westminister or elsewhere" and the chancellor and lord privy seal with the assent of six of the court, upon information presented to them, could initiate process under the privy seal or the great seal. Accusations had to be brought within six months of the offense and the case had to be completed within eighteen months "next after the same offence." The court could inflict imprisonment and fine

3. 1 Edward VI, c. 12.

and was empowered to diminish the penalties specified in the proclamations as they saw fit. The statute also specified that no offender would "incurre the daunger and penaltye" of a proclamation unless it had been proclaimed in his shire before the offense was committed. Another section of the statute ordered sheriffs or other officials to proclaim the proclamations directed to them in four market towns within fourteen days after receiving them, "to the entent the Kinges subiectes shulde not be ignorant of his proclamations."[4]

Four years later, when a revision of this structure became necessary, it was also done by statute. The preamble to 34 & 35 Henry VIII, c. 23 explained that the court had been busy and that it had proved difficult to achieve the quorum specified in the Statute of Proclamations within the time limit of eighteen months:

divers and soondrie Informacions have been given and had for the King againste the same Offendoures before the saide honourable Counsaill mencioned in the saide Acte, according to the tenor and effecte of the same Acte; and the same Informacions after Issue joyned and witnesses publisshed, have taken no effecte ende or perfecte determynacion within the tyme lymited by the same Acte, for and in defaulte that there hathe not been present so manye of the Kinges saide moste honorable Counsaill as be lymited and appointed by the same Acte: and so therebye Offendoures have been and be lyke hereafter to be unpunisshed, to the greate encouraging of all suche lyke Offendoures.[5]

In order to resolve the problem, the statute provided that as long as nine persons including at least two of the great officials mentioned in the Statute of Proclamations were present, any judgment or decree given by them was to have the full force

---

4. 31 Henry VIII, c. 8. The other members were the archbishop of Canterbury, the lord steward or grand master, the lord chamberlain of the king's household, two bishops appointed by the king from his council, the secretary, the treasurer and the controller of the king's household, the master of the horse, the master of the rolls, the chancellor of the Duchy of Lancaster, the chief baron of the Exchequer, the under treasurer of the Exchequer, and the treasurer of the king's chamber. See Elton, *Tudor Revolution*, 340–41 for an analysis of the personnel of the court.

5. 34 & 35 Henry VIII, c. 23.

of law. The closing sentence of the statute limited its duration to the life of Henry VIII.

The actual functioning of this court can be reconstructed from the surviving records preserved among the Star Chamber Proceedings in the Public Record Office.[6] For the present study fifteen cases have been located which were specifically addressed to this court. Their bills are easily recognizable from their unique address:

To the right honourable the Lord Archebishoppe Caunterbury the lord chauncellor of England, the lord Treasourer of England, the lord president of the Kynges most honourable Counsell, the lord pryvy Seale, the greate Chamberleyne of England and other the Kynges most honourable Counsell namyd and appoynted by an Acte of Parlyament made at Westminister the xxviijth day of Aprell in the xxxj yere of the reigne of our sovereign lord Kynge Henry the eight for the heryng and determynacion of the contemptes and offences commytted and don by any person or persons contrary to the Kynges highnez proclamacions sett furthe made and proclaymed by the Kynges highnez and his most honourable Counsell namyd in the seid Acte or the most part of them by vertue of the said Acte.[7]

The bills continued by a careful formula to reveal their reliance on the authority of the Statute of Proclamations. They specifically quoted a portion of the Statute of Proclamations and the proclamation upon which the accusation rested. They maintained that the proclamation was based on the authority of

6. Public Record Office (PRO) Star Chamber Proceedings, Henry VIII (St Ch 2). Although these cases are calendared, the calendar is not completely trustworthy for locating all cases based on proclamations and does not reveal which ones were addressed to the statutory court. *P.R.O. Lists and Indexes No. XIII List of Proceedings in the Court of Star Chamber Preserved in the Public Record Office, I, (1485–1558)*. Leadam has included two cases in his Selden Society volume; however, he does not include all the documents available in one of those cases. In *Smythe and Barnes* vs *Valentyne and others*, he includes only the bill. The answer, depositions, and interrogatories are omitted. Leadam, *Star Chamber*, II, 225ff; 277ff. See PRO St Ch 2/17/195 for the bill and 2/19/209 for the remainder of the case.

7. PRO St Ch 2/1/153. The remaining bills are found in 2/2/168; 2/2/170; 2/2/210; 2/17/195; 2/20/188; 2/23/7; 2/23/183; 2/23/208; 23/23/248; 2/24/310; 2/28/14; 2/28/24; 2/29/96; 2/29175. Two other surviving cases may also have been addressed to the Court. One is so badly mutilated that the full address is lost. *Ibid.*, 2/8/150, and the other consists merely of a series of depositions which dealt with an offense against a proclamation. *Ibid.*, 2/2/22.

the statute and that it was proclaimed in the defendant's county on a specific date before the offense took place. They then stated that the alleged offense was in violation of a proclamation and ended by requesting a writ of subpoena for the defendant to appear and answer the charges usually before "your lord-shipps"; however, one bill mentioned "the Kynges Courte of the Starre Chamber." [8]

The surviving bills cited offenses against four proclama-tions. The vast majority, twelve out of the fifteen, alleged offenses against a proclamation dated February 16, 1541, for-bidding unlicensed exports. No extant copy of this proclamation has been discovered; however, a portion of it can be recon-structed from the bills in the Star Chamber Proceedings. The proclamation rested on the authority of the Statute of Proclama-tions. It forbade unlicensed export of corn, grain, meal, billet, timber, tanned leather or hides upon pain of forfeiture of the items shipped and "all other their goodys and cattalles and also to have imprisonment at the Kynges maiestyes wyll and pleasure." It threatened mariners who transported the goods with loss of their ships and also the goods and chattels of the mariners on the ships.[9] Customers, controllers, or searchers who allowed the export would forfeit their offices as well as their goods and chattels.[10] Although the enforcement section of the proclamation is not included in the bills, a portion of it can be determined from another source. 34 & 35 Henry VIII, c. 9 referred to the proclamation. It threatened offenders against one section of the statute with forfeiture of the grain

8. *Ibid.*, 2/28/24. Some bills also alleged violation of statutes: "agaynest the tenor and forme of the sayd proclamacion as agaynest the forme and effecte of dyvers statutes and provysyons." The case was, however, based on the proclamation probably both because the proclamation carried a more severe penalty and also so it could be heard by the court set up by the Statute of Proclamations. *Ibid.*, 2/28/14.

9. *Ibid.*, 2/23/183. Some of the bills read only "other their goods and chattels" but the majority include the word "all."

10. *Ibid.*, 2/2/170. Since the bill from which the text in the printed edition of Tudor royal proclamations was taken did not accuse port officials of allowing illegal export that portion of the proclamation was not included in the bill and is therefore not provided in the edition by Paul L. Hughes and James F. Larkin. *Tudor Royal Proclamations I: The Early Tudors (1485–1553)* (New Haven, 1964), III, No. 197.6, pp. 280–81.

shipped and of their ships if they failed to enter into security with the customer at Bristol not to transport the goods abroad, "whereof the King our Soveraigne Lorde to have three partes therof and the partie that will sue for the same the fourthe partes before the Kinges moste honorable Counsaill according to the Kinges Proclamacion in that behaulf made and provided." [11]

Two of the remaining bills rested on a second proclamation dated April 4, 1542, prohibiting the stealing or keeping of hawks' eggs or the raising of certain kinds of hawks. The penalty decreed was an incredibly large fine of £100 of which informers were to receive £40. [12]

The last of these fifteen bills involved no fewer than three proclamations. Baldwyn Smythe and Richard Barnes accused Sebastian Danckerd and Henry Pyntill of shipping cheese and butter in violation of a proclamation of January 7, 1544, which temporarily forbade all export of a series of food items until provision could be made for England. They also accused the port officials of Ipswich and Colchester of collusion. This proclamation decreed forfeiture, imprisonment, and fine for offenders and £100 fine for port officials who allowed the export. [13] In the same bill they accused a number of persons of violating a proclamation of May 20, 1541, which had modified the earlier proclamation of February 14, 1541, to allow victualling of Calais. However, it specified that if anyone maintained he was going

11. 34 & 35 Henry VIII, c. 9. Section ii of the statute enacted that no person was to load grain on the Severn between Gloucester and Bristol before entering into security with the customer at Bristol not to transport the goods abroad.

12. Corporation of London Record Office (CLRO), Journals of the Common Council, XIV, 319; British Museum (BM) Harleian MS, 422, 141; Hughes and Larkin (eds.), *Royal Proclamations*, I, No. 211, pp. 309–10. The date given by Hughes and Larkin is probably the date when the proclamation was proclaimed. Both bills cite the proclamation as being made on April 4, and the proclamation title, included on the copy in the London records gives the same date. The text printed by Hughes and Larkin specifies that the informer will receive "one tenth" of the fine; however, the manuscript reads £40.

13. BM Harleian MS, 442, 153; Hughes and Larkin (eds.), *Royal Proclamations*, I, No. 225, p. 324. The bill maintained that the proclamation was based on the Statute of Proclamations; however, the surviving manuscript copy of the proclamation does not make a reference to the Statute of Proclamations.

to ship to Calais and then went elswhere, he would incur the penalties of the earlier proclamation.[14]

Each of the cited proclamations carried an unusually severe penalty and therefore promised a substantial reward to the informer who introduced the case. Whether the full penalty threatened was actually exacted or was simply used as a threat to deter offenders poses another problem which will be dealt with elsewhere in this study. Undoubtedly they were meant in part to attract private prosecution since the government did not have the machinery to enforce penal laws by public process. The surviving bills confirm that they were successful. Information was brought by the attorney general, William Whorwood, in only three cases, and two of them accused port officials of corruption. Three were introduced by John Mascy, searcher for Chester, probably primarily interested in his own reward, and the remainder came from private bills.Clearly, among the private prosecutors, there were professional informers.[15]

The bills, if the accusations were true, suggest some corruption among port officials. In three cases they were specifically accused of allowing illegal export. In three other cases, although no specific charge was made in the bill, it is quite clear that, if the defendants were guilty, the port officials were certainly implicated.[16] The bills are usually almost impossible to date precisely, but the offenses were always specifically dated. Six offenses occurred in 1541, seven in 1542, and one in each of the two following years. Fortunately, two stem from the period after the revision of the Statute of Proclamations so it is at least possible to make some comparisons and to try to determine if the enactment of 34 & 35 Henry VIII, c. 23 actually improved the efficiency of the court.

14. Hughes and Larkin (eds.), *Royal Proclamations*, I, No. 201, pp. 298–99.
15. PRO St Ch 2/2/168; 2/2/170; 2/2/210 for the attorney general's bills; *Ibid.*, 2/24 /310; 2/28/14; 2/28/24 for Mascy's bills. Henry Sayer, who brought two bills, was extremely active in the Exchequer as an informer. In Easter Term, 1545, alone, he brought at least eight accusations to the Exchequer. PRO E159/324, Easter, 24; 29; 64; 65; 665; 67; 68; 71. Baldwyn Smythe, who brought one bill, also appeared frequently as an informer in the Exchequer.
16. PRO St Ch 2/22/217; 2/29/96; 2/29/175.

Answers survive in ten cases. Generally they alleged that the information was untrue and "insufficient in the lawe" and that the defendant was, therefore, not compelled to answer. This response, which was standard form in answers in conciliar courts, was in each case followed by a formal answer to the charges in the bill. Some of these answers are especially revealing, because they indicate that the Statute of Proclamations may have at times even hindered enforcement by providing the defendant with a convenient technical point on which to rest at least part of his defense. One defendant argued that the bill had not alleged "that the said proclamation was made at four severall markett townes accordyng to the tenor of the said estatute [Statute of Proclamations]."[17] John Dankerson, accused of exporting grain in violation of the proclamation of February 14, 1541, maintained that the offense had taken place before the proclamation was actually proclaimed in his county.[18]

Possibly the most interesting answer was that given by Robert Vawdrey, deputy customer of Chester. Vawdrey was accused by the attorney general of allowing illegal export of grain. He maintained that he did not have to answer because he was a deputy customer, and the proclamation specified only customers, comptrollers, and searchers. This portion of his defense is so remarkable that it is worth repeating verbatim:

the worde of the proclamacion recited in the seid informacion extendes by especiall worde to Custumers, Comptrollers or Serchers and not to any Deputis of any Custumer Comptroller or Sercher as by the same proclamacion playnly apperith. And therefore and forasmuche as it apperith by the seid informacion that the seid Robert Vawdray at the days and tymes of the suposed offence spicfied in the seid informacion allegged to be done was but deputie Custumer and no Custumer, Comptroller nor Sercher, he is not charged nor chargeable by the seid proclamacion for that that the same proclamacion is to be taken and construed in like maner and forme as a estatute peynalty which ought not be construed by any equitie but directly accordyng to the Word in the same conteyned.[19]

17. *Ibid.*, 2/23/248.
19. *Ibid.*, 2/2/211.

18. *Ibid.*, 2/29/175.

He went on to answer further and to deny the charges, but his plea seems to have been taken seriously, for in the interrogatories efforts were made to establish that even if he was a deputy customer, he still did the same work and had the same responsibilities as a customer.[20]

Replications survive in three cases, and a rejoinder is available in one. Usually they fail to provide any new information; however, one replication is of considerable interest, because, at least indirectly, it illustrates that lack of a quorum may have been a common plea on the part of defendants. The bill was probably submitted late in 1542 before the revision of the Statute of Proclamations had taken place. John Hogges accused Thomas Isakke of keeping goshawks contrary to the king's proclamation. Isakke admitted keeping the hawks, but maintained that the proclamation had not been proclaimed in his vicinity, and he, therefore, had no knowledge of the proclamation. Hogges asked in his replication that he be awarded the decision because Isakke had confessed that he kept the hawk, "in this honerable court beyng fully furnisshed with such nombre of the Kinges most honerable counsell as be mencened in the seid Acte [Statute of Proclamations]."[21]

Depositions were taken both in and out of court. In one case it can be documented that depositions were definitely taken in the Court of Star Chamber. A note at the end reads: "The said John Spodill came into the Court of Sterr Chamber" and depositions were taken by Thomas Eden, the clerk of the Star Chamber.[22] In three cases commissions were utilized to take depositions in the county. A commission of *dedimus potestatem* was utilized in one post-1543 case possibly, since was not unusual in Star Chamber proceedings, to lighten the burden on the court. The commissioners were ordered to arrest the ship and goods seized and to call the parties before them and if "it shall appere to them the same corne to be forfayt," they were given

20. *Ibid.*, 2/2/212.   21. *Ibid.*, 2/23/248.
22. *Ibid.*, 2/19/209. The appearance of the documents seems to provide evidence of where the depositions were taken. Depositions taken in court are generally on a small folded sheet, while those taken by commissions are usually on a long roll with either the signatures of the commissioners or a statement by them at the end.

214   R. W. Heinze

full power to keep the ship to the king's use and to sell the
corn. They were also instructed to make a report of their actions
"in this Court of Sterr Chamber." [23] Unfortunately, we do not
know if they utilized that authority. In one case the interrogatories are especially interesting, because they reveal that
the informer took seriously the penalty of forfeiture of all goods
and chattels specified in the proclamation. One of the questions
he submitted was "of whatt substance in gooddes, money, plate
and other thinges is the seid defendaunt woorth?" [24]

Although the evidence from the surviving documents so
far discussed reveals a good deal about the procedure and the
functioning of the court, the answers to the more important
questions are elusive since the most crucial documents have
not survived. If the decree books were available, one would
be able to find more convincing answers to such questions as:
How effective was the court? How swift was its procedure?
Were the severe penalties decreed in the proclamations actually
carried out? Did 34 & 35 Henry VIII, c. 23 have any significant
impact on the effectiveness of the court? Lacking the documents
necessary to provide more definitive answers, one is forced
to utilize evidence from a variety of sources to suggest, at least,
likely answers to these questions.

Fortunately, the surviving records provide a good deal
more than is evident at first glance. First, one can say something
about the time that elapsed between the last offense cited and
the taking of depositions in five cases. Since three of them
were probably heard before the quorum of the court was
changed and two were certainly heard afterwards, some comparisons are possible.

The longest period between the offense and the depositions
occurred in one of the cases involving John Mascy. Mascy cited
an offense which took place on July 19, 1542, and depositions
were not taken until May 12, 1544, almost twenty-two months
later.[25]

23. *Ibid.*, 2/22/217.   24. *Ibid.*, 2/29/96.
25. *Ibid.*, 2/2/174–76; 2/28/14.

A large number of documents survive for another case in which Henry Sayer accused James Flechar of illegal export on July 12, 1542. A commission was sent out on June 20, 1543. The depositions were returned on October 4, 1543, signed by the commissioners, who reported that they only had depositions on the part of Flechar, because Sayer did not bring any witnesses before them. They also submitted written evidence from the customer's and comptroller's books establishing that George Trappe rather than Flechar had shipped the goods in the ship named in the bill on the date specified. Sayer, however, had already produced witnesses in court and the depositions taken on his part are dated June 7, 1543. In this case there must have been at least a six-month delay between the bill and the commission. The offense took place in July, 1542. By the limitations imposed in the Statute of Proclamations information had to be brought by January, 1543. Yet the commission was not sent out until at least five months after the last possible date for the bill, and the report did not come back until four months later.[26] The attorney general was more fortunate. He brought his accusations against Robert Vawdrey and others for offenses committed in June and August of 1541. Depositions were taken on July 4, 1542, thirteen months after the first offense cited.[27]

The two cases heard after the enactment of 34 & 35 Henry VIII, c. 23 moved much more quickly. John Lysse seized a ship in which Symond Edwards was illegally exporting on November 11, 1543. The bill can be dated specifically, because the commission made reference to it. He submitted the bill on November 29, 1543, and the commission was sent out the same day with orders to decide the issue and report back by January 20, 1544.[28] Baldwyn Smythe and Richard Barnes were not so fortunate, but possibly the blame rests on them for bringing such a complex case. In one bill they alleged a series of five offenses committed

26. *Ibid.*, 2/29/96. This case spanned the period when 34 & 35 Henry VIII, c. 23 was enacted.
27. *Ibid.*, 2/2/210–12.
28. *Ibid.*, 2/22/217; 2/23/183. This is the only surviving case where the commissioners were actually directed to hear and to decide the case.

between July 13, 1544, and September 12, 1544, by seven different men. Depositions for the informers were taken in court on February 29, 1545, and those for two of the defendants are dated April 23, 1545, nine months after the date of the first offense.[29]

None of this, of course, tells us anything very specific about the full time involved in the case, because we normally do not know the actual date of the bill, or of the final decree. However, if the three cases heard before the enactment of 34 & 35 Henry VIII, c. 23 are not an exception, certainly they suggest that the preamble to that statute was not exaggerating when it maintained that it was difficult to acquire convictions within the time limit of eighteen months. Furthermore, the average interval that elapsed between the offense and the depositions in the cases heard before 1543 was significantly longer than in those heard after that date. Even assuming a wide variation in the time between the offense and the submitting of the bill, there is at least some evidence that the court acted more swiftly after the quorum requirement was changed.

Unfortunately, it is more difficult to learn anything about the actual results of the cases or if the full penalties of the proclamations were in fact carried out. Some information on at least the second question can be obtained when it is possible to trace the careers of defendants after the decision must have been given. John Mascy, the searcher of Chester, who must have had a notorious reputation and who had been accused by the attorney general, either was not convicted or the full penalty of the proclamation was not applied. He was still searcher at Chester on July 29, 1546, four years after the alleged offense.[30] Robert Vawdrey, who had presented that clever

29. *Ibid.*, 2/17/195; 2/19/209.
30. John R. Dasent, and others (eds.), *Acts of the Privy Council of England (1452–1628)* (London, 1890–1907), I, 499. John Mascy was also accused of misconduct on October 17, 1539, PRO SP/1/154, 37; on June 7, 1545, the inhabitants of Chester complained to the Council that he had seized certain Spanish wines from a merchant and he was ordered by the Privy Council to restore them. Dasent, *Acts of Privy Council*, I, 184.

defense to the attorney general's information, certainly was not ruined professionally even if he lost the case. In October, 1545, he was made serjeant-at-law at Chester.[31] Finally Sebastan Danckard and Giles Hostman, two of the merchants accused by Baldwyn Smythe and Richard Barnes of shipping butter and cheese in violation of the proclamation of January 7, 1544, were allowed by the council in August, 1546, to convey cheese with the remainder of their license, because they had not been able to use the full amount specified as a result of the restraint imposed by the proclamation.[32] All of this implies that, if the men were actually convicted, the full penalties were not carried out.

Fortunately for one case, a decree is available as the result of a unique recording on the king's remembrancer memoranda rolls in the Exchequer. This finally makes it possible to discuss a case in its entirety.

The bill, answers, and depositions are found among the Star Chamber Proceedings. The bill was addressed to the court established by the Statute of Proclamations in the normal manner. Henry Sayer accused Peter Henryksen of shipping wheat, malt, and barley on March 31, 1541, in a ship owned by Jasper Cornelisson in violation of the proclamation of February 16, 1541. He also accused Harmar Artson of shipping malt and barley in a ship owned by John Dankerson on the same day. Sayer revealed that he had seized the ships and goods and left them in the hands of Edward Baker, the mayor of Lynn. The defendants answered that the goods were bound for an English port and that they had signed an obligation with the customer of Lynn to that effect. In addition they maintained that they had shipped before the proclamation had been proclaimed at Lynn. The replication, rejoinder, and interrogatories do not survive, but the interrogatories can be surmised from the depositions. One set of depositions, taken in

31. *Letters and Papers, Foreign and Domestic of the Reign of Henry VIII* (London, 1862–1919), XX(2), No. 706 (21), 319.
32. Dasent, *Acts of Privy Council*, I, 509, 513.

the county by three commissioners, was sent back to the court on July 4, 1541. The interrogatories must have dealt with the basic facts of the case and the defendants' effort to establish that they had shipped before the proclamation had been proclaimed in Lynn on March 28, 1541. Nine witnesses testified, including Edward Baker, who held possession of the goods and ships. Most of them maintained that the goods had been shipped before the proclamation, although one stated that Artson had shipped after the proclamation, "by reason he could not take hit in before for fowlenes of wether."

The second set of depositions were those for Sayer taken on June 18, possibly in 1541, although the year is not given. These reveal a possibility that officials may have been bribed. The interrogatories must have asked whether the defendants had entered their destinations in the customers' records and whether recognizances had been taken. In addition they must have sought to establish that the customers were bribed and that when Sayer asked to see the recognizances he was told by the deputy customer, Abraham Polson, that there were none. The three men questioned—Edward Baker, John Pace, the customer, and Abraham Polson—all maintained that bonds were taken before the proclamation and recorded in the customer's book. Although Baker said he knew nothing about the questions dealing with bribes, both Pace and Polson firmly argued that they had "never receyved any reward nor any was promised," and that Polson did not say there were no bonds. They did admit that Sayer had asked to see the customer's books, but they maintained that Pace had asked Sayer if he had a commission from the king's council. When Sayer answered negatively, Pace said he would not be allowed to see them unless he had such a commission.[33]

Although he seems to have been hampered in his efforts by the port officials, Sayer persisted and in the end received a reward which must have made worthwhile all the energy he had expended. The case was transferred to the Exchequer

33. PRO St Ch 2/29/175.

after the decision in order to collect the sums due to the king, and the Exchequer record provides us with information on the remainder of the case. On November 17, 1544, the king directed a writ to the treasurer and barons of the Exchequer enclosing both, "Tenorem cuiusdam decreti & judicij coram nobis and consilio nostro in Camera stellata apud Westmonastarium," and an account made by Edward Baker to the same court. The names used for the court clearly indicate that the decision was given in the Court of Star Chamber. The writ called the court, "consilio nostro in Camera stellata" and in the decree the court called itself, "the honorable court of Sterr Chamber." [34]

The decree and the account of Baker reveal certain further steps in the case. Baker stated in his account that he was called to London by subpoena three times during the case, "one tyme xii dayes, one other tyme xi dayes and the third tyme xx dayes," possibly indicating long delays in the procedure. The decree finally came on June 14, 1543, after the defendants failed to appear at the final hearing. The court reported the event in part as follows:

and for asmoche as at the heryng and discussyng of the seid informacion none of the seid parties apperid ne yet also any person of any attorney auctorised and instructed apperid for them to make aunswere in the same matter and for asmoche also vppon the deliberate examinacion and heryng of the same matter ther aperid a playne and evident intent to convey and transporte ouer into the parties of beyond the see all the seid corne and grayne mencioned in the seid informacion contrary to the kynges maiesties proclamacion.[35]

The court, therefore, decided against the defendants and declared the grain and ships "forfeyted vnto the Kynge." The penalty was severe, but the full penalty of the proclamation, forfeiture of all goods and chattels, was not carried out, and the customs officials, who must have been involved, if the defendants were actually guilty, do not seem to have been punished. Baker, who was present at the time of the decision, was bound

34. PRO E159/322, Michaelmas, L.   35. *Ibid.*

by recognizance to yield an account for the grain sold by him and for the ships. His account reveals that the grain was sold for a total price of £139. 9s. 4d. and he had taken recognizances for the ships which were valued at £72. He deducted his expenses incurred in connection with the case and for storing, hauling, and measuring the grain. This left a total of £129. 7s. 9d. from the sale of the grain and £72 in recognizances for the ships. In accordance with the proclamation one-fourth, £50. 6s. 11¼d., was awarded to Sayer and the remainder, £151. 0s. 9¾d., went to the king.

After examining the account, the Exchequer ordered Baker to be bound to make satisfaction to both the king and Sayer for their share of the money received for the sale of the grain and to deliver the obligations made for the ships. Baker delivered the obligations on November 20. They had been taken on July 26, 1541, and August 16, 1541, almost two years before the decision was given, from the owners of the respective ships and four other men. The validity of each obligation had been made dependent on the outcome of the case. Each was to become due when the ship was "judged or deamed a lawfull forfeiture by reason of the seid seasure" or else it was "to be voide or of none effect." The Exchequer record ends with the order of the court for the men who had made the obligations to appear. Two men appeared, in neither case the original owner of the ship, and they made new obligations to pay three-fourths to the king and one-fourth to Sayer.[36]

The court, at least in this case, had proved a useful instrument for enforcing royal proclamations, and the informer, after a two-year wait, was handsomely rewarded for his efforts.[37] Nevertheless, the full penalties of the proclamation had not been imposed, and despite the fact that the goods had been seized, it took a long time before a decision was rendered. The

36. *Ibid.*, Ld.
37. Compare Sayers gain of £50 6s 11¼d. in one case with George Whelplay's gain of £21 11s 8½d. in a series of actions in the Exchequer for over a period of three years. Elton, *Star Chamber Stories*, 86.

interval between the offense and the depositions was only three
months, but the decree was not given until twenty-three months
later, in violation of the time limit set by the Statute of Proclamations. Clearly the lamentations of the preamble of 34 & 35
Henry VIII, c. 23 were not an exaggeration even though in
this case the defendants were convicted. One wonders, however,
if they would have had more success, had they appeared at
the final hearing and reminded the court of the eighteen-
months limitation.

Thus the Statute of Proclamations did have a significant
effect on the enforcement of royal proclamations, but it is not
always clear how effective that impact was. The conciliar court
was utilized rather extensively, and the bills introduced as well
as the defenses offered relied heavily on the specific wording
of the Statute of Proclamations which at times may have even
hindered the process of prosecution. Furthermore, the time
limit imposed by the Statute seems to have caused difficulties
at least before 1543. On the other hand there is no indication
in the surviving materials that the court functioned as a body
separate from the Court of Star Chamber. One bill requested
appearance before the "Kynges Courte of the Starre Chamber,"
depositions were taken in the "Court of Sterr Chamber" by
the clerk of the Star Chamber, and commissioners were ordered
to report to the "Court of Sterr Chamber." Even the single
surviving decree indicates that the decision was given by "the
honorable Court of Sterr Chamber." The procedure of the
court was identical with Star Chamber procedure with the single
exception that proclamations cases were addressed in a different
manner from normal Star Chamber cases, and they relied so
heavily on the Statute of Proclamations for their authority.

Even the formal address does not seem to have been necessary to have cases heard before the court. Sometimes plaintiffs
seem to have become confused and addressed their bills in
the normal Star Chamber manner. In one case two bills survive.
One was addressed to the chancellor with a brief reference
to the Statute of Proclamations and the second was addressed

in the formal fashion of a proclamations case.[38] George Whelplay, whose extensive activities as an informer between 1538 and 1541 Professor Elton has described, brought twenty three bills between 1541 and 1543 based on violations of the proclamation of February 16, 1541, forbidding unlicensed export.[39] None of them were addressed in the normal manner used for other proclamations cases. Rather all were addressed to the king as was common for Star Chamber cases. They followed two different set forms. Fifteen bills followed a short form in which the bill simply cited the proclamation and asked for a writ of appearance "before the lordes of your most honorable councell at Westminister."[40] Eight bills used a longer form, which was distinguished from the other by a reference to the condition which resulted in the proclamation and ended with a request that the accused be summoned to appear before "your honourable counceill in Starre Chaumber." [41] For three cases additional documents survive which reveal that the court took action on these bills. They do not, unfortunately, reveal anything further about the court. In one the depositions at least provide some dates. The offense alleged against a certain William Hyll for export of beans took place on April 21, 1543, and the depositions were taken on November 16, 1543, seven months later.[42]

If in practice no distinction was drawn between the court established by the Statute of Proclamations and the Court of Star Chamber, the major impact of the Statute of Proclamations on the enforcement of royal proclamations must have been to encourage proclamations cases to be handled by the Court of Star Chamber.[43] However, it must have been the Court of

38. PRO St Ch 2/23/208−210.
39. *Ibid.*, 2/18/149; 2/27/32; 2/27/40; 2/27/42; 2/27/63; 2/27/64; 2/27/80; 2/27/87; 2/27/90; 2/27/91; 2/27/93 (twelve bills); 2/27/118.
40. *Ibid.*, 2/27/63; 2/27/90; 2/27/32; 2/27/40; 2/27/42; 2/27/64; 2/27/87; 2/27/91; 2/27/118; 2/27/93 (six bills).
41. *Ibid.*, 2/18/149; 2/27/80; 2/27/93 (six bills).
42. *Ibid.*, 2/27/63.
43. This conclusion is not new. Professor Elton, who cited two of the cases heard in the court noted: "There is nothing to show that this conciliar committee ever dealt with Mascy's and Sayer's bills. The indications are that the complaints were handled

Star Chamber fettered by the quorum requirements and the time limit specified in the Statute of Proclamations for the preamble of 34 & 35 Henry VIII, c. 23 certainly clearly states that this was a problem, and the evidence gleaned from the surviving cases confirms this. Even the single case for which one can document a successful prosecution exceeded the time limit set by the Statute of Proclamations.

Thus the Statute of Proclamations seems only to have resulted in proclamations being enforced in a court where historians have generally maintained they were already being enforced before 1539.[44] One naturally is led to inquire why the government initiated such a procedure. A facile solution might be that offered by Professor Adair: the government sought enforcement in common-law courts and the Commons were responsible for the substitution of the conciliar court. Unfortunately he offered no documentation in support of this conclusion, and there is evidence that proclamations could, nevertheless, be enforced in common-law courts after 1539.[45]

Furthermore, "the setting up of such a statutory body is too clearly in line with other early-Tudor practice to come from anyone but the government." [46] Finally there are additional reasons why government initiation seems a more plausible solution.

---

like all others received by Star Chamber." Elton, *Star Chamber Stories*, 94. Leadam was more cautious. Although he puzzled over the similarity with the Court of Star Chamber, he maintained: "The two informations, the Attorney-General v Danby and others and Smythe v Danckerd are rather cases before the Council in Star Chamber to use the words of the Act of 1539 on which they are laid, than cases heard before the Court of Star Chamber proper." Leadam, *Star Chamber*, II, xix–xx.

44. Robert Steele, *A Bibliography of Royal Proclamations of the Tudor and Stuart Sovereigns ... with an Historical Essay on their Origin and Use*, Vol. V, *Bibliotheca Lindesiana* (Oxford, 1910), xxx–xxxi; Adair, *English Historical Review*, XXXII, 41–42; Theodore Plucknett, *A Concise History of the Common Law* (5th ed.; London, 1956), 183; G. R. Elton, *The Tudor Constitution* (Cambridge, 1960), 22.

45. Adair, *English Historical Review* XXXII, 43; Rudolph W. Heinze, "The Pricing of Meat: A Study in the Use of Royal Proclamations in the Reign of Henry VIII," *Historical Journal* XII (1969), 594. Three proclamations issued between 1539 and 1547, which specifically cited the Statute of Proclamations, allowed enforcement in common law courts. Hughes and Larkin (eds.)., *Royal Proclamations*, I, No. 218, p. 319; No. 231, p. 333; No. 242, p. 344.

46. Elton, *English Historical Review*, LXXV, 212.

Contrary to the generalizations mentioned earlier, the Court of Star Chamber does not seem to have been very active in enforcing royal proclamations before 1539. Only two proclamations issued before that date ordered enforcement there,[47] while, in contrast, at least seven specifically or by inference allowed enforcement in the court established by the Statute of Proclamations between 1539 and 1547.[48] In addition, although forty-five cases alleging violations of royal proclamations have been found among the Star Chamber Proceedings for the reigns of the three Tudor kings, only three can definitely be dated outside of the period when the Statute of Proclamations was in effect. In each of these cases the complaint came to the Star Chamber only after local efforts to enforce had failed, and resistance to local officials or their failure to enforce was an important concern in each of the bills.[49]

47. Hughes and Larkin (eds.), *Royal Proclamations* I, No. 118, pp. 172–74; III, No. 118.5, pp. 274–75. No. 118, dated November 12, 1527, ordered commissioners to "visit and search the barns, graners, ricks, and stacks" and "to compel" individuals having surplus grain to bring it to market. Offenders were to be reported to the "Council in the Star Chamber." PRO St Ch 2/26/159 reveals that the commissioners actually made those reports. No. 118.5, which cannot be dated, ordered that grain hoarders be reported to the council and that the council in Star Chamber punish local officials who failed to carry out the statutes on vagabonds and unlawful games.

48. Hughes and Larkin (eds.), *Royal Proclamations*, I, No. 231, p. 333; No. 242, p. 344 specifically permit informers to sue for their share of the forfeiture, "in any of the King's Courts of his Exchequer, King's Bench or Common Pleas, or else before such of the King's most honorable council as be appointed to hear and determine the same by authority of the said act [Statute of Proclamations]." *Ibid.*, No. 232, p. 334. makes the same statement, but it is probably a duplicate of No. 231. Other proclamations are not as specific but one can assume that those proclamations specifically based on the Statute of Proclamations provided for enforcement in the statutory court by their reference to the Statute of Proclamations. *Ibid.*, No. 218, p. 319; No. 211, p. 310; Nos. 217, p. 318; Nos. 201, p. 299; III, No. 196.7, p. 280–81.

49. In the earliest case, dated January 1528, James Newby was accused of not selling grain according to the king's proclamations and not obeying the bailiff when he was ordered to do so. He was accused before the commissioners but still would not obey. In addition he played at unlawful games and resisted all efforts at correction; therefore, the constables and bailiffs of the town accused him before the Star Chamber. PRO St Ch 2/22/240; Leadam, *Star Chamber*, II, 168ff. In a second case the inhabitants of Yaxley and Holme accused Thomas Alward and Christopher Branston of engrossing and forestalling. The citizens maintained that they had complained to the justice of the peace, but he would take no action and threatened them with imprisonment if they molested the accused. Complaints at the sessions also resulted in no action; so the citizens asked Wolsey to consider their complaint. PRO St Ch 2/17/344; Leadam, *Star Chamber*, II, 178ff. A third bill was heard in 1530. The Constable and Bailiff of the town of Taunton accused John Combe of playing at unlawful games contrary

To my knowledge the only other surviving evidence of enforcement of proclamations in the Court of Star Chamber is found in the Ellesmere manuscripts. Eight cases based on violations of proclamations are listed specifically. Two of them are most certainly references to cases already discussed. Three others were heard between 1539 and 1547 and only three can be dated before the enactment of the Statute of Proclamations.[50] All involved violations of a proclamation of June 22, 1530, forbidding certain religious books and bible translations. Persons having these books were to be reported "to the King's highness and his honorable council, where they shall be corrected and punished."[51] They were, in fact, "corrected and punished," but the account reads more like the council acting in a quasi-judicial fashion rather than a decision of the court of Star Chamber. John Croker was sent "to the flete for havinge a new testament contrary to the proclamacion, the boke to remayne her," John Borstick was sent to the Tower, and John Parsecke and others were "Iudged to ryde openly with papers and with ther own handes to throw the boks into the fyre."[52]

to the proclamation. Efforts by town officials to enforce the proclamation were resisted and as a result other persons in the town had begun to resist their authority, and good order could not be maintained. PRO St Ch 2/18/307. A final case involving proclamations, which concerned a religious offense, cannot be dated precisely, but it was probably heard at the time of the enactment of the Statute of Proclamations or shortly thereafter. *Ibid.*, 2/16/91.

50. Henry E. Huntington Library (HEH) Ellesmere MS 436; MS 2652. 15 mentions Robert Danby and Edward Baker in cases involving illegal export of corn. Both names are mentioned in cases addressed to the statutory court on approximately the same date. Another case dated April 10, 1544, involved a violation of the proclamation on keeping hawks. The final two are more difficult to place. One, dated October 27, 1545, reads, "Richard Stode to the flete for pleadange his fathers cause at the barre agaynst the proclamacion in that behalfe," *Ibid.*, MS 2652, 5d. The other, in the first year of Edward VI's reign, probably involves the same offense. *Ibid.*, 15. They may have been based on a proclamation of June 28, 1546, "Requiring Certification of Barristers in Crown Courts," but the information given is too limited to be precise. Hughes and Larkin (eds.), *Royal Proclamations*, I, No. 270, pp. 371–72. Ellesmere MSS 436 and 2652 contain extracts from the Star Chamber books of orders and decrees made during the reign of Elizabeth.

51. Hughes and Larkin (eds.), *Royal Proclamations*,. No. 129, pp. 193–97.

52. HEH Ellesmere MS 2652, 15. The council also punished offenders in this fashion during the period when the Statute Proclamations was in effect. The council register includes a number of examples dealing especially with forbidden books and printing offenses. Dasent, *Acts of Privy Council*, I, 107, 117, 120.

After the repeal of the Statute of Proclamations the Court of Star Chamber does not seem to have been actively involved in the enforcement of royal proclamations. Only one proclamation issued in Edward VI's reign ordered enforcement there, and no proclamations cases have been found in the Star Chamber Proceedings for either the reign of Edward VI or Mary after 1547.[53] Evidence of more extensive utilization of the Court of Star Chamber for enforcing royal proclamations comes primarily from the reigns of Elizabeth I and James I.[54] All that can be said for the period before 1539 is that, although some cases alleging offenses against royal proclamations did reach the Court of Star Chamber, it was an unusual rather than a common occurrence. The same seems to be characteristic of the reign of Edward VI.

If this is true, then the enforcement clauses of the Statute of Proclamations take on a new significance. One of the primary efforts of the Statute may have been to provide statutory authority for enforcing royal proclamations in a conciliar court in order to improve the efficiency of enforcement and the effectiveness of proclamations.[55] The court was deliberately distinguished from the Court of Star Chamber by the inclusion of many nonmembers of the Privy Council possibly to "free the leading councillors from the heavy task of judging breaches

53. Hughes and Larkin (eds.), *Royal Proclamations*, I, No. 365, p. 500. One case involving illegal export of wool, brass, and hides contrary to "lawes, statutes and proclamations" was heard shortly before the repeal of the Statute of Proclamations. It came to the Star Chamber in a rather unusual way. The defendants were indicted "in your graces Court of Admyralte," but since the value of the goods could not be known "without the confession of the said parties offenders vpon due examynacion" the plaintiff requested the Star Chamber to direct a commission "to examyn the said offenders." PRO St Ch 3/1/46.

54. William Hudson, *A Treatise on the Court of Star Chamber*, 108, Vol. II of Francis Hargrave (ed.), *Collectanea Juridica* (London 1791). Haward's reports contain a number of cases based on violations of proclamations. John Hawarde, *Les Reports del Cases in Camera Stella* ed. William P. Baildon (N. p., 1894), 78–80.

55. One of the lamentations of the preamble to the Statute of Proclamations was that proclamations were "wilfully contempned and broken . . . for lack of a directe statute and lawe to cohart offenders to obey the saide proclamations." Therefore it was necessary "that an ordynarie lawe shulde be provided by thassent of his Majestie and Parliament, for the due punyshment correccion and reformacion of suche offense and dysobedyences." 31 Henry VIII, c. 8.

of proclamations" so that they could attend to administrative matters.[56] If the Star Chamber had dealt regularly with proclamations cases before, this might not have been necessary, but the expected influx of a significant number of new cases necessitated an arrangement that would relieve the privy councillors. Moreover, it was not intended to be the sole method of enforcing proclamations.[57] Obviously one court could not deal with all offenses against proclamations. Most proclamations continued to order local officials to enforce, and a number of them specified other central courts in addition to the conciliar court. The court must have been intended to deal primarily with those problems which were most critical and those offenses which were most difficult to correct by ordinary methods of procedure.

The proclamation of February 16, 1541, prohibiting unlicensed export, upon which almost all of the surviving bills were based, provides an excellent example. Attempts to curb this practice were constantly hampered by the many subterfuges the offender could use to evade the law, the corruption of port officials and the often ineffective procedure of the Exchequer which dealt with most of these cases.[58] As early as August, 1531, Henry VIII had given instructions to Thomas Cromwell to make an effort to improve enforcement of the export regulations: "That all obligacons for conveyeng of corne and other greyn may be called out of the handes of the customers and also that serche may be who hathe caried corne and greyn aswell vncustomed as agenst the kynges commaundement and restraynte and sharpe proces to be made agenst them for the same withoute any delaye." [59] Cromwell tried valiantly for four years but apparently without much success.[60] In May, 1538,

56. Elton, *Tudor Revolution*, 343.
57. During the period 1539–47 the Exchequer heard an unusual number of cases dealing with proclamations. PRO E159/319, Easter, ii; Trinity, xxii; 320, Easter xxviii; Michaelmas, xxiv; 321, Easter lvii; Michaelmas, iiid; 322, Hilary, xvi; xx; 323, Easter, ix; Michaelmas, v; ix; xxi; 324, Hilary, vii; xid; lxxix; lxxxiv; 325, Michaelmas, xv; xix.
58. Elton, *Star Chamber Stories*, 149ff.
59. B.M. Cotton MS Titus BI, 486.
60. *Ibid.*, Titus BIV, 108. Cromwell's letter to John Gostwick, outgoing auditor of

a commission, set up to inquire "concernynge aswell conveynge of corne beoffes muttons, vealles, porkes, butter, cheese, talloo as other victualles to any parties of beyond the see," warned Cromwell:

if all such forfatures of victualles as corne beoffes muttons vealles porkes butter cheysse talloo & other vytals or any of them by vertue of this commyssion nowe forfated be not brefly and consequently executed or called aponn after presentment had into the kinges Exchequer and the fynes wherof quyckly levyed such offendours and trespassours woll not regard dred nor fere but rather have more comfurth in ther wronngfull vsaunces to the evyll example of others.[61]

In October of 1540 George Whelplay reported to the council that out of 3,750 quarters of corn exported from Yarmouth, 1,800 had been carried overseas, and he submitted the names of the major offenders.[62] Late in 1540 he also brought a whole series of accusations to the council alleging serious malfeasance of duty by port officials. The council took the accusations seriously enough to ask the duke of Norfolk to investigate and told him that the king "taketh" the matter "very earnestly." [63] Norfolk replied in an angry fashion reminding the council of Whelplay's reputation. Nothing seems to have come of the matter, but Whelplay stubbornly brought further accusations on November 6, 1540.[64] Certainly the problems involved in enforcing previous export legislation and the suggestions that port officials were guilty of negligence or outright corruption must have had an effect on the drafting of the proclamation of February 16, 1541, which was issued just three months after Whelplay's last recorded accusations. The severe penalties, both for exporters and port officials, may have been utilized in a desperate effort to deter violations. Most important, the use of the conciliar court was probably introduced to assure speedy and certain punishment.

---

the Exchequer on October 20, 1535, reveals that he had given up hope of collecting most of the money outstanding on obligations.
    61. PRO S.P. 1/132, 136.   62. Ibid., 1/243, 169–70.
    63. Nicholas H. Nicolas (ed.), Proceedings and Ordinances of the Privy Council of England (1386–1542) (London, 1837), VII, 57, 60–61.
    64. Ibid., 78.

The enforcement procedure set up by the Statute of Proclamations may have seemed an excellent theoretical plan, but it failed to work in practice. From the evidence submitted, it seems the government's hopes were not realized. The court could not be constituted as originally envisioned, and the cases were heard by the Star Chamber hampered by the quorum requirement. Therefore 34 & 35 Henry VIII, c. 23 was enacted to correct some of the problems. Whether or not Parliament originally had some questions about the establishment of the conciliar court in 1539 cannot be determined from the available evidence, but when the government attempted to improve the effectiveness of that court in 1543, there are reasons to believe that Parliament resisted.

On March 3, 1543, 34 & 35 Henry VIII, c. 23 was introduced in the House of Lords as a "Billa for certain of the King's Majesty's Council to give Judgment, and take Order against Offenders and Breakers of Proclamations" and was given its first reading on that date.[65] No mention is made of the bill in the *Journal of the House of Lords* until April 18, six weeks later, when the reading of an "Act for the Authorizement of the King's Majesty to make Proclamations and the same so made to stand in no less Strength than if the same had been enacted by Authority of Parliament" is recorded.[66] This was clearly not the bill introduced on March 3, for on the following day, the original bill reappeared and was given its second reading: "Item lecta est Billa pro secunda vice against Breakers of Proclamations." [67] The other act must, therefore, have been the original Statute of Proclamations, for the title leaves no other possibility. At the next meeting of Parliament, on April 21, the bill was given its third reading and sent to the Commons, but the *Journal* records a dissenting voice: "Item 3 vice lecta est Billa against breakers of Proclamations cui omnes Proceres assenserunt, preter Dominum Mountjoye." [68] The Lords obviously had some concerns about the bill, for they had the Statute of Proclamations read before proceeding to the second reading,

65. *Journals of the House of Lords*, I, 212.   66. *Ibid.*, 224.
67. *Ibid.*, 225.   68. *Ibid.*

possibly to assure that there were adequate safeguards on the question of penalties, and even then at least one of the members opposed the bill. The bill now disappeared in the Commons until May 8 when it was returned to the Lords, "with new Words thereunto annexed."[69] Thus the Commons, too, had enough concern about the bill to amend it. Fortunately, the nature of this amendment can easily be determined by even a cursory glance at the original bill in the House of Lords Record Office. The act is written in a very precise clerk's hand with no additions or corrections until the very last sentence, which is in an entirely different hand. This must have been the amendment added by the Commons. The sentence reads: "This Acte to endure during the Kinges Majesties lief which our lord long preserve."[70]

The Commons had enough objections to limit the duration of the statute and this limitation may have proved quite significant. With the death of Henry VIII the statute was no longer in effect, and, therefore, Edward VI's councillors were faced with the same unwieldy court that had originally stimulated the revision of the Statute of Proclamations. This could explain its repeal in Edward's first Parliament.[71] Somerset might have attempted to extend 34 & 35 Henry VIII, c. 23, but he must have been aware of the opposition in 1543 and that the Commons had been responsible for limiting the statute to the lifetime of Henry VIII. Without 34 & 35 Henry VIII, c. 23 the conciliar court was certainly less effective; and, consequently, the Statute of Proclamations may now have seemed more of a hindrance than a benefit.[72] Furthermore, by repealing what seems to have been an unpopular statute, Somerset was able both to gain

69. *Ibid.*, 230.

70. House of Lord's Record Office MS 34 & 35 Henry VIII, c. 23.

71. 1 Edward VI, c. 12. 34 & 35 Henry VIII, c. 23 was also repealed in this statute, but it must have only been a formality, for the act was clearly limited to the lifetime of Henry VIII. Adair, relying entirely on the preamble of 34 & 35 Henry VIII, c. 23 surmised a connection between the failure of the statutory court and the repeal of the Statute of Proclamations: "in the failure of this special court to justify its existence lies the secret of the repeal of the Statute of Proclamations." Adair, *English Historical Review*, XXXII, 43.

72. The Statute of Proclamations forbade the use of proclamations in violation

greater freedom in the use of proclamations and possibly win the gratitude of Parliament.

A. F. Pollard once commented that the striking thing about the Statute of Proclamations was the degree to which it remained a "dead letter."[73] In some respects he was correct. The period during which the act was in effect witnessed no significant changes in the use of proclamations. In fact, only nine of the surviving proclamations issued during the period even refer to the statute. However, he failed to investigate the question of enforcement, and in that area one must make some significant qualifications. The impact of the statute is noticeable primarily in its effect on the enforcement of royal proclamations, but not as the government had originally intended. The devised machinery failed to work in practice, and as a result the Court of Star Chamber, which before 1539 had seldom tried offenses against royal proclamations, was forced to carry the burden intended for a special conciliar court. The quorum requirement and the time limit imposed by the statute made it difficult for the court to function effectively, and in 1543 a revision attempted to correct some of the problems. Whether this succeeded cannot be clearly ascertained, although the evidence suggests the court acted more swiftly after 1543. What is certain is that the death of Henry VIII meant a return to the earlier ineffective procedure. Somerset preferred not to renew a statute which Parliament had originally questioned, and it is likely that the "Act that Proclamations made by the King shall be obeyed" was repealed when it no longer served as a useful instrument for achieving that goal.

---

of an act of parliament. Somerset's injunction, issued on July 31, 1547, which ordered the reading of Cranmer's Homilies, was in violation of 34 & 35, Henry VIII, c. 1 which forbade teaching contrary to the King's Book. Gardiner reminded Somerset of the limitations imposed by the Statute of Proclamations in a letter written shortly after the injunctions were issued. Hughes and Larkin (eds.), *Royal Proclamations*, I, No. 287, pp. 393–403. James A. Muller (ed.), *The Letters of Stephen Gardiner* (Cambridge, 1933), 390–92.

73. A. F. Pollard, *The Evolution of Parliament* (London, 1926), 266.

Louis A. Knafla

Che Matriculation Revolution and Education at the inns of court in Renaissance England[1]

The lawyers of Tudor England, like those of any age, were members of a tightly knit profession. They shared similar educational backgrounds, social and economic status, and professional views. Standing together in a privileged relationship to the crown and the institutions of government, they were beginning to form the largest sector of the ruling class. The lawyers were educated at the four Inns of Court—the institutions for common-law studies that were located in London within the vicinity of the courts of law. The Inns, however, were far more than law schools. They represented—with the addition of Serjeants Inn—professional organizations for the senior members

1. Much of the research for this essay was made possible with the aid of a Canada Council Research Fellowship and a University of Calgary Sabbatical Leave, 1970–71. Some of the statistics and the ideas were included in papers for Professor Toby Milsom's seminar in English Legal Processes at the Institute of Historical Research, London, May 10, 1971; and Professor James Cockburn's seminar in English Law and Government at the Folger Shakespeare Library, Washington D.C., October 14, 1971. I would like to thank them and the people who attended for their comments, criticisms, and suggestions.

and governors of the law profession, and for the judges of the realm.

The middle decades of the sixteenth century, from the 1530's to the 1560's, witnessed a number of developments which deeply influenced the Inns of Court. The expansion of grammar schools and universities, the social and cultural awakening of the gentry and the middle class, agricultural and commercial growth, and the revolutionary implications of the legislation of the Reformation Parliament had a considerable cummulative impact upon the Inns. The impact, which became decisive in the third quarter of the sixteenth century, prompted numerous innovations: a matriculation revolution, a change in the educational background of the entrants, the advent of humanistic studies, and the unfolding of complex legal problems which led to a rebirth of the law. These subjects deserve examination not only for what we can learn about the students and the Inns, but also for the knowledge we can discover concerning the law and the legal profession, and some of the interests and attitudes of the governing class.

The purpose of this essay is to explore three areas of development in the history of law students and the Inns of Court in Tudor England. The first is an account of the expansion of the Inns in the Elizabethan period. The matriculation revolutions of 1579–83 and 1593–1608 comprise one of the major developments to occur among institutions of higher learning. A study of these revolutions indicates the response of the Inns to the social and educational demands of the period. The second area of development is the changing educational background of law students that begins in the second decade of Elizabeth's reign. Occurring prior to the expansion of the Inns and extending beyond it, the cultural, intellectual, and political interests of new students fresh from the universities had a considerable impact on the law schools which they attended. These broad interests, together with the technical ones of a profession in the midst of a legal renaissance, deeply affected the life style of the Inns and the course of study. The third area consists of a description of the academic interests of the lecturers in the late sixteenth century. Based on a partial examination of student notes on the lectures, or readings, at the Inns of Court, the new concerns of the law profession revealed the pervasive influence of the English renaissance and the statutes of the Henrician Parliaments on law and society in Tudor England.

A major expansion of the Inns of Court occurred in the second half of the sixteenth century that was part of an educational revolution throughout the institutions of higher learning. A previous study of this revolution—based on five- and seven-year moving averages of entrants to the universities and the Inns of Court—stated that there was a uniform pattern of matriculation in all institutions of higher learning for the era of 1560–1640.[2] The study indicated for the Elizabethan age that the years from 1560 to the late 1570's witnessed a growth in the number of students admitted to colleges and Inns of approximately 17 percent. A second period, from the late 1570's to the late 1580's, had a constant rate of matriculation. The third period, from the late 1580's to 1596, had a rapid decline in the number of entrants that almost fell to the previous admissions level of 1560. This cycle of rise and decline was reenacted in the remaining years of Elizabeth's reign, 1596–1603. Afterwards, admissions accelerated dramatically in the first decade of James's reign, rising by more than one-third. The study concluded that a matriculation revolution had occurred in the early years of the seventeenth century, oversupplying society with professional graduates who contributed to the "alienated intellectuals" of early Stuart England.[3]

The moving averages that were calculated in that study for the four Inns of Court formed part of the evidence for those conclusions. It was shown that there was a decline in the admissions to the Inns of approximately 22 percent from

2. Lawrence Stone, "The Educational Revolution in England, 1560–1640," *Past and Present*, No. 28 (1964), 54–57, and especially Table III.

3. Mark H. Curtis, "The Alienated Intellectuals of Early Stuart England," *Past and Present*, No. 23 (1962), 25–43.

1560 to 1568, a leveling off in the years 1568–72, and then the greatest rise of admissions in the century: from *c.* 140 per annum in 1572 to *c.* 230 per annum in 1582. This prominent increase tailed off in a sharp decline to *c.* 165 in 1590. The cyclical pattern was reenacted in the ensuing decade, reaching *c.* 240 in 1597 and subsiding to *c.* 200 in 1600. From this date a third major increase began that reached a peak of *c.* 285 in 1608.[4]

The sources of the admissions figures for the four Inns of Court do not support the account that has been summarized above on the dating and the extent of the matriculation revolution either among institutions of higher learning or for the Inns of Court. The annual matriculation figures from the original records do not lend themselves easily to moving averages and to the quantitative method of statistical analysis. At Gray's Inn, for example, the admissions for the years 1568–72 were 59, 20, 40, 69, and 45. Sharp contrasts such as these are manifest in figures for all the Inns. For example, in the decade of the 1560's the high and low annual figures at Gray's Inn were 62 and 20; Middle Temple, 65 and 8; Lincoln's Inn, 57 and 8; and the Inner Temple, 80 and 1.[5]

Discrepancies such as these are due partially to lackadaisical registrars, but also to local conditions. Years of plague and famine and of economic depression would have an unusually depressing influence on particular years. The figures for isolated years of human catastrophe, once combined with the totals for other years, would not represent a trend that would be meaningful for an understanding of admissions. Likewise, if a particular Inn did not follow the pattern of others, the matriculation figures of that Inn when included with those of its sister institutions would inhibit our ability to interpret the direction and patterns of their growth. The importance of statistics in history—once they are used—is to discover the reality of the world from which they are derived, and the causes of

4. Stone, "Educational Revolution," 51–53, particularly Graphs II–III.
5. Tables I–IV, respectively.

their inception. In this instance we can learn more by looking at the annual totals, by accounting for discrepancies, and in attempting to interpret these figures in conjunction with other sources.

A study of the annual admissions for 1560–78 reveals that these years constituted a genuine historical period in the history of three of the Inns of Court: Gray's Inn, Middle Temple, and Lincoln's Inn. The Inner Temple alone experienced widely fluctuating numbers unconnected with local developments, and a gradual decline in entrants.[6] After discounting several exceptional factors, the registration figures demonstrate that matriculations from 1560 to 1578 seldom rose or declined by more than 10 percent of the 1560 figure. The numbers deleted are those for years that were affected by a virulent strain of bubonic plague in 1563, by the plague, typhus, and famine outbreaks of 1568–70,[7] and for the Inner Temple. Thus the period 1560–78 was one of relative normality, years in which the history of the Inns experienced a rather consistent level of admissions.[8]

The first period of significant growth came suddenly in 1579, when the matriculations to the three Inns rose from a total of 127 to 198, a dramatic rise of more than 50 percent. High figures such as these remained general for a further five years. The annual average had leaped from 124 in the years 1572–78, to 183 in 1579–84. Even the admissions to the Inner Temple turned upwards as the Inn recovered from its former decline in 1578–86. A revolution in admissions had taken place. The following years of 1585–93 comprised a short period of consolidation. The matriculations dropped to 156 in 1585, and continued at an average annual rate of 155 through 1593.[9]

6. Table IV. The decline is evident in the manuscript register. The extreme fluctuations can be attributed in part to the half-hearted and faulty registration of students in this period, a conclusion that can be made from the confusion of the manuscript and the printed registers (see n. *d*).

7. J. F. D. Shrewsbury, *A History of Bubonic Plague in the British Isles* (Cambridge, 1971), 188–94, 203–206.

8. Table V.

9. The rise in enrollments occurred after the new buildings at the Inns had been completed; see *infra*.

The last decade of Elizabeth's reign represented the second major expansion in the number of law school admissions. In 1594 the entrants to the three Inns that had exhibited new growth patterns rose from a previous average of 155 to a single figure of 247, and the students continued to enter in these large numbers in the following year. However, the outbreak of a new epidemic of bubonic plague in 1596 interrupted the continuation of this pattern, and the pattern could not be maintained in the following decade of plague, famine, inflation, and rebellion.[10] But the three Inns continued to enroll some of their largest annual admissions of the century. The absence of human and economic dislocation in the first decade of James's reign allowed the extraordinary enrollments of 1594–95, 1597–98, 1600, and 1602 to become constant,[11] comprising the second period of high growth that occurred in the law schools in Elizabethan times.

Two prominent features can be discerned in the history of matriculations to the Inns of Court in this era. First, there was a measure of consistency in the annual admissions within prescribed levels. Secondly, when expansion occurred it was significant. Thus one can conclude that the period 1560–78 had a constant rate of matriculation, and that the years 1579–84 comprised the first period of highly accelerated growth. Likewise, the years 1585–93 can be interpreted as years of consolidation, from which a second period of accelerated growth began in 1594.[12]

While the history of the Inns of Court in Tudor England has yet to be written, a possible explanation of this expansion can be suggested. First, the assumption is that the governors and benchers were men who planned the administration of their institutions.[13] The explanation is that the planning of

10. Shrewsbury, *Bubonic Plague*, 222–30, 264–70.
11. Table V, excluding the totals for the years that have been placed in brackets.
12. The two periods of growth were also distinguished by the increased number of Irish Catholic admissions: Donal F. Cregan, "Irish Catholic Admissions to the English Inns of Court, 1558–1625," *Irish Jurist* (1970), 95–114, especially App. II.
13. That the judges and benchers controlled the calls to the Bar, and the number

size—both in terms of catering for the budding gentleman and the prospective lawyer—was related first to the increased attractiveness of the Inns as educational institutions, and secondly to the expansion of the forms of action and the growth in jurisdiction of the common-law courts. The almost geometrical increase in proceedings before the common-law courts in the last three quarters of the sixteenth century was a unique experience in the history of the law.[14] So too was the appointment of numerous clerks and attorneys and the growth in authority and prestige of the solicitor and attorney general.[15]

The matriculation evidence for the growth of the Inns of Court in the periods of 1579–84 and 1594–1608 can be substantiated by a partial examination of the history of their physical plant. The two Inns in which the increase in admissions was most pronounced were the Middle Temple and Lincoln's Inn. In the Middle Temple a number of major building projects were begun in 1565–68, and completed in the mid-1570's. These included the Plowden buildings, Brick Court, the Herbert chambers, and the Great Hall—a magnificent edifice that was medieval in structure with a renaissance decorative style.[16] A building program at Lincoln's Inn was in progress during these same years. The chief projects included the Irishmen's chambers, the Draper and Coke buildings, and the so-called "new

---

of attorneys practicing before the courts has been suggested by Michael Birks, *Gentlemen of the Law* (London, 1960), 95–100.

14. For example, a survey of the docket books for the plea rolls of the Court of King's Bench, civil side, for the following periods illuminates the sheer growth of civil business before the court in the sixteenth century: 1500–1505, average of 594 membranes per year (Public Records Office, KB Ind. 1327–28); 1553–58, 941 mbs. *p.a.* (PRO, KB Ind. 1338); 1590–95, 3256 mbs. *p.a.* (PRO, KB Ind. 1351–52); and 1605–10, 8323 mbs. *p.a.* (PRO, KB Ind. 1357–58). A similar pattern has been discovered for the assizes: James Cockburn, *History of English Assizes, 1558–1714* (Cambridge, 1972), 99–104, and Fig. III.

15. J. H. Baker, "A History of the Order of the Serjeants at Law" (Ph.D. dissertation, University College Faculty of Law; London, 1968), 295–97, 398–404.

16. *Middle Temple Records: Minutes of Parliament*, ed. C. T. Martin (London, 1904), I, cited hereinafter as *M. T. Minutes*. The references are, respectively: 152, 155, 183; H. H. L. Bellot, *The Inner and Middle Temple* (London, 1902), 277; *M. T. Minutes*, 195, 207; and *ibid.*, 148, 153, 158–59, 174.

buildings" that cost over £1000.[17] A number of extensions and additions were planned in the 1580's and raised by the early 1590's. Moreover, another large group of "new buildings" was constructed in 1596–1602 which included new chambers for the benchers.[18]

The evidence of admissions which indicates that the Inner Temple was not a partner in the expansion of the law schools in the Elizabethan period can be corroborated by the history of its building programs. Fuller's buildings and Hare Court were first constructed in the 1560's and Hurleston's chambers and the Leicester buildings were completed by the mid-1570's.[19] In 1577–79 numerous orders were issued by the Inner Temple Parliament to tear down existing chambers and rebuild them anew. These instructions were followed by an order of July 5, 1579, that no more building licenses would be issued in the future.[20] It appears that at this date—the year in which the other Inns expanded, the Inner Temple either by unfavorable circumstances or by intention had called a halt to the expansion of accomodations at the Inn. The rebuilding of the existing plant, however, was continued. A few major projects were undertaken later, and most of them were concerned with pulling down decayed structures and raising new ones to replace them.[21] This was the manner in which the Crompton buildings were constructed in the 1580's, although the Caesar buildings were newly raised in the 1590's.[22]

The governors and benchers of the Inns both encouraged

---

17. *The Records of the Honourable Society of Lincoln's Inn: The Black Books*, ed. W. P. Baildon (London, 1897), I, cited hereinafter as *L. I. Black Books*, at 344; 346; and 354–55, 448.
18. *Ibid.*, I, 428–29, 431 for the plans of the 1580's; and II, 50, 59, 63, 69, 72 for the construction in 1596–1602.
19. *A Calendar of the Inner Temple Records*, ed. F. A. Inderwick (London, 1896), I cited hereafter as *I. T. Records*, at 221–23, 225, 229, 237–38; 244–46, 281; 264–65; and 286–87, 289, 293.
20. The seven groups of orders are in *ibid.*, 289, 291, 295, 298, 299. The order of July, 1579 is at p. 300.
21. *Ibid.*, 350–52, 364, 366, 368.
22. *Ibid.*, 310, 312–14, 323–24; and 411–13, 426.

and promoted plans to accelerate the construction of the Inns in the midst of London's boom years.[23] Initially, the motive could well have been one to require more students to reside in chambers. Formal attendance was increasing during the stable years of 1560–78. By 1574—on the eve of the matriculation revolution—there was still a shortage of accomodation, particularly at the Middle Temple.[24] This situation appears to have been alleviated by 1585/6.[25] The building programs that were completed by the end of the sixteenth century made possible the culmination of the matriculation revolution, and they had a lasting influence on the physical makeup of the law schools.

The governors and benchers also enlarged the bureaucracy of the Inns in order to cope with their expansion. The minutes of the meetings of the benchers include many administrative orders to officials both old and new, orders which refer to the creation of new posts and to the enlargement of existing staff.[26] But the history, and the actual effectiveness of the administration remains to be studied. One can surmise that there was no thorough reorganization of the administration, and that the management of the Inns did not become particularly efficacious. Perhaps the administrative history of the Inns in the late sixteenth century mirrored some of the failures that occurred within the departments of state.

The increased numbers of students affected the statutory requirements for advancement within the profession. For example, the benchers drafted more formal qualifications for calls to the Bar, and the pressure to evade them was intensified. Such pressure also encouraged the advent of patronage and

23. Many contemporary comments were based not on observation, but on the accounts of previous writers. For example, John Stowe's account, which is based on that of Sir John Fortescue: British Museum, Harleian MS 542, fols. 125–40. Most later antiquarian studies have proved to be either too vague or inaccurate. The only modern attempt to discuss the physical growth of the Inns is the preliminary work of Elijah Williams, *Early Holborn and the Legal Quarter of London* (London, 1927), 487–91, 690–92, 1175–88, 1458–73, but it is not very informative. The general account of London in this period is Martin Holmes, *Elizabethan London* (London, 1969.) We can, hopefully, know much more when Professor Bindoff completes his major study of the city in the sixteenth century.

24. PRO, SP 13/95/91, a survey of the chambers dated May, 1574.

25. BM, Lansdowne MS 47, fols. 113–15, compared with the admissions figures.

26. In particular, *L. I. Black Books*, I; and the *M. T. Minutes*, I–II.

the politicization of the law profession. The ability of readers and benchers to admit one son free of fees, other students at half-price, and to prefer and stymie the advancement of particular individuals are examples illustrative of how the rulers of the Inns relied increasingly on the influence of family and patronage in the educational system.[27] By the end of the century the more conservative patriarchs of the legal profession such as Anderson, Egerton, and Walmesley could complain and lament of the excessive numbers of undistinguished lawyers advanced by the profession.[28]

The substantial growth of the Inns of Court in the Elizabethan period was not solely a quantitative development; it also comprised significant qualitative forces which changed the educational backgrounds of its entrants. The foundation of new grammar schools in the Edwardian and early Elizabethan age made possible the education of the sons of yeomen and merchants who previously had lacked the training to undertake more advanced professional studies. The growth of the grammar schools had a significant impact on the universities, and the enrollment at Oxford and Cambridge increased at least significantly in the third quarter of the sixteenth century.[29] The university colleges had an undoubted influence on the schools of the common law.

The impact of the universities on the Inns of Court was made quite prominently in the decade of the late 1560's to the late 1570's. The evidence of this influence can be derived

27. By "politicization" and "influence" I am referring to Professor Wallace MacCaffrey's development of the terms in his study of *The Shaping of the Elizabethan Regime* (Princeton, 1968). An excellent example of the implications of patronage for the government of the Inns is that provided by Sir Thomas Bromley and the Inner Temple. Bromley, having contributed many favors to the Inn, gained the privilege (or seized it) of calling men to the Bar (*I. T. Records*, I, 316, 320, 332, 343). Several benchers opposed this unsuccessfully, threatening to disbar men so preferred (*ibid.*, 316, 329-32, 343). Bromley tested the occasion by securing the reversion to the office of chief cook against the wishes of the incumbent, and despite additional opposition he never relinquished his influence (*ibid.*, 321, 362-63). Patrons, however, were important to the professional success of an Inn. It was the growing loss of such influence which caused Gray's Inn to petition the Privy Council in 1579: BM, Lans. MS 59, fol. 117.

28. Summed up by Egerton in his tract on law reform: "Memorialles for Iudicature," Huntington Library, Bridgewater and Ellesmere MS 2623, fol. 1.

29. Joan Simon, *Education and Society in Tudor England* (Cambridge, 1966), 179-96, 223-44, 299-332, 369-83.

from a study of the collegiate origins of every student admitted to the Inns in the years of 1561, 1571, 1581, and 1601.[30] The percentage of university students who enrolled at the law schools in 1561–81 rose more than threefold, from 13 percent to 42 percent of the annual admissions. This revolution in the educational origins of law students occurred precisely during those years in which the annual matriculations to the Inns remained constant. Only after this revolution did Gray's Inn, Middle Temple, and Lincoln's Inn embark on their accelerated rates of growth.

Equally significant is the fact that in the following periods of consolidation and further expansion, the proportion of entrants from the universities did not decline but continued to rise in a gradual, consistent pattern. Each of the four law schools, moreover, enrolled university students at almost equal rates of increase. The proportion of university students among all entrants to the Inns continued to rise from 42 percent in 1581 to 49 percent in 1601.[31] Thus one could suggest that the revolution in the educational origins of law students during years of constant admissions, prior to the physical and human expansion of the Inns, and the continued entrance of students from the universities was tied irrevocably to the cultural and professional development of the institutions of higher learning.

The movement, or recruitment, of university students to the Inns of Court was an attainment that bore a close relationship to the internal expansion of the universities in the sixteenth century. Collectively, the enrollment of the universities increased in the decade 1566–76, precisely the period in which the admission of university undergraduates to the Inns rose in such large proportions, from a total of 26 in 1561 to 103 in 1581. Admissions to Cambridge increased in the decade of

30. Table VI.

31. Year	Gray's Inn	Middle Temple	Lincoln's Inn
1571	30%	23%	33%
1581	64%	40%	51%
1601	54%	50%	49%

1555–65, and the Cambridge students accounted for between 67 percent and 100 percent of university entrants to Gray's Inn, Middle Temple, and Lincoln's Inn from 1551 to 1571. Matriculations to Oxford, on the other hand, increased in the later period of 1570–83. This was the period in which the number of Oxford students rose and eventually surpassed those who had entered the Inns from Cambridge. Admissions from Cambridge and Oxford numbered 40 and 21 in 1571, 55 and 48 in 1581, and 51 and 65 in 1601, respectively.[32]

The revolution in the educational origins of matriculants to the Inns also followed lines of development that can be affixed to individual colleges. At Gray's Inn, for example, 40 percent of all university students admitted came from one of five colleges: Trinity, Christ's, Caius, and Queen's College, Cambridge, and Magdalen College, Oxford. Moreover, the admission of Cambridge students continued to outnumber Oxonians at the end of the century by nearly two to one. At Lincoln's Inn, nearly one-half of all university students came from one of five colleges: St. John's, Christ's, and Trinity College, Cambridge, and Magdalen, Trinity, or Hart Hall, Oxford.[33] Just as individuals forged personal ties in the grammar schools and universities in the early decades of the Elizabethan period,[34] similar ties were formed in the universities and the Inns of Court.

The membership of the Inns was also tied to geographical areas and to status groups in the social hierarchy of English society. Demographically, a sampling of the place-name origins of matriculants to the Inns in the second half of the sixteenth century demonstrates a clearly recognizable pattern. It seems that Gray's Inn drew students largely from Kent, East Anglia, the Home Counties, and the eastern Midlands; the Middle Temple from the South and the South-West; Lincoln's Inn from

32. See n. *e*. Table VI provides only cummulative totals for the universities.
33. Table VII. These were also colleges—with the exception of Hart Hall—that had major increases in admissions during the 1560's and 1570's.
34. For example, in Dr. J. T. Cliffe's illuminating study of *The Yorkshire Gentry: From the Reformation to the Civil Wars* (London, 1969), 68–76.

London, East Anglia, the western Midlands, Wales, and Ireland; the Inner Temple from Kent, Middlesex, Wales, and the North.[35] These generalizations also corroborate a sample of the law students who came from the universities.

That an Inn of Court should draw most of its membership from particular geographical areas accords with an understanding of the life style of the law profession in this period. The dynasticism of legal families and the comital basis of legal practice at the bar placed an important traditional emphasis upon the recognition of an Inn in particular areas. This emphasis was buttressed by the rise of patronage in the Elizabethan era. Legal personalities emerged who were influential in attracting students from their counties to attend the Inn of their renown. The records of the Inns have copious entries recording the impact of rather famous lawyers and judges on their growth and expansion.[36]

The membership was tightened by degrees of social status and the fellowship of local status hierarchies. A sample of the social origins of law students in the Elizabethan period has revealed several conclusions.[37] Gray's Inn, for example, was unmistakeably the law school for the elite. The largest Inn, it contained the highest proportion of the sons of the nobility and the gentry. Its students also comprised the largest proportion of eldest sons; in fact, 50 percent more elder than younger

35. The only complete references to places of origin for the period are the admissions registers of the Middle and the Inner Temples. The registers of Lincoln's Inn are complete on this subject from 1570, and Gray's Inn from 1582. Different conclusion for the later period, overlapping with this one, were reached by Wilfrid Prest, *The Inns of Court, 1590–1640* (London, 1972), 32–38.

36. The careers of a number of prominent lawyers, writers, and judges proved instrumental in the development of their Inns. For example: Sir Nicholas Bacon, Sir William Cecil, Sir Francis Walsingham, and Sir Francis Bacon at Gray's Inn; Sir John Popham, Sir James Dyer, Edmund Plowden, and Sir John Doddridge at the Middle Temple; Sir Henry Hobart, William Lambarde, Sir Thomas Egerton, and William Hakewill at Lincoln's Inn; and Sir Thomas Bromley, Sir Edmund Anderson, Sir Edward Coke, and Sir Julius Caesar at the Inner Temple.

37. Only the Middle Temple records are complete for this information in the Elizabethan period. The Inner Temple records are complete from 1569, Gray's Inn from 1581, and Lincoln's Inn not until 1612. Different conclusions for a somewhat later period have been reached by Prest, *Inns of Court,* 27–32.

ones. The prestige of Gray's Inn was also reflected by the large number of honorary admissions usually given to unlettered nobles and upper gentry who had attained office in the Privy Council or in the departments of state.

The three other Inns were primarily schools for the sons of gentlemen. The Middle Temple catered largely for the eldest sons of the gentry, while Lincoln's Inn and the Inner Temple attracted the younger ones. Lincoln's Inn, for example, had five times more younger than elder sons of gentlemen from 1589–1603, while the Inner Temple had eight times more younger sons in the same period. The admissions registers are not very exact in noting the sons of yeomen and merchants prior to the 1590's. A much more thorough analysis of the registers and other records will be required before any generalizations on social origins can be made substantially for the sixteenth century.

The students who attended the Inns of Court in the second half of the sixteenth century were motivated by a variety of reasons. One of the most important ones was the general attraction of aspiring to the tenets of courtly humanism. The royal colleges that were endowed for the laity in the 1540's—Trinity College, Cambridge, and Christ Church, Oxford—became the academic palaces of Elizabethan England. Formed in part for the promotion of courtly humanism—the study of the classics, "right learning," prose and poetry, and the fine arts, these educational institutions were constructed to serve church and state. They fulfilled in the eyes of their founders the dreams of Sir Thomas More, Sir Thomas Elyot, and Sir Thomas Smith for the creation of an intellectual elite that would mold a new society.[38] First the colleges, and later the Inns became the repositories of orderly social achievement and political advancement. By the third quarter of the sixteenth century, university students of gentle status proceeded to the Inns of Court in order to extend and to complete the process of humanistic

38. The studies especially of Joan Simon, James McConica, H. C. Porter, and Douglas Bush.

education. This process came to include a broader range of social and cultural activities, a knowledge of political affairs, and new contacts for employment among the circles emanating from the central courts and the departments of state. The sons of yeomen and merchants, nurtured in an age of agricultural and commerical expansion and excluded increasingly from the universities, entered the Inns as a more inexpensive way to achieve gentle status.[39] But admission meant much more than that.

Students particularly became attracted to London in the later sixteenth century. The capital city had become a metropolis, a city of social and cultural importance. London, moreover, was the center of the royal court, and the patronage at the disposal of the queen and her courtiers had surpassed even that of her Tudor predecessors. The Inns of Court adapted irrevocably to their new environment, and thus they came under the direct influence of the social, cultural, and intellectual circles that prospered in Elizabethan London. Students not only took an active part in such activities, but a few of them became poets, dramatists, and prose writers.[40] Lawyers and the law formed a central place in their literature, and the legal profession was brought into the mainstream of English literary life. An age of fictional characters emerged which brought to posterity caricatures such as Clerk Brainworn, Attorney Littlewit, Serjeant Pettyfog, and Judges Overdo and Eitherside.[41]

The Elizabethan era also saw the development of another corruption of classical humanism, a movement which can be

39. Some of these matters are discussed by Simon, *Education and Society,* 268–98, 353–58; and by Wilfrid Prest, "Legal Education of the Gentry at the Inns of Court, 1560–1640," *Past and Present,* No. 38 (1967), 20–39. While I have not determined the number of yeomen and merchant sons, their admission to the Inns is not in dispute.

40. John Lehmann, *Holborn* (London, 1970), 26–38; and Fritz Caspari, *Humanism and the Social Order in Tudor England* (Chicago, 1954), 132–56. A narrative account of the history of the drama at the Inns in this period is that of A. Wigfall Green, *The Inns of Court and Early English Drama* (New Haven, 1931), 40–153.

41. For a catalogue of examples, see Bertil Johansson, *Law and Lawyers in Elizabethan England* (Stockholm, 1967).

referred to as "antihumanism."[42] Closely allied in the Edwardian period with the "commonwealthmen," and afterwards with "puritanism," antihumanism was man's quest to determine personally and for himself the ends for which he existed, and to work within the system to attain them. Antihumanism was temperate, humble, and modest. Devoted to the work ethic, it was aggressive in wrestling with the problems of this life. Critical of existing policies and institutions, it preferred the new to the old: puritanism to episcopacy, contemporary to classical authors, achievement to heredity. The purpose of education, to paraphrase John Cheke and Richard Mulcaster, was to put the learning and experience of the past to the service of life in the present.

Antihumanism was practical and economic. Job-oriented, it was especially well suited to the study of the common law and to the professional man. It embraced a number of the leading educationalists of the 1560's–80's, men such as Laurence Humphrey, president of Magdalen College, Oxford.[43] Some of the leading families of the Elizabethan nobility (Bedford, Huntingdon, and Leicester), and of the gentry (Bacon, Knollys, and Walsingham) attempted to put this gospel into action, and their work influenced Parliament, the Privy Council, and the institutions of government.

To achieve an understanding of the common law was an arduous task, and the years of difficulty and despair that were required to learn it prompted the more ambitious men to seek advancement in the profession. The Inns where these men studied throughout the learning seasons were situated not only close to London's social and cultural playgrounds, but also near centers of practical instruction. London, in another and very

42. The concept has been explored by Hiram Haydn in his essay on "The Enigmatic Elizabethans," in *The Counter-Renaissance* (New York, 1950), 1–26. The term as it is used in this essay regards "anti-humanism" as a school of humanistic studies: the antithesis of "courtly humanism," but not of "humanism."

43. Hugh Kearney, *Scholars and Gentlemen: Universities and Society in Pre-Industrial Britain, 1500–1700* (Ithaca, 1970), 38–45.

different sense, was becoming a city of small, independent schools specializing in subjects such as science, medicine, mathematics, geography, astronomy, cosmography, engineering, mining, and ordnance.[44] Thus the study of conveyancing, writs, the forms of action, and legal processes was not alien to the city's practical, professional climate. In fact, some law students even became interested in scientific problems.[45]

While the Inns of Court embraced some of the major developments that grew out of early Tudor humanism, the interests and attitudes of the graduating law student can not be summarized easily. Each graduate probably represented a different blend of elements, and the students who entered the law profession became professional men. Bound together in an occupational group, they prospered in success, wealth, and prestige. As the institutions and policies of Tudor government matured, the common lawyers began to dominate legal practice before the prerogative and the common-law courts, the assizes, local commissions, the commissions of the peace, and eventually the proceedings in the House of Commons.[46] By 1600 they had been lumped together as a financial group for the royal purposes of gathering forced loans and additional levies.[47] But professional comraderie did not prevent the unfolding of different outlooks within the law profession. The experiences of their apprenticeship would not be lost, and questions concerning the preservation and renovation of church, state, and society affected the law profession as deeply as they entangled and embroiled the members of the local communities.

A discussion of legal education in the later sixteenth century

44. George Buck, *The Thirde Universitie of England* (London, 1612); Simon, *Education and Society*, 383–403; and Kearney, *Scholars and Gentlemen* passim.
45. [Paul Hentzner] *A Journey into England in the Year M.D. XCVIII*, ed. Horace Walpole (repr.; Edinburgh, 1881), 29.
46. J. S. Cockburn, "Seventeenth-Century Clerks of Assize—Some Anonymous Members of the Legal Profession," *The American Journal of Legal History*, XIII (1969), 315–32; J. H. Gleason, *The Justices of the Peace in England, 1558 to 1640* (Oxford, 1969), 83–95; and J. E. Neale, *The Elizabethan House of Commons* (London, 1949), 301–308.
47. The list in the *Acts of the Privy Council of England*, ed. John R. Dasent, XXXI (1599–1600), 28–32.

belies a common assumption as to the ineffectiveness of the Inns of Court in Elizabethan England. The assumption is that the curriculum of the Inns was in decay, and no longer useful for the study of the common law. In fact, some writers have gone so far as to declare that one need not have attended the Inns at all; that a person could have read books to be called to the Bar.[48] The system of court attendance, quasitutorials, bolts, moots, and readings—in addition to individual study—was not altogether effective. But the deficiencies of the system were not alleviated by the legal literature of the period. The printing revolution in law books in the early decades of the sixteenth century had made available collections of the Year Books, statutes, and books of precedents.[49] But the expansion of the forms of action and the development of new legal doctrines in the later sixteenth century made redundant some of the applicability of this material.[50]

The publication of the Year Books in the sixteenth century was one of the greatest feats of the printing industry. Their value to the study of the common law was inestimable.[51] But these collections of sources were limited, particularly with reference to the new developments of action on the case for trover and conversion, defamation, and *indebitatus assumpsit*. Neither did the Year Books or the older texts provide much instruction and thought for the emerging doctrines of negligence and strict liability, promise and consideration, conversion and misconduct, and private and public morality; nor for contemporary problems concerning wills, uses, fraudulent conveyances, the common

48. The views particularly of Sir William Holdsworth, *A History of English Law* (3rd ed.; London, 1945), V, 340–55, 393–96; Kenneth Charlton, *Education in Renaissance England* (Toronto, 1965), 174–87; and Birks, *Gentlemen of Law*, 103–106.

49. These are surveyed in Henry S. Bennett, *English Books and Readers, 1475–1557* (2nd ed.; London, 1969), 76–81.

50. Louis A. Knafla, "The Law Studies of an Elizabethan Student," *The Huntington Library Quarterly*, XXXII (1969), 221–40; and Samuel E. Thorne, *Readings and Moots at the Inns of Court in the Fifteenth Century, I*, Selden Society, LXXI (London, 1954), xvii.

51. Dr. John Baker of St. Catherine's College, Cambridge, is currently preparing a reprint—with an introduction and bibliography—of a small-folio collected editions of the Year Books.

recovery, leases, and rents.[52] Meanwhile, the law reports—and especially the printed ones—seldom provided full accounts of recent cases. In a period of rapid legal change recent cases would be of essential importance to a fledging young practitioner.[53] Only in the late sixteenth century did the profession begin to produce extensive manuscript collections of annual law reports and printed editions of statutes.

The law students by the 1570's had an impressive and expanding number of printed and manuscript sources at hand for the study of the common law.[54] While many of them were critically edited and accurately published, and adequate textbooks were still lacking. This suggests that the law was in such a state of change and incertainty that textbooks could not be satisfactorily written. The abridgments of Brooke and Fitzherbert, Littleton's *Tenures,* Phaer's *Presidents,* and Rastell's *Entrees* were the major published tools for the study of the land law in the late sixteenth century.[55] However, most contemporary lawyers could use them effectively only by massive cross-references to the "modern" reports of prominent judges such as Edmund Plowden and Sir James Dyer.[56] Their own efforts to compose study manuals for personal use appear confused to us;[57] except, perhaps, for specialized legal studies.[58] It has

52. S. F. C. Milsom, *Historical Foundations of the Common Law* (London, 1969); Samuel E. Thorne, "Tudor Social Transformation and Legal Change," *New York University Law Review,* XXVI (1951), 10–23; C. H. S. Fifoot, *History and Sources of the Common Law* (London,1949); and Ralph Sutton, *Personal Actions at Common Law* (London, 1929).

53. Essential in terms both of legal procedure and thought. J. H. Baker, *An Introduction to English Legal History* (London, 1971), 92–94, 107–108.

54. Henry S. Bennett, *English Books and Readers, 1558–1603* (London, 1965), 156–66.

55. Sir Anthony Fitzherbert, *La Nouvelle Natura Brevium* (London, 1553); Thomas Littleton, *Litleton's Tenures* (London, 1557); Thomas Phaer, *A Boke of Presidentes Exactly Written in Maner of a Register* (London, 1550); William Rastell, *A Colleccion of Entrees* (London, 1566); and Sir Robert Brooke, *La Graunde Abridgement* (London, 1573).

56. Knafla, "Law Studies," 225–33.

57. For example, those of Richard Morrison (BM, Royal MS 11. A. XVI); Robert Bowyer (BM, Lans. MS 98–99); Roger Owen (BM, Harl. MS 969); Thomas Machen (BM, Lans. MS 77, 79); and the anonymous tract in BM, Harl. MS 980.

58. The manuscript tracts, for example, which were written on the interpretation of statutes: that of Sir Thomas Egerton *A Discourse upon the Exposicion & Understandinge*

been suggested that the governors and benchers of particular Inns worked to influence the preparation and publication of legal texts that would incorporate the vast accumulation of legal learning and the growth of new doctrines; furthermore, that the Inns became the clearing houses for legal literature printed in the later Tudor period.[59] The publication of legal sources was perhaps the initial stage of this development. The publication of the first modern textbooks in the early seventeenth century could well have marked the concluding stages.[60]

Given an inadequacy of texts, the study of the common law relied increasingly upon printed source materials, actual attendance at court, and expert guidance. The readings, or lectures at the Inns of Court—few of which have ever been published[61]—contain a very substantial source for the interests and learning of the utter barristers who became the most acknowledged legal scholars in the kingdom. Readers, in the first half of the sixteenth century, were still involved in the accepted custom of lecturing on a cycle of medieval statutes. As late as the second half of the reign of Henry VIII, 90 percent of the lectures were on pre-Tudor statutes, and most of those lectures were on the statutes of the thirteenth century. A change in subject matter came gradually in the third quarter of the century. The scheduled lectures, torn from the cycle of designated statutes by midcentury, had assumed a new shape of

of Statutes, ed. Samuel E. Thorne (San Marino, 1942); and the one attributed to Sir Christopher Hatton, *A Treatise concerning Statutes, or Acts of Parliament, and the Exposition thereof* (London, 1677).

59. Howard Graham, "The Rastell's and the Printed English Law Book of the Renaissance," *Law Library Journal*, XLVII (1954), 12–25; and Lewis W. Abbott, *Law-Reporting in the Sixteenth Century* (London, 1972), Chap. 2.

60. The textbooks especially by William Fulbeck, *A Direction or Preparative to the Study of the Lawe* (London, 1600); Sir Henry Finch, *Law, or a Discourse Thereof* (London, 1627); Sir Francis Bacon, *The Elements of the Common Lawes of England* (London, 1630); Sir John Doddridge, *The English Lawyer* (London, 1631); and the *Institutes* of Sir Edward Coke (1628–44).

61. The only original bibliography of readings in print was that contained in Edward Brooke, *Bibliotheca Legum* (London, 1777), in a section on miscellaneous reports and treatises at pp. 12–17.

their own. Readers, free to choose their subjects, chose statutes that reflected the problems, practices, and interests of the law profession which formed in their totality the educational background of the humanist lawyer.[62] The lecture had become a partial substitute for the textbook.

From 1558 to 1579, 70 percent of the lectures were devoted to enactments of Henry VIII, and 30 percent to earlier statutes. By the late sixteenth century the statutes of the thirteenth century were no longer considered relevant for lecture material. The readings of 1580–1603 were based chiefly on Henrician (45 percent) and Elizabethan (36 percent) statues. The momentous changes in the land law effected by the Reformation Parliament, and the later statutes that were passed for revision and modification had influenced decisively the topics of study at the Inns of Court. The transformation of the readings complemented the publication of current editions of reports and statutes. The law lecture, in helping to fulfill the criteria of a text, had also become contemporaneous.

The compilation and identification from student notes of 152 individual manuscript readings on statutes delivered in the period 1529–1625, provides an initial collection of rich source material.[63] As legal literature, the readings mirror many features of the few significant, printed legal works of the period. The lectures, especially from the late 1560's, often placed the statute in a historical context. An acquaintance was made with the important law writers of the past. The lecturer was careful in assessing the intentions and expectations of the legislators and the contemporary decisions of the courts. Roman law principles were often given as additional evidence to illustrate the perspicacity of particular common law precedents, especially on vexatious questions which concerned the crown and the Church. Divisive social, political, and religious questions were

62. Other examples and comments in Prest, *Inns of Court,* 119–30.

63. The sources are given in note *g.* I would like to thank the Canada Council for its financial support of this project, and my research assistant, Ms. Maria Cioni of Girton College, Cambridge.

discussed rather than ignored when they were pertinent to an issue. The Elizabethan reader appears to have had few prescriptions in setting out the context of a legal problem, and would arrive occasionally at controversial conclusions.[64]

The lectures were designed to explore in an intricate and comprehensive manner the meaning, intentions, interpretations, and application of individual statutes or numbered sections. Occasionally a reader's lecture would assess the positive and negative aspects of the act; instances where the law was clear, where there were doubts, and where one could discover nice evasions.[65] The reader would warn the listener to be indifferent to absolute standards of truth, to search diligently into the records, to expand his powers of memory, and to develop dexterity of argument. Readers appeared to devote their energies to some of the methods and intentions which contemporary jurists such as Sir Francis Bacon and Sir Edward Coke objected to publicly in the early seventeenth century.[66] In this regard the evidence suggests that the readings at the Inns of Court are not best assessed by the occasional polemical comments of excessively ambitious jurists.

Two conspicuous historical facts emerge from this partial collection of lectures at the Inns of Court in the age of the renaissance. Firstly, of the 152 collected readings on statutes for the period 1529–1625, 55 percent were addressed to legislation which was composed during the Henrician revolution in government, 1529–42.[67] Moreover, nearly half of these readings were devoted to the statutes on uses, wills, leases, tenancy, and fraudulent conveyances. Delivered largely in the period 1565–

64. For a different view, based largely on secondary literature, see Kenneth Charlton, "Liberal Education and the Inns of Court in the Sixteenth Century," *British Journal of Educational Studies,* IX (1960), 25–38. An initial comparison can be made from the earlier readings edited by Professor Thorne: *Readings and Moots, I.*

65. For the evolution of the reading, and a comparison of the law school and the university lecture, see Thorne, "The Early History of the Inns of Court," *Graya,* No. 50 (1959), 79–96.

66. The *Works of Francis Bacon: Literary and Professional Works,* ed. James Spedding (London, 1868–69), VII, 396; and Sir Edward Coke, *The First Part of the Institutes of the Lawes of England* (2nd ed.; London, 1628), fol. 28ov.

67. Table VIII.

1619, the lectures on these enactments were models of complexity. Many were devoted to specific speciality branches: to subjects such as dower and jointures, security of title, leases for years and for life, rents and taxes, and enclosures.

While the legislation of the Reformation Parliament is known largely for its impact on religion and the Church, the fact remains that the great bulk of its legislation was directed to social, economic, and legal problems.[68] So too was the business of its successor. The acts which proposed economic regulation and legal change comprised the most hotly contested issues of those Parliaments. A new kind of society in a country astir with bureaucratic change could hardly come to easy agreement on subjects which touched the manner in which the landed classes carved out their existence in the countryside. The legislation of 1529–42 was part of the "administrative revolution." Affecting deeply the economic wealth and configuration of society, the lack of study on this legislation is illustrative of how much we still have to learn.[69]

The second conspicuous historical fact concerns the new legal interests which appeared in the late 1570's and the early 1580's. Statutes concerning advowsons, simony, pluralities and nonresidence, lay appropriation of tithes, usury, the rights of women, the dissolution and sale of college and chantry land, the decay of towns, the powers of corporations and local commissioners, and elections begin to turn up in the lecture titles of readers in late Elizabethan England, and more fully in the lectures of the early seventeenth century.[70] The reader's rostrum was not only reserved for the analysis of the revolution in the land law that was instigated by the legislation of Henry VIII, but it came to be used increasingly for difficult legal questions concerning the Church, corporations, and local authorities

68. Stanford E. Lehmberg, *The Reformation Parliament, 1529–1536* (Cambridge, 1970), 249–53 and *passim*.

69. G. R. Elton, *The Tudor Revolution in Government* (Cambridge, 1953), 415–27; and *"The Body of the Whole Realme:" Parliament and Representation in Medieval and Tudor England* (Charlottesville, 1969), 45–57.

70. The most popular statutes lectured on were the Statutes of Leases (13 Eliz.), Recoveries (14 Eliz.), Fraudulent Conveyances (27 Eliz.), Elections (31 Eliz.), Simony (31 Eliz.), Decay of Towns (39 Eliz.), and Chantries (43 Eliz.).

which would become crucial questions of state by the turn of the century.

The lectures of the late sixteenth century also revealed the contentious nature of life in late Elizabethan England. In an age of sharp disagreement and acid controversy, the reading became a means to publicly express professional or personal dissent. Some lecturers turned from the statute to attack a recent authority,[71] and others lectured on a statute to assail an earlier reading by one of their colleagues.[72] The lecture, however, was couched in gentle language. Confrontation was more cutting and biting than slashing and tearing. These readings also illustrated the extent to which lecturers were trained in rhetoric, reflecting the changes in methodology and oratory that accompanied the advent of humanistic studies.[73] They had begun to espouse the historicism, the speciality, and the critical acumen that had come to mark the study of the law on the Continent in midcentury.[74]

The law profession was influenced decisively by the social and intellectual developments of the sixteenth century. The sons of yeomen and merchants as well as those of the gentry and nobility contributed to the social mobility of a notwithstanding conservative age. Attending grammar schools, halls or colleges, and the Inns of Court, they participated in the matriculation revolution. Becoming lawyers and officials, they were men whose knowledge of legal problems and the law would influence the way in which society would interpret the past and shape its existence in the future. Profoundly affected by the rebirth of the common law, they had become by the end of the sixteenth century fascinated with the fabric and substance of human society.

71. William Fleetwood on Littleton's *Tenures*, in BM, Harl. MS 5225, fols. 8r–14v; and James Ley on Rastell's *Tenures*, in Cambridge University Library, MS Dd. 5.50, fols. 24r–25v and MS Dd. 11.87, fols. 170r–8or.

72. Phillip's attack (CUL, MS Ee. 4.5, fols. 78r–79r, 87r–v) on Richard Marsten's reading in the Middle Temple on the statute of 14 Eliz. (CUL, MS Ee. 4.5, fols. 88r–90r), chap. 8 on Recoveries.

73. R. J. Schoeck, "Rhetoric and Law in Sixteenth-Century England," *Studies in Philology*, L (1953), 110–27; and D. S. Bland, "Rhetoric and the Law Student in Sixteenth Century England," *Studies in Philology*, LIV (1957), 498–508.

74. Donald R. Kelley, "The Rise of Legal History in the Renaissance," *History and Theory*, IX (1970), 174–94.

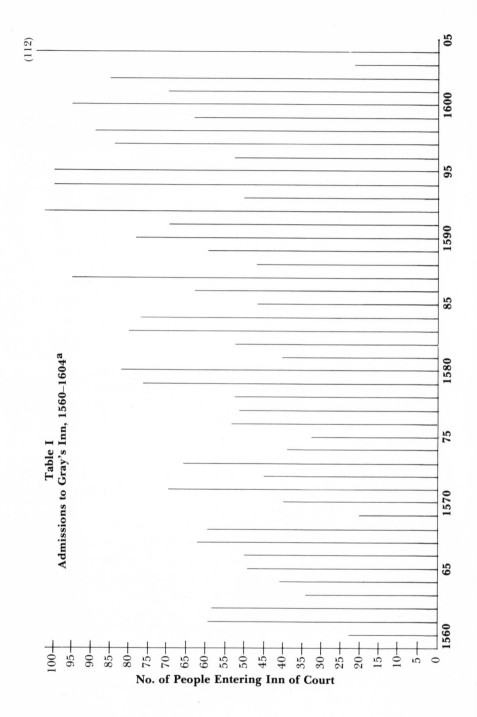

Table I
Admissions to Gray's Inn, 1560–1604[a]

No. of People Entering Inn of Court

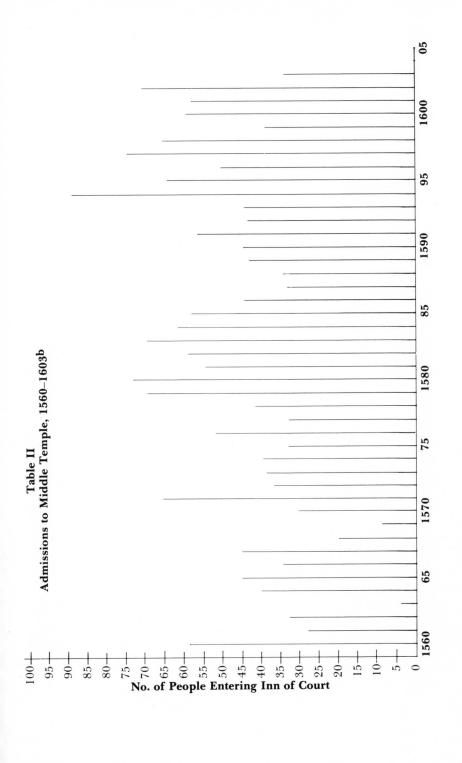

Table II
Admissions to Middle Temple, 1560–1603b

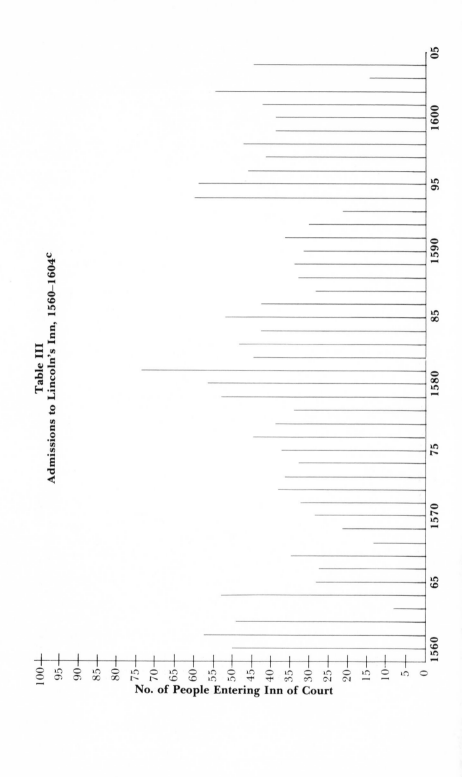

Table III
Admissions to Lincoln's Inn, 1560–1604[c]

No. of People Entering Inn of Court

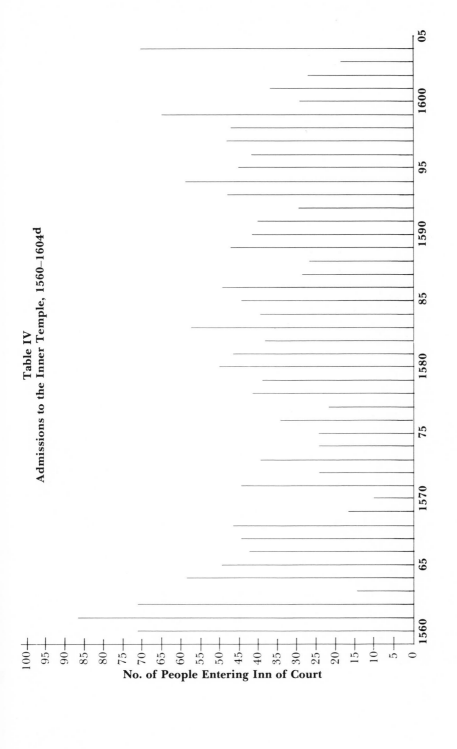

Table IV

Admissions to the Inner Temple, 1560–1604d

Table V
Total Admissions: Gray's Inn, Middle
Temple, and Lincoln's Inn, 1560–1603

Year	Admissions	Year	Admissions	Year	Admissions	Year	Admissions	Year	Admissions
1560	131	1570	99	1580	199	1590	153	1600	201
61	133	71	166	81	169	91	161	01	168
62	139	72	119	82	156	92	166	02	210
63	45	73	139	83	197	93	114	03	58
64	134	74	110	84	181	94	247		
65	122	75	102	85	156	95	221		
66	111	76	149	86	162	96	148		
67	142	77	122	87	156	97	199		
68	92	78	127	88	129	98	200		
69	61	79	198	89	135	99	140		

Table VI
Matriculations from the Universities, 1561–1601[e]

Inn of Court	1561			1571			1581			1601			Totals: No's	% from Univ.	% with Degree
Gray's Inn															
Matriculants	51			73			85			93			302		
From Univ.		6			21			34			46		107	35%	
With Degree			4			6			3			14	27		25%
Middle Temple															
Matriculants	28			67			55			68			218		
From Univ.		3			15			21			33		72	33%	
With Degree			1			5			5			12	23		32%
Lincoln's Inn															
Matriculants	54			39			61			39			193		
From Univ.		6			12			30			19		67	35%	
With Degree			0			3			8			6	17		25%
Inner Temple															
Matriculants	81			45			45			36			207		
From Univ.		11			13			18			18		60	30%	
With Degree			4			1			2			3	10		17%
TOTALS	214	26	4	224	61	15	246	103	18	236	116	35			
Percent from Univ.	13%			28%			42%			49%					
Percent with Degrees	32%			24%			17%			30%					

Table VII
University and Collegiate Representation
at the Inns, 1561–1601[f]

Item	Gray's Inn	Middle Temple	Lincoln's Inn
Matriculations from each University	Camb.–68; Oxf.–36	Camb.–26; Oxf.–45	Camb.–39; Oxf.–27
Percent of entrants from largest college rep'd.	Trinity, C. 11%	Queen's, O. 8%	St. John's, C. 12%
Percent from top five Colleges	Christ's, C. Caius, C. Queen's, C. Magdalen, O. 40%	Clare, C. Hart Hall, O. Magdalen, O. Broadgate's Hall, O. or Trinity, C. 37%	Christ's, C. Trinity, C. Magdalen, O. Hart Hall or Trinity, O. 49%
Percent from top eight Colleges	Emanuel, C. Brasenoze, O. St. John's or Clare, C. 55%	St. Alban's, O. Lincoln, O. 51%	Peterhouse, C. Queen's, C. 65%
Total number of Colleges represented	27	31	24

Table VIII
Readings on the Statutes of Henry VIII, 1529–1542⁵

21 Hen. VIII c. 3. Plaints in Assize (2). Harl. 5265, f. 1r–26r; Harg. 88, f. 4r–23v.
21 Hen. VIII c. 13. Pluralities (4). Harg. 91, f. 196r–319v; Harg. 91, f. 338r–50r; Harl. 1692, f. 80v–82r; Ee. 6.3, f. 57r–58v.
21 Hen. VIII c. 15. Recoveries (3). Harg. 92, f. 41r–56r; Harl. 5225, f. 15r–19r; Dd. 5.50, f. 35r–38v.
21 Hen. VIII c. 19. Avowries (4). Lans. 1134, f. 19v–31r; Harl. 6722, f. 2r–53v; Hh. 2.1, f. 107r–19v. Harg. 92, f. 18r–20v.
23 Hen. VIII c. 5. Sewers (2). Dd. 5.3, f. 1r–43v; Ll. 5.9, f. 1r–173r.
27 Hen. VIII c. 10. Uses (13). Harl. 829, f. 29r–48v; Harl. 1853, f. 90r–167r; Harl. 5265, f. 135v; Lans. 119, f. 83r–85r; Lans. 1122, f. 39r–47r; Harg. 33, f. 138r–59v; Dd. 11.87, f. 11r–19v; Dd. 11.87, f. 46r–47r; Dd. 11.87, f. 55v–67r; Ee. 4.5, f. 1r–11r; Ee. 4.5, f. 78r–79r, 87r–v; Ee. 4.5, f. 88r–90r; Kk. 6.42, f. 2r–24r.
27 Hen. VIII c. 16. Enrollments (4). Lans. 1134, f. 31v–45v; Dd. 5.50, f. 26r–27v; Dd. 11.87, f. 20r–39v; Ee. 6.3, f. 33r–48v.
31 Hen. VIII c. 1. Partitions (1). Hh. 2.1, f. 121r–26r.
32 Hen. VIII c. 1. Wills (6). Add. 3295, f. 54r–58v; Harg. 402, f. 34r–59r; Harl. 4556, f. 2r–15v; Harl. 829, f. 18r–28v; Lans. 1141, f. 2r–79v; Hh. 2.1, f. 71r–80v.
32 Hen. VIII c. 2. Limitation of Prescription (4). Lans. 1119, f. 95r–99r; Harl. 5265, f. 148r–51r; Harg. 33, f. 160r–73v; Ee. 4.5, f. 12r–17v.
32 Hen. VIII c. 5. Debts (3). Harg. 22, f. 22r–62r; Dd. 5.50, f. 55v–56r; Dd. 11.87, f. 94v–98r.
32 Hen. VIII c. 7. Tithes (3). Harg. 92, f. 104r–107v; Harg. 372, f. 4r–15v; Harl. 5265, f. 27r–56v.
32 Hen. VIII c. 28. Leases (5). Harg. 92, f. 63r–84r; Lans. 1119, f. 43r–60r; Lans. 1134, f. 46r–82v; Ee. 4.5, f. 80r–81r; Ee. 6.3, f. 60v–67v.
32 Hen. VIII c. 30. Jeofaile (2). Harg. 199, f. 2r–21r; Dd. 5.51, f. 135r–37v.
32 Hen. VIII c. 32. Leases (6). Harl. 5225, f. 8r–14v; Harl. 5265, f. 157r–58v; Harl. 1692, f. 9r–14r; Dd. 11.87, f. 68r–75v; Hh. 3.7, f. 30v–34v; Ll. 3.12, f. 479r–536r.
32 Hen. VIII c. 34. Conditions (4). Harg. 92, f. 108r–118v; Dd. 5.51, f. 154r–58v; Ee. 6.3, f. 69r–80r; Hh. 3.7, f. 75r–103v.
32 Hen. VIII c. 36. Fines (2). Harg. 33, f. 174r–98r; Lans. 1121, f. 2r–20v.
32 Hen. VIII c. 37. Rents (4). Harg. 26, f. 10r–12v; Harl. 5265, f. 154r–56v; Ll. 3.12, f. 1r–15v; Ee. 4.5, f. 82r–86v.
33 Hen. VIII c. 39. Debts (1). Harl. 1692, f. 21v–23v.
34 Hen. VIII c. 5. Wills (7). Harl. 4990, f. 88r–123v; Harl. 5225, f. 41r–v; Dd. 5.51, f. 22r–26v; Ee. 4.5, f. 35r–53v; Ee. 6.3, f. 122r–152r. Lans. 1119, f. 70r–81r; Harg. 89, f. 4r–20v.
34 Hen. VIII c. 20. Land in Tail (2). Harl. 1692, f. 64v–66v; Ee. 4.5, f. 28r–34v.

Notes to Tables

a Tabulated from *The Gray's Inn Admission Register, 1521–1889* (London, 1889). There appear to have been no consistent procedures for the admission of new students to Gray's Inn. Entries are for the calendar year beginning January 1. For different charts and figures for admissions to the Inns, see Prest, *Inns of Court*, 11, 15, 243–44.

b From *The Register of Admissions to the Honourable Society of the Middle Temple*, ed. H. A. C. Sturgess (London, 1949), I. The record of admissions is probably accurate from 1557, when the benchers had to give assent in full council to the admission of entrants to the Inn.

c *The Records of the Honourable Society of Lincoln's Inn: Admissions, 1420–1893*, ed. W. P. Baildon (London, 1896), I. The record of admissions appears to be accurate from 1573, when the benchers introduced a separate admissions book.

d *Members Admitted to the Inner Temple, 1547–1660*, ed. W. H. Cooke (London, 1878). Matriculation lists were entered into the records by the Treasurer annually from 1547. But this printed register can not be relied upon as it is extremely faulty. It has been used here with the typescript copy of the manuscript register in the Inner Temple Library, fols. 23–291. In all cases of contradictory evidence the manuscript has been given precedence.

e This table represents the conclusion of looking up the entrants to the Inns of Court for specified years in the registers of Oxford and Cambridge universities. Honorary admissions have been excluded, and therefore the totals here do not in every case equal the figures in Tables I–IV. The records used for the Inns are those cited in notes *a–d* above.

The university registers are not adequate for statistical study until 1571 at the earliest. The registers which formed the basis of this study were J. and J. A. Venn, *Cambridge Matriculations and Degrees, 1544–1659* (Cambridge, 1913); A. Clark, *Register of Oxford, 1571–1622* (Oxford, 1887), I–II; and J. Foster, *Alumni Oxonienses* (Oxford, 1891–92), I–IV. The primary consideration in allowing a matriculation from the university to an Inn of Court to be counted was the provision of sufficient evidence. The errors in making such decisions, especially prior to the 1570's, are chiefly in the range of understatement. The problem of the universities failing to secure the formality of matriculation from their students would cause more entrants to the Inns to go unnoticed, than noticed for their collegiate background. A partial assumption of this study for the statistics prior to 1580 is that the failure to register matriculations at the universities was so general that the proportion of entrants to the Inn would be relatively constant even if better evidence had existed.

I would like to thank Dr. James McConica for bringing these and other problems in the use of the university registers to my attention. Ms. Maria Cioni of Girton College, Cambridge, assisted in the major part of the research.

f Based on the information compiled for Table VI. Students whose college was not designated were omitted entirely for the purposes of this list. Students who attended university after matriculating to an Inn were also excluded. For a student who attended more than one college, the second college attended was used for his collegiate designation: the college from which he matriculated to the Inn.

g The list of 83 readings was compiled from the manuscript collections at the British Museum and Cambridge University Library. The references beginning with double letters are from the CUL; all other references are from the BM. Most of the lectures were identified for reader, Inn, and year of lecture. The reference given is to the fullest account of the lecture. Many lectures were found in multiple copies, and hopefully an edited bibliography of lectures from all manuscript repositories in Britain and North America can someday be prepared.

G. R. Elton

The Rule of Law in Sixteenth-Century England

Interest has recently revived in a slightly old-fashioned problem, the essential character of the Tudor state. The problem is less artificial than might be supposed. Of course, there is always something artificial about any attempt to establish a generalized identity for over a hundred years of history; there is danger in any formulation which necessarily ignores the changes brought by time; and there may well be deficiencies in an analysis which turns away from the realities of social relationships to the abstractions of legal and political thought. Nevertheless, I believe that we are right to inquire by what title the system of government under the Tudors should be described. For one thing, in doing so we attend to matters about which a good many people who lived under that system were concerned to think and write. For another, we need to have a firm grasp of these concepts—the sixteenth century's concepts, not ours—if we are to see the events and personalities of the age aright. Just because it follows more closely the lines of thought that engaged the sixteenth century itself, the discussion is actually nearer the heart of any sound understanding than are even those important inquiries about social structure and mobility, economic transformation, or the role of education which have rightly attracted so much attention of late. What the true relation should be between power and law, by what right kings reigned, how far obedience was due to them, how a commonwealth should be—and how England was—governed: these are questions we should continue to debate if we want our minds to remain attuned to the age we study.

At the same time it is true that the sixteenth century has suffered more than most from historians' predilection for concise description and memorable labels. At one time (not so long ago) Tudors and despotism went unquestioningly hand in hand. The tally of headless victims and the violence of royal passions seemed to make no doubt of that. But Pollard argued powerfully that Henry VIII was a constitutionalist, happy in meetings of Parliament, and Neale demonstrated that Elizabethan governments had to take serious account of the House of Commons; Tudor rule was redefined as essentially constitutionalist and limited. Before this, I have endeavored to clinch the point when I tried to persuade anyone who would listen that even that Machiavellian figure Thomas Cromwell was really the champion of law and Parliament and limited monarchy. However, a few years ago Professor Dunham discovered and raised a paradox in Tudor constitutional thinking: he discerned in it both a convinced deference to the sovereign law and a steady augmentation of a lawful regal power superior to the law. More recently still, Professor Hurstfield firmly reopened the whole question by reviving the notion of Tudor despotism. It therefore seems desirable to consider whether they have in fact succeeded in undermining the newer orthodoxy of Tudor constitutionalism.

Mr. Dunham was troubled by what seemed to him like contradictions.[1] He recognized that Tudor theorists believed

1. William H. Dunham, Jr., "Regal Power and the Rule of Law," *Journal of British Studies*, III (1964), 24–56. Hereinafter cited as Dunham.

themselves to be living in a system in which law ordered each man's place, rights and duties, and that the theory, at least, put similar restrictions on rulers and ruled alike. But it seemed to him that the developments of the sixteenth century both reinforced an inherited respect for the rule of law, and by changing that law, constantly added to the power of the crown, till a possible conflict existed between what he calls the *lex parliamenti* and the *lex coronae*. He thought that the problem was shelved by the Elizabethan jurists because in their pragmatic approach they felt no need to raise it, but that it remained to become the issue between the Stuarts and their Parliaments. In this, of course, he was sufficiently orthodox: that the Tudor failure to resolve the theoretical conflict between the rule of law (the rule of the common law) and the lawful powers of divine-right monarchy led to the confrontations between the Stuart kings and constitutionalist parliamentarians is one of the oldest of explanations for the breakdown of government in the seventeenth century. I also find it one of the least convincing, if only because at least down to 1640 the debates continued to be conducted precisely in Tudor terms. That is to say, all sides remained agreed that (to quote Mr. Dunham) "government according to procedures duly recognized as having validity of law" was the proper constitution of the realm of England.[2] If the Elizabethans failed to inquire which law it was that should authorize these procedures, then so, too, did the subjects of the first two Stuart kings. Actually, I think that they were all quite clear about the law they had in mind and that Mr. Dunham sees a distinction which is not there. Their arguments failed not because they advanced from different positions but because in fact they shared a common position by that time irrelevant to the real problems of the state. What put an end to the traditional discussion was the discovery that the rule of law, by itself, was no longer enough either in practice or by way of a concept.

Mr. Dunham defines his paradox as arising from the fact that "statutes strengthened both political law and regal

2. Dunham, 56.

authority; and many an act of Parliament expressly enlarged, but at the same time limited, the regal power." [3] His point, it would seem, is that Tudor statutes often added to the personal power of kings, with the result, for instance, that Henry VIII in the end had a position close to "that Free Monarchy whose True Law James I was to describe." [4] Note that we are here dealing with innovation and addition, not with that "regal power" which medieval jurists readily enough ascribed to the most constitutionalist of kings. Now it seems to me that Mr. Dunham has tended to confuse things that should be kept apart. In the first place, he treats the extensive powers granted to the crown by statute as though they in some way established a legislative authority in opposition to statute. But so long as the king's right to annul attainders, enforce or disallow acts of Parliament, or bequeath the crown by will rested on statute, so long the exclusive legislative authority of Parliament was maintained and nothing was added to the free or prerogative powers of the crown. One common and frequent purpose of all law-making is to encourage and promote action by adding powers to the executive, and the new laws of Henry VIII's day certainly did a lot of this, as indeed does much modern legislation. Yet none of this in any way detracts from the ultimate supremacy of the body which makes the law, or from the fact that such powers are defined and settled by law. To say that Henry VIII "was not too proud to use the regal powers that statute had bestowed" is surely to mistake the ordinary relationship between legislature and executive.

Secondly, by a contrary confusion, Mr. Dunham, in trying to depict a vastly growing power in the crown, fails to note how rarely these statute-granted powers were in fact used. They did not remain dormant, but their application was sparing. This underlines the basic fact behind the first point, behind the readiness of statute to delegate powers to the crown: an

3. *Ibid.*, 29. Mr. Dunham never defines what he means by "political law," but it would seem to mean the whole body of constitutional rules which determined the rights of government and subject. Unfortunately, no one in the sixteenth century had risen to any such concept, and the term remains somewhat unreal.
4. *Ibid.*, 30.

age of intermittent Parliaments, employing statute in a novel way to carry out large political programmes, simply had to leave a good deal of flexibility to the empowered agent. That is to say, royal power increased but it did not do so as regal power. So far from being liberated, the prerogative (necessarily the actor in any executive steps) was repeatedly placed upon parliamentary authority: and in theory (which is what matters here) this represents a form of restraint. The dominant doctrine was both consistent and uniform: England was ruled by law and law-determined processes; that law comprehended the powers of the crown; those powers could be altered only by the action of the supreme legislator. If Elizabethan jurists failed to debate a conflict of laws it was not because they willfully overlooked the reality but because they recognized and accepted the real truth. There was no conflict between *lex parliamenti* and *lex coronae*, two terms which I do not remember encountering in the Tudor authorities. Their use confuses the argument by putting on a par two very different aspects of the concept *lex*. The law of Parliament was the law made by Parliament; the law (or prerogative) of the crown was the law-established power of the crown. The first was sovereign in the act of legislation; the second comprised the special rights of the chief executive. The first was capable of adding to itself; the second could not breed. The first therefore controlled the second, even though that control may frequently have been used in a beneficial and procreative manner. That this was indeed the accepted relationship between the two shall be shown in a moment.

With Professor Hurstfield we are in a less rarified atmosphere, among some of the facts of power rather than among the theories.[5] Admittedly he offers a definition of despotism: an authoritarian rule in which government enforces its will, suppresses dissent, and rules a society whose members have few means of influencing major decisions.[6] But while he is right in saying that a really rigorous definition of despotism

5. J. Hurstfield, "Was there a Tudor Despotism after all?," *Transactions of the Royal Historical Society* (1967), 83–108. Hereinafter cited as Hurstfield.
6. Hurstfield, 86.

would—because men are not perfect even in their more evil intents—free even harsh regimes from that label, his own definition would seem to pull in the majority of regimes dead or living. A definition which could apply equally to the rule of Henry VIII and of Joseph Stalin, of Augustus Caesar, King Solomon, and the younger Pitt, and which occasionally looks accurate also for modern Britain and the United States, would seem to be altogether too generous. However, Dr. Hurstfield's argument centers upon two more specific issues. First, he wishes to reassert the old view that Thomas Cromwell (and by implication Henry VIII as well) meant to create a monarchic rule free of traditional restraints; and second, he holds that the notion of parliamentary consent had so little reality in the sixteenth century that government by statute was simply a more efficient way of promoting despotism. The problem of considering these views is complicated by Dr. Hurstfield's admission that he has "not mentioned a single new document," [7] a claim which in itself constitutes no virtue when a good many old documents are also not mentioned, important additional ones could be found, and the ones used are treated as though they had not before this been thoroughly and frequently discussed. It will therefore be advisable to consider the fundamental issues involved before turning to Dr. Hurstfield's particular arguments.

The issues raised in the debate are important though hardly novel. In essence they are three: the relationship between law and prerogative, the king's position with respect to the making of law, and the political question of consent (the reality of the parliamentary process).

The first problem—the prerogative and the law—comes first because it describes the manner in which these matters appeared to Tudor writers. What concerned them, and should therefore concern us, was not perhaps the freedom of parliamentary elections or the politics of consent, but the relation-

7. *Ibid.*, 107.

ship of the royal prerogative to the ordinary processes of the law. Was the prerogative superior or additional to the law, or was it comprehended in the law?

On this central point the best opinion was quite clear. William Staunford wrote his treatise on the prerogative in 1548, but half a century later his authority was still supreme. Reviewing the theorists of the law in 1600 for the benefit of students, William Fulbecke described him thus: "In Master *Staunford* there is force and weight, and no common kind of stile; in matter none hath gone beyonde him, in method, none hath ouertaken him; in the order of his writing hee is smoothe, yet sharpe, pleasant, but yet graue; famous both for Iudgement in matters of his profession, and for his great skill in forraigne learning, And surely his method may be a Law to the writers of the Law which succede him." [8] What this paragon had to say about the prerogative was quite unequivocal. The term comprises privileges vested in a given person and more particularly in a "soueraine gouernor of a realm"; it includes a variety of special rights at law (the holder of prerogative cannot be sued, or disseised, or dispossessed, his goods cannot be taxed or distrained, etc.). Prerogatives are many, but they are precise and have in part been summed up in a statute (the spurious act *de prerogitiva regis*). "Howbeit, this parlament maketh no part of the kinges prerogatif, but long time before it had his being by th'order of the common law." [9]

This opinion was delivered at the end of Henry VIII's reign when, on the showing of both Mr. Dunham and Dr. Hurstfield, one might have expected a less "common law" view of the prerogative. It was thoroughly borne out in judicial pronouncements in two cases in Elizabeth's reign, reported by Plowden. In *Williams* v. *Berkeley* (Trinity term, 4 Elizabeth I), Brown J. said: "The King cannot do any Wrong, nor will his Prerogative

8. William Fulbecke, *A Direction or Preparative to the Study of the Law* (London, 1600), fol. 28.

9. William Staunford, *An Exposicion of the Kinges Prerogatiue* (London, 1567), fol. 5.

be any Warrant to him to do an Injury to another . . . If he
should take the whole, he would do a Wrong to the other,
which his Prerogative will not suffer him to do . . . The Estate
was the cause of the Act, and is restrained by the Act, which
the King cannot enlarge by his Prerogative without another
Act of Parliament, but in taking the Estate he is restrained
along with the Estate." In other words, the prerogative is subject
both to the common law (which will so interpret it that, there
being no legal remedy for wrong done by the king, no injury
shall result from its exercise) and to statute which where it
applies governs the actions of the king as much as of anyone
else. And even in the *Case of Mines* (9 & 10 Elizabeth I), in
which the existence of prerogatives not listed in the spurious
statute was stressed, it was explicitly stated that all these are
rights "allowed to the King by the Law."[10]

Tudor lawyers, therefore, regarded the royal prerogative
as a department of the common law, definable but not establish-
able by statute. They seem to have held that no new prerogatives
can be created, while all those known were "allowed by the
law." Thus it would seem that the legislation of Henry VIII
followed strict common-law principles *(modo Cromwelliano)* when
it attempted to give statutory recognition to the prerogative
power of issuing proclamations; it may even have gone a bit
further, as Sir Roger Twysden saw, when another act of 1539
laid down the precedence of the lords in Parliament and thereby
limited the undoubted prerogative of granting honours and
establishing an order among them.[11] This is a very legal and
legalistic concept of the prerogative, and one might perhaps
expect it to weaken in the face of the crown's expanding political
power. Did opinion swerve from Staunford? Mr. Dunham discovered in William Lambarde's *Archeion* an exposition of the
potentialities of conflict between the ordinary positive law and
the "regality, prerogative or judicial power" of the crown,
together with an attempt to resolve the conflict by subjecting

10. *Plowden's Reports* (ed. 1779), 246–48, 322.
11. 31 Henry VIII, c.10; cf. Roger Twysden, *Certain Considerations upon the Government of England,* ed. J. M. Kemble (London, 1849; Camden 1st ser., Vol. XLV), 21.

both to a third entity to be called "the rule of law."[12] Unfortunately, by quoting him out of context, Mr. Dunham has misrepresented Lambarde's argument which is not about these issues at all. He ascribes to Lambarde a high view of the prerogative, in the manner of the later Stuarts; but so far from calling (as is alleged) the king's power "absolute and unbridled" Lambarde supposed that others might mistakenly understand him to think of it in those terms.[13] For himself, he was concerned solely with a possible conflict between the ordinary courts and the prerogative courts over the provision of justice. His argument turned not on the prerogative as such but on the king's right to dispense justice outside the ordinary courts; he emphasized that it was pressure from suitors that called forth such action; what worried him was no conflict of laws but the prospect of excesses in practice–the readiness of the royal Council to go beyond the "prefixed limits" of their power, and the impatience of "the *Common Man* . . . to have his Causes determined either at the *Councell-board* without open hearing, or by absolute authoritie, without prescribed rule of ordinary proceeding."[14] The *"Contrariety* of *Law"* of which he spoke consisted solely of a conflict of jurisdictions applying the same body of law; his resolution of this *Antinomia* does not demand the establishment of a separate and superior rule of law, but describes the existing practice by which extraordinary jurisdiction was reserved for cases in which the common-law courts, for one reason or another (and he lists them), could not settle matters.[15] Lambarde's "Law absolute and ordinary" are not the prerogative and statutory authorities which Mr. Dunham reads into them, but the two forms of procedure in court, one by the rules of process defined in the common law and the other without them (absolved from them). Nowhere in his treatise does he come within hailing distance of the problems which engage us here.[16]

---

12. Dunham, 53–54.
13. William Lambarde, *Archeion*, ed. C. H. McIlwain and Paul L. Ward (Cambridge, Mass., 1957), 62.
14. *Ibid.*, 65.   15. *Ibid.*, 66–68.
16. That Mr. Dunham has perverted the sense of Lambarde's remarks by citing them out of context may be briefly shown. Lambarde speaks of the king's *"Regalitie,*

On one occasion in the sixteenth century the possibility seems to have been mentioned that the absolute power of the crown may not be subjected to adjudication by the law. The case is peculiarly documented but worth citing. At some time in the reign of Elizabeth, a dispute was argued in a court (probably Common Pleas) between the queen's printer, Christopher Barker, and the University of Cambridge, touching the former's claim to a monopoly of bible-printing.[17] On Barker's behalf it was argued: "The privilege to appoint printers, and to allow what books they should print, is a matter of absolute prerogative and is not to be ordered by rule of law nor disputable by the same; therefore, her majesty making her special grant to Mr. Barker, that only stands good and none else." To this counsel for the University replied: "It is true that the matter is a matter of prerogative; but when it has pleased her majesty's progenitors to interest any corporate body or natural person in the said prerogative, then is the same to be censured by the law and to be ordered by the rule of the same." He was relying on the argument that Henry VIII's grant to the university of July 20, 1534, which empowered the chancellor, masters, and scholars to appoint printers and license books, created not an authority in the university but an interest because it implied "a matter of profit or benefit." We do not know the decision

---

Prerogative, or Iudiciall Power" used in summoning defendants into court and points out that it in no way offends "the free course of the *Common Law"* (p. 73); Mr. Dunham collects the first part of the sentence together with others equally mishandled to suggest a concept of prerogative law. When Lambarde mentions "a certaine soveraigne and preheminent *Power,"* he explicitly has in mind nothing but the power to remedy defects in the common law and modify its rigour (p. 43); Mr. Dunham uses the phrase to underpin his contention that Lambarde regarded the king's prerogative as a power separate from the common law. Mr. Dunham says that Lambarde "paradoxically" made the law itself fall under the law; but the point made by Lambarde, no paradox at all, is the perfectly sound and sensible one that trial at law has the advantages of *"ruled law* and bounded *jurisdiction,"* whereas trial in Star Chamber leaves the party without any certainties of procedure: even counsel will be bewildered.

17. This is vouched for by a copy of a report, now preserved among the archives of the Cambridge University Press (deposited in the University Archives, Cambridge). The copy is undated and probably incomplete, but it reads like a proper account in translation. I have not tried to track the case in the uncharted wastes of the plea rolls, especially since the court that heard it has to be conjectured.

of the court. If the printer had won, it would have been held that a patent of monopoly might not be disputed in the courts because it derived from the "absolute prerogative." But as the university continued to print the Bible it must be supposed that the court rejected this submission and accepted the view that by making a grant the prerogative subjected itself to the control of the law. This is equal to saying that the prerogative, however absolute, becomes law-governed when it embodies itself in action; or, to put it another way, that any prerogative to be called absolute is free of legal restraint only so long as it remains dormant. Such doctrine would ingeniously defeat the whole concept of an absolute *(legibus soluta)* power in the crown and exclude the rule of law only from those operations of the monarch's authority which do not touch the subject's interest.

In fact, I know of no decision under the Tudors which contradicts Staunford's definition of the prerogative as governed by the law, indeed as a department of the law. For a different opinion we have to wait for the reign of James I, but even then it is suspect. Dr. John Cowell, in his *Interpreter,* certainly put forward a totally opposed view, calling the prerogative "that especiall power . . . that the King hath in any kind, ouer and aboue the ordinarie course of the common lawe, in the right of his crowne." He agreed that some of the rights involved had been defined in the law, but maintained that most were not and that even the "custom" of England, by which the king allowed Parliament to participate in the making of laws, rests on his "benignitie" only.[18] He derived his interpretation from the axiom "that the king of England is an absolute king, And all learned politicians [writers on politics] doe range the power of making lawes *inter insignia summae & absolutae potestatis.*" A splendid piece of *a priori* reasoning influenced by Bodin. In passing, it is worth noting that Cowell ascribed no legislative authority at all to the king's proclamations which

18. Cowell made the point several times, *sub verbis* king, Parliament, Prerogative *(The Interpreter,* Cambridge, 1907).

276 G. R. Elton

to him were only notices "publikely giuen of any kind of thing, whereof the king thinketh good to aduertise his subjects."

Cowell's absolutist views sprang from his learning as a civilian, and he quotes extensively from non-English laws and precedents. As is well known, both Parliament and James I agreed readily in condemning the book just because of his statements on the prerogative, a plain acknowledgment of what the right doctrine was thought to be. But in 1607, when Cowell wrote, he had a recent judicial pronouncement on his side. Chief Baron Fleming was a common lawyer who in his notorious judgment in Bate's case (1606) defined the prerogative as "double, ordinary and absolute," asserting that only the former was "guided by the rules of the common law," while the latter were better termed "policy and government." [19] Though in a way he was only echoing Bracton's distinction between *jurisdictio* and *gubernaculum,* the 350 years since Bracton's day had altered the meaning of many terms, and Fleming clearly opened a road to the discovery that the king's prerogative included powers superior to the law. That, however, Fleming and Cowell (if the former had any clear notion whither he was tending) were not typical even of early-Stuart opinion emerges plainly enough from the views of that rabid royalist, David Jenkins, one of Charles I's judges and a prisoner in Newgate when he wrote his treatise on the prerogative in 1647.[20] He was not perhaps trying to curry favor with his jailers: the book is a violent attack on the Parliament and a vigorous defense of the king. Yet the table of contents states simply: "The King's Prerogative, and the Subject's Liberty, are determined and bounded by the Law." And in the text he explains with perfect clarity that both these terms are defined ("admeasured") by the "written law." "We do not hold," he adds, "the King to have any more power . . . but what the Law gives him." [21] As Twysden, a less determined

19. *The Stuart Constitution,* ed. J. P. Kenyon (Cambridge, 1966), 62–63.
20. *The Works of the Eminent and Learned Judge Jenkins upon divers Statutes concerning the King's Prerogative and the Liberty of the Subject* (n.d.).
21. *Ibid.,* 61. This phrase almost exactly repeats the opinion of several judges and councillors, given in 1610 (cited W. Notestein, *The House of Commons 1604–1610* [New Haven, 1971], 396).

royalist, put it about the same time: prerogatives "are not numberlesse, but conteyne in themselves matter of prescription"—that is, are defined in law.[22]

Thus, in the crucial century between Staunford and Jenkins, authoritative opinion held that the royal prerogative was a set of rights defined in the law and subject to its rule, and that this rule is to be found in the common law and in explicatory acts of Parliament. It follows that the king was still, as in the thirteenth century, held to be under the law, though the growth of the law had resulted in producing more specific limitations to royal action than Bracton ever knew. The rule of law—observance of its substantive and procedural rules —governed both monarch and subject.

As the seventeenth century was to discover, there were two weaknesses in this apparently clear-cut and satisfactory position. It held good without difficulty only so long as the law was somehow regarded as fixed: what was the king's position with reference to the making of new law? And it did not exclude the possibility that the lawful prerogatives of the crown included powers which might affect the law itself. We turn to the second of our issues in debate.

The first point, in fact, posed no real problem until alien views of the need for a single, undivided legislative authority penetrated into England. Lawmaking was the province of Parliament, and the king alone could give to nothing the force of statute. Neither, of course, could the Commons or the Lords. The point, which is commonplace throughout the literature, was most neatly employed by John Aylmer in 1558. He was trying to counterblast John Knox's *First Blast of the Trumpet,* and he set himself to prove the innocuousness of a woman ruler in a constitutionalist regime like that of England. Even twenty years later he would no doubt have sung Eliza's praises, but at the start of her reign he could only maintain that the common harmfulness of a woman on the throne was in England exorcized by her inability to do anything on her own. "She

22. Twysden, *Certain Considerations,* 87.

maketh no statutes or laws but the honourable court of Parliament." What harm can she do? "If . . . the regiment were such as all hanged upon the king's or queen's will and not upon the laws written; if she might decree and make laws alone, without her senate; if she judged offences according to her wisdom and not by limitation of statutes and laws; if she might dispense alone of war and peace; if, to be short, she were a mere monarch and not a mixed ruler, you might peradventure make me to fear the matter the more." [23] An admirable description of the commonplaces of the rule of law, for once from a nonlawyer. Exactly the same kind of monarchy was still regarded as characteristic of England by Twysden, nearly a century later: English government rests entirely upon the common law, and the English monarchy is "restrayned," that is limited in power. The king must govern by the laws he has sworn to maintain; he cannot by himself alter old law or make new; and he cannot proceed except in the established courts by the known law.[24]

All this is ordinary enough—in which fact lies its importance. I claim no special excellence or wisdom for any of these writers; the point is that they state the generally agreed assumptions. Their testimony is the more valuable, much more valuable than the words of deeper thinkers like Hooker, Bacon, or Hobbes. And all agreed that the rule of law under which they conceived themselves to be living extended also to the making of law. Equally, as I have shown before this, the royal prerogative to issue proclamations did not enfranchise any personal legislative authority in the crown, before, under or after the act of proclamations. Proclamations were best defined in the words of the *Discourse upon the Statutes,* possibly written by Thomas Egerton in his student days: they were good if made "in supplement or declaracion of a lawe," but "for anie thinge that is in alteracion or abrydgement they have no power." [25] There is no prerogative power of making new laws or abrogating old;

23. *The Tudor Constitution,* ed. G. R. Elton (Cambridge, 1960), 16.
24. Twysden, *Certain Considerations,* 17, 87.
25. *A Discourse upon the Exposicion & Understandinge of Statutes,* ed. S. E. Thorne (San Marino, Calif., 1942), 105, 107.

legislation is the function of the king in Parliament, the united action of the whole realm, and the rule of law is thus capable of being maintained in full, even in the process of changing that law. Such was the theory, and such (which is more) the practice.

Nevertheless, a further word is needed on the act of proclamations because it continues to trouble both Mr. Dunham and Dr. Hurstfield. The former reads the phrase in its preamble which mentions "what a king by his royal power may do" as offering an explicit description of regal greatness. In fact, however, it has no such general meaning; rather it specifically refers to one aspect of prerogative action, recognized by the law—the issuing of proclamations and their just claim (ignored by wicked men) to be obeyed. So far was this much maligned act from wishing to augment the king's power that, rather surprisingly, it expressly asserted the opposite intention: one reason for legislative action on that occasion is stated to be the fear that in his eagerness to make people behave themselves the king might "extend the liberty and supremacy of his royal power." This expansion beyond the limits set by the law the statute treats as undesirable, and it therefore must be regarded as limiting. Dr. Hurstfield, who (like all of us today) accepts that the act as passed did not increase the power of the crown because it merely gave statutory expression to powers which the prerogative already possessed at common law,[26] nevertheless continues to think that the bill originally introduced was a different matter altogether. We do not know its terms, and he may be right in ignoring my attempt to reconstruct the bill's history in which I endeavored to show that the Commons were probably responsible for forcing the restrictive second clause into the act, that the Lords showed themselves sensitive on the issue of parliamentary authority, and that the final outcome is unlikely to have been profoundly different from the original bill.[27] But how does he arrive at his own vision of that bill?

26. Hurstfield, 93.
27. G. R. Elton, 'Henry VIII's Act of Proclamations,' *English Historical Review*, lxxv (1960), 208–22.

For his assessment of the government's extreme intentions —namely that it wanted an act which would make unlimited legislation by proclamation possible—Dr. Hurstfield relies on the memories of opposition and the terms of the preamble. On the first, I have nothing much to add: I have before this shown that opposition existed and what it amounted to. I might just note that the replacement of one bit of paper or parchment by another in the passage of the bill, traditionally supposed (in this case) to demonstrate the violent changes needed (but really necessitated by the addition of an internal clause embodying the safeguards asked for and promised)[28] occurred quite commonly in Henrician Parliaments and proves nothing about the intensity of opposition or the character of the original bill.[29] The preamble, however, needs a further word. It does not deserve Dr. Hurstfield's profound suspicions or his curious comparison with Hitler's enabling law. Those, to him, ominous phrases about "unity and concord" or "the good and quiet of his people" are not broad hints of enlarged ambition but explicitly refer to what the king in his government has done

28. Dr. Hurstfield says (95–96) that Gardiner thought the government wanted more than they got. But what Gardiner said (*The Tudor Constitution*, 24) was that after "liberal words" a "plain promise" was given that proclamations would not do "anything contrary to an act of Parliament or common law," which—since it concerns the content and not the constitutional position of proclamations—offers no support for the view that the original bill meant to replace parliamentary by prerogative legislation.

29. Mr. J. I. Miklovich has kindly supplied me with a list of bills (1536–1547) which the Commons amended so drastically that they drew a new version which they sent up together with the rejected old one. These are: the bill for Robert Sherborne's pension (28 Henry VIII, c.23: L[ords'] J[ournals], I. 93a), the bill enabling ex-religious to hold lands (31 Henry VIII, c.6: *LJ* i.121a), the bill for proclamations (31 Henry VIII, c.9: *LJ* i.122b); the bill protecting various forms of game (31 Henry VIII, c.12: *LJ* i.124b), the bill concerning tithes (32 Henry VIII, c.7: *LJ* i.155a), the bill for titles of nobility (32 Henry VIII, c.9: *LJ* i.148a), the sanctuaries bill of 1540 (32 Henry VIII, c.12: *LJ* i.149b), the bill for the breed of horses (32 Henry VIII, c.13: *LJ* i.149b), the bill for the honor of Wallingford (32 Henry VIII, c.53: *LJ* i.161b), the attainder of Thomas Cromwell (32 Henry VIII, c.62: *LJ* i.149b), the abortive bill for customers' registers (*LJ* i.227b). It is worth noting that the 'tractable' Commons of 1539–40 were far more active in this way than any other House. In addition, two bills were replaced by new drafts after committal in the Lords, as also happened to the proclamations act at one stage (those for Canterbury, 34 & 35 Henry VIII, c.18 [*LJ* i.232b], and for the preservation of woods, 35 Henry VIII, c.7 [*LJ* i.259b]). It would be hard to divine major political problems in most of these cases; manifestly, procedural consequences of routine disagreements and amendments are more likely to be the explanation.

in the past; they are perfectly correct historical statements on the use of proclamations. The preamble is solemn and pompous, in the best Cromwellian manner, but it utters no novel claims or disturbing threats. All that it says is this: the king has been issuing proclamations which wicked people have disobeyed; the absence of statutory authority has made enforcement difficult; the needs of public affairs often demand regulations at short notice which it might be disastrous to have to put off to the next Parliament; [30] it is undesirable that the crown should, by public misbehaviour, be driven to an arbitrary extension of its powers; the king, by the advice of his Council, should be able to issue proclamations; and an act of Parliament should be provided to supply means of enforcement. There is not one word in all this that conflicts with the act as passed, and it is not possible to argue from the preamble that the original bill would have replaced statute by proclamation or given "the Crown in its own person" freedom to legislate—which, as Dr. Hurstfield rightly says, would have been despotism.

But Cromwell in 1535, as we are once more reminded, told the duke of Norfolk how delighted he was to hear from the judges that the king could by proclamation stop the export of coin from the realm. The lord chief justice even said that such an order would be "of as good effect as any law made by parlyament or otherwyse," a phrase to be echoed four years later in the act. Dr. Hurstfield thinks that this shows Cromwell pleased at being able to use proclamations instead of statutes.[31] It shows only that he was unfamiliar with the power of proclamations at common law, with the massive precedents for the use

30. Dr. Hurstfield's gloss on this passage really will not do. The phrase reads: "considering also that sudden causes and occasions fortune many times which do require speedy remedies, and that by abiding for a Parliament in the mean time might happen great prejudice to ensue in the realm." This was a commonplace experience in the sixteenth century. To suggest (Hurstfield, 97) that after all it took only a few weeks to get a Parliament together and that in reality the crown wished to avoid the discussions of "emergency—or controversial—measures" in Parliament is to apply suspicion rather than analysis and to suggest, absurdly, that every single emergency (a sudden need to attend to some prices, for instance) should have led to the calling of a Parliament.
31. Hurstfield, 97–98.

of proclamations touching coin, and with a relevant statute of Richard II's. There were many gaps in Cromwell's legal education, but none in his constitutionalism. We have recently learned how his regime really used proclamations: in support and execution of statutes, not in replacement of them. To quote Dr. Heinze's conclusion of his study of meat price proclamations: [32] "The whole pattern documents Thomas Cromwell's preference for legislation by statute wherever possible. . . . When the Statute of Proclamations is viewed in this context, it is difficult to conclude that the governments had any surreptitious intent." This is indeed so. Statutory authority was sought and found for the crown's common-law prerogative of issuing proclamations, and the effect of this was restrictive rather than 'expansive. At any rate, Somerset, who repealed the act, issued far more and far more ominous proclamations than Henry VIII had done, with or without the act.[33] Cromwell's purposes are perhaps better deduced from the effect of his legislative program and his known support for Thomas Starkey's constitutionalist views on government, than from his pleasure at being able to prohibit the export of coin without having to draft a new statute.[34]

32. R. W. Heinze, "The Pricing of Meat: A Study in the Use of Royal Proclamations in the Reign of Henry VIII," *Historical Journal*, XII (1969), 583–95.

33. Dr. Hurstfield (95) once more uses Somerset's repeal to suggest that "this innocent piece of legislation" had left a nasty taste in the mouth. I must remind him once again that without the repeal Somerset would have needed the constant consent of twelve other councillors to make his lavish proclamations policy legal. On this policy, see my article, "The Good Duke," *Historical Journal*, XII (1969), especially 705–706.

34. Cromwell wrote his letter to Norfolk in 1531, not 1535. This is proved not only by its extraordinarily deferential tone, very different from that which by 1535 he was using to the duke, but also by its contents. It is concerned with preventing the export of coin from the realm, and the committee of legal advisers wished to rest the necessary proclamation on an act of Richard II. The proclamation which resulted was published on July 18, 1531 (*Tudor Royal Proclamations,* ed. Paul L. Hughes and James F. Larkin, I, no. 133). There was no proclamation on the subject in 1535. This redating has some consequences. Cromwell's apparent ignorance of the power of proclamations is explained now that we know he expressed it early in his official career, while the eight years between this letter and the act of proclamations make quite sure that he did not, in consequence of what he had learned, lay up a thought of substituting proclamations for statutes throughout the time of his ministry. The date of 1531 makes the letter entirely useless for Dr. Hurstfield's purposes. It may also be noted that the lord chancellor who presided when that allegedly dangerous opinion was given was not Thomas Audley, but Thomas More.

It thus remains true that the Tudor crown neither could make law in its own right nor ever wished to acquire the power to do so. Yet this still leaves the question whether the king could not perhaps control the law made by the mixed legislative sovereign in such a way as to render his theoretical subjection to that legislative sovereignty in effect meaningless. As is well known, the crown had the power to exempt individuals from the operation of statutes by licenses *non obstante*. Such licenses could be authorized in the act or they could rest solely upon the prerogative. Mr. Dunham may be right in saying that "in politics" such action, even when based on statutory authority, "subordinated statute law to regal power," but the distinction is essential: statute-authorized licenses preserved the principle of the superiority of the king-in-Parliament over the king *solus*, while prerogative licenses demonstrated the existence of an occasional power in the king to control statute. The problem has not been much discussed, and this is not the place to explore so large a topic fully. The one investigation so far made of it has shown that the prerogative was in this function as in others closely controlled by the law which admitted the power in the sphere of the king's administrative responsibility but denied it in cases where a subject's rights at law might be affected.[35] As is well known, the question was raised in the monopolies debate in 1601, because, as Francis Bacon said, these licenses applied particularly to penal statutes of the kind proposed for the restraint of monopolists, so that any act made would remain subject to the crown's power to grant exemptions from it.[36] He used this argument because he favored an approach by petition which might be less offensive to the queen. Others who also wished to proceed in this fashion agreed with him on the liberty of the prerogative.[37] But all of them had

35. Paul Birdsall, "Non Obstante"—a study of the dispensing power of English kings," *Essays in History and Political Theory in Honor of Charles Howard McIlwain* (New York, 1936), 37–77.
36. Simonds D'Ewes, *The Journal of all the Parliaments of the Reign of Queen Elizabeth* (London, 1682), 645.
37. Francis Moore (*ibid.*, 646), George Moore (*ibid.*, 647), and Mr. Spicer (*ibid.*, 649).

a reason for pressing the point and may have exaggerated. In this same debate, Henry Montague pointed out that the queen's license could "not alter the law, which cannot be but by Act of Parliament"; the license could only dispense a man from the penalty of the law.[38] As he explained, judicial opinion had held that "a grant to the hurt of the subject is void" and also that "law and prerogative are the same thing"—that is, as I have shown, that the prerogative was treated as part of the law; and from this he drew the conclusion that a bill could not be said to touch the prerogative because "there is no rule of prerogative but the laws of the land." In law, he seems to me to have been absolutely correct. Licenses *non obstante* rested either on the authority of the statute to which they were applied or on the law-restrained prerogative. In either case they left the law untouched; in either case they were controlled by judicial interpretation; in neither case did they equip the crown with powers superior in statute.

However, as Montague's argument suggests, this theory could still have left the facts of the case quite different: what virtue is there is a law when in a given case its sole sanction can be rendered nonexistent? Did the prerogative of licensing exemptions from the law in practice enable the Tudor crown to disallow statute? The example of James II comes to mind: the dispensing power could be used in very drastic fashion. This is a question which requires massive research and lengthy exposition; at present I can only offer a provisional conclusion that the practice of the Tudors did not transgress the conventions of the law. We must take note of the real purpose of penal statutes. Intended to regulate, they could not be totally rigorous; flexibility was meant to be there from the first because absolute rigor would have been self-defeating. The acts stated general rules which, if enforced, would often have led to stagnation or else total evasion. The administrative structure (and the weaknesses) of the Tudor state made it necessary, on the

38. Cited in J. E. Neale, *Elizabeth I and her Parliaments 1584–1601*, (London, 1959), 382.

occasion that some attempt was made to control an area of public or private life, to proceed by general prohibitory acts to be articulated by means of licensed exemptions. This means that one is bound to find some licensing; I am almost prepared to argue that acts never exempted from by *non obstante* patents were acts never enforced. But, secondly, we know far too little so far about the licensing policy of the crown, and much of the little we have been told was said by scholars who erroneously supposed that every license was an evasion of at least doubtful propriety. I once made a sample check in the reigns of Henry VII and Henry VIII: and there I found surprisingly few such licenses. Of those found, the main bulk dealt with trading at the ports (sometimes under the navigation act which had to be so operated if it was to have any meaning at all, and sometimes under the prerogative power to control trade), or with dispensations for clerical pluralism and nonresidence specially provided for in the relevant act. Potentially dangerous licenses, exempting from penal statutes, amounted to one in the years 1495–1500 and to twenty-six in the years 1531–1538.[39] I therefore have my doubts about Henry VII's dozens and Henry VIII's hundreds alleged by Mr. Dunham.[40] The situation would not appear to have changed markedly in the reign of Elizabeth, though an increasing population and additions to the statute book should have resulted in more lavish licensing. The index to the last published volume of the *Calendar of Patent Rolls* lists over six hundred licences for the four years 1569–1572, but the bulk of these touch alienation of lands and only twenty-one would appear to have been *non obstante;* and not one of these last turns out on inspection to be objectionable. Licenses need a lot of analysis, and a crude use of figures could mislead badly.

39. G. R. Elton, "State Planning in Early-Tudor England," *Economic History Review*, 2nd Ser., XIII (1961), 433–39; see p. 438.

40. Mr. Dunham relies on E. F. Churchill's highly misleading discussion ("The Dispensing Power and the Defence of the Realm," *Law Quarterly Review*, XXXVII [1921], 412–41) which is shot through with false assumptions but at this date hardly worth criticizing any longer. However, even Churchill mentions only one dozen for Henry VII and one hundred for Henry VIII.

When all the conditions are taken into account—the necessary principle of proceeding by statute-cum-license, the licenses authorized by statute, and the very small number of licenses which actually put aside an act by the exercise of the prerogative—it may appear that the theoretical subordination of the prerogative to Parliament's legislation was supported by what actually happened.

Thus the conclusion must stand that Tudor thinking and practice on the law subordinated everybody, the king included, to the rule of law which defined rights and duties, and defined the processes by which these could be obtained or enforced. The law could be altered only by its own doing (judicial decision) or by legislation in which the whole realm was deemed to participate, and the whole Parliament certainly needed to act in harmony. This is the truth of the law: and it means that insofar as sixteenth-century England had a justifiable doctrine concerning its constitution this was neither despotic nor divided between the concepts of statutory authority and regal power. The doctrine—unitary, single, and conscious—spoke in terms of the rule of law and the lawmaking monopoly of Parliament.

Such was the general and effective theory, but it now becomes necessary to turn to the fundamental objection raised by Dr. Hurstfield, namely that the political structure of Tudor England made nonsense of these theoretical positions. In his view, Thomas Cromwell in particular wanted nothing to do with a Parliament that might obstruct the free making of law by the king; he despised the institution. Dr. Hurstfield once more uses Cromwell's well-known letter which wittily lambasts the futile labors of the 1523 Parliament:

I amongst other have endured a Parliament which continued by the space of seventeen whole weeks, where we commoned of war, peace, strife, contention, debate, murmur, grudge, riches, poverty, perjury, truth, falsehood, justice, equity, deceit, oppression, magnanimity, activity, force, attemprance, treason, murder, felony, conciliation, and also how a commonwealth might be edified and also continued within our realm. Howbeit, in conclusion we have done as our predecessors have been wont to do, that is to say, as well as we might and left where we began.[41]

Let me once more try to lay this ghost. Dr. Hurstfield at least agrees that the letter is amusing, but he regards it as "the comment of a bored, impatient, cynical man" to whom the whole session was a waste of time and who simply despised Parliaments.[42] Cromwell, who "wanted legislation, not deliberation," clearly saw nothing but nonsense in those assemblies; contrary to what I had once suggested, he did not here show himself fascinated by and involved in their often tedious processes. Is that so? I offer the following quotations:

The House of Commons has nothing to do and can scarce make a house to adjourn. The last money bill is before your lordships, and the Speaker will not let it pass, till the session is at an end, that he may have some pretence for the flourish about the Close.[43]

My lords, we have it from the highest authority that in the multitude of counsellors there is safety; but we in this nation may from experience say, that in the multitude of legislators there is confusion; . . . every member of the other House takes upon him to be a legislator. . . . The other House, by their being so numerous . . . are too apt to pass laws which are either unnecessary or ridiculous, and almost every law they pass stands in need of some new law for explaining and amending it.[44]

As we have got more members, and more space to put them in, we shall want more hours to talk in, more clerks to attend their business, and so to patch up the constitution of the Chair, and of the Table, that they may be able to go through twice the fatigue that was required of their predecessors.[45]

No more the disciplined array of traditionary influences and hereditary opinions. . . . That is all past. For these the future is to provide

41. R. B. Merriman, *Life and Letters of Thomas Cromwell* (Oxford, 1902), I, 313 (spelling modernized).
42. Hurstfield, 92–93.
43. British Museum, Add. MS 35423, fol. 23.
44. *Parliamentary History*, XV 724–39.
45. Cited in O. C. Williams, *The Clerical Organization of the House of Commons 1660–1850* (Oxford, 1954), 206.

us with a compensatory alternative in the conceits of the illiterate, the crotchets of the whimisical, the violent courses of the vulgar ambition that acknowledges no gratitude to antiquity—to posterity no duty.[46]

[He] spoke of the immense multiplication of details in public business and the enormous task imposed upon available time and strength by the work of attendance in the House of Commons. He agreed that it was extremely adverse to the growth of greatness among our public Men.[47]

A Parliament is nothing less than a big meeting of more or less idle people. In proportion as you give it power it will enquire into everything, settle everything, meddle in everything.[48]

[The virtue of patience] seems to me essential for one who has to undergo the tedium of long debates, much repetition, and many irrelevancies. I frequently used to inculcate upon the clerks at the Table ... that it was of no use repining, and that come weal, come woe, we would have to remain at our posts until the middle of August, with the additional prospect of an autumn session, and that we could do nothing towards a more rapid expedition of business.[49]

The session of 1887 was the most arduous of my recollection. . . . There was no limitation to the length of our sittings. . . . For those who, like myself and probably a majority, were busily engaged in their own affairs during the day, the stress was such that only youth, and an ironclad constitution, could withstand.[50]

And who were these "bored, impatient, cynical" men who so despised the time-wasting, pointless and frustrating business of Parliament—men whose agonies surely persuaded them to seek other ways of making a career? Who were these agents of legislation who clearly would have wished to remove from the body politic an instrument of so little practical virtue? They were Henry Pelham, writing to Lord Chancellor Hardwicke in 1746; Hardwicke himself in the Lords a little later; John Hatsell, clerk of the House of Commons in 1800; Disraeli,

---

46. Cited in Monypenny and Buckle, *The Life of Benjamin Disraeli* (London, 1914), III, 108.

47. Cited in John Morley, *Life of Gladstone* (ed., 1905), I 299.

48. Walter Bagehot, *The English Constitution* (standard ed.), 180.

49. J. W. Lowther, Viscount Ullswater, *A Speaker's Commentaries* (London, 1925), II 298.

50. H. H. Asquith, *Fifty Years of Parliament* (London, 1926), I 168–69.

speaking in the House in 1848; Sir Robert Peel, in conversation with Gladstone in 1846; Bagehot writing his comments in the 1850's; Speaker Lowther recalling the first decade of the twentieth century; and H. H. Asquith who stayed in the Commons for some thirty-five years after his ironclad constitution had been first undermined by the absurdities of parliamentary business. This is the voice of the old House-of-Commons man—exasperated, resentful, this-is-the-last-time-y, but ever fascinated by the strange institution which brings him to the center of affairs and determined to use it to rule the state or promote such lesser ambition as may move him.

In all this, Cromwell's letter differs from the rest only by being a good deal wittier and perhaps also a little more perceptive. I doubt whether there are many things said by Mr. Gladstone which would have extracted a nod of agreement from Thomas Cromwell, but I think he would have applauded the G.O.M.'s reaction to an impertinent lecture from Thiers on representative institutions: "When they talk to us about the House of Commons, there is a reply which but for the proprieties would be best: 'Teach your grandmother to suck eggs.' "[51] To the evidence collected elsewhere for Cromwell's activities as a parliamentary statesman,[52] I may add a small but revealing detail. In the Reformation Parliament, certain members opposed the government's policy, and one of them at least, Sir George Throckmorton, followed the guidance of a group of politicians out of Parliament, led by Fathers Peto and Reynolds. Their counsels and long custom maintained his views, and Cromwell, well aware of the situation, confined himself to frequent warnings not to listen to such advice.[53] Thus, in a matter of some delicacy, Cromwell's behavior, far from displaying impatience with tiresome elected bodies or eagerness

51. *The Political Correspondence of Mr. Gladstone and Lord Granville 1868–1876*, ed. Agatha Ramm (London, 1963; Camden 3rd ser., Vols. 81–82), I 129.

52. G. R. Elton, "The Political Thought of Thomas Cromwell," *Transactions of the Royal Historical Society* 5th ser., VI (1956), 69–92.

53. *Letters and Papers . . . of Henry VIII*, XII ii,. 952.

to bully troublesome men, was characteristic of a parliamentary manager, a "leader of the House."

Cromwell's supposed despotism, though worthy of refutation, is a relatively minor issue. The crux of Dr. Hurstfield's argument lies more weightily in his discussion of the problem of consent. He agrees that Tudor government legislated by statute but holds that the evidence will not sustain the assumption "that the use of statute is somehow hostile to despotism." [54] A good point. Perfectly legal means have been used before this to produce an overthrow of the law. But what is in question here is not whether this or that tyrant (especially whether Dr. Hurstfield's chosen example, Hitler) so used legal means, but whether the Tudor use of legislation by Parliament disguised despotic action. Here Dr. Hurstfield leaves me bewildered. He reminds us at length that Tudor Parliaments were elected on a narrow franchise and under a system of patronage. If there was consent, it was therefore the consent "of a minority of the minority of the population." [55] (Surely it should be a majority of that minority?) True enough: the sixteenth century did not practice democracy or manhood suffrage. The universal consent, which all Tudor writers on the subject agree was represented in Parliament, concerned the consent of the members of the realm (shires, cities, boroughs), not of individuals who were, however, deemed to be present because their community was represented. In practice, it is fair to say that consent was a reality even for individuals (as much of a reality as in most modern democracies), provided they belonged to what we have learned to call the political nation, Sir Thomas Smith's "them that beare office"—and let us remember that Smith included among them not only noblemen and gentlemen but also citizens, burgesses, and yeomen.[56] By sixteenth-century standards, the English political nation was exceptionally large, as indeed the House of Commons was far and away the biggest representative assembly in Europe, especially in proportion to population.[57]

54. Hurstfield, 98.   55. *Ibid.*, 102.
56. *De Republica Anglorum*, Book I.
57. These points are elaborated in G. R. Elton, "The Body of the Whole Realm:

But no, Dr. Hurstfield continues, their free consent, too, is a double fiction. In the first place, Parliaments were packed. It is nice to see this skeleton brought out of its cupboard again. Dr. Hurstfield still cites Edward Hall's remark that the 1529 House of Commons contained a majority of king's servants, though this charge was disproved over a hundred years ago by the discovery of a membership list of that Parliament. He once again treats the unique case of Cromwell's dictatorial handling of the 1536 Canterbury election as typical, without heeding the strong hint in the evidence that what we do not know in the story might very probably remove the odium from Cromwell's action.[58] And he makes much of Cromwell's promise to Henry that the 1539 Parliament, the elections for which involved much display of conciliar management, would produce a "tractable " House ("tractable" being glossed as "subservient," which is not the same thing)—even though it was this allegedly subservient body that allegedly forced the king to abandon his allegedly despotic intent to substitute proclamations for statutes. There are some misapprehensions here. Cromwell, I fear, as is the habit of electoral managers, overstated his achievement, but no doubt he had some success in organizing returns, while his very boast proves that tractability was not to be taken for granted in Henrician Parliaments. "Good government," says Dr. Hurstfield, "as he [Cromwell] indicated to Henry VIII, required a subservient parliament." [59] No such thing: any system of government which involved the presence of a representative assembly with the taxing and lawmaking powers of the sixteenth-century Parliament required methods designed to make executive and assembly capable of working together, though the perfect machinery for this was not worked out till the emergence of true democracy and very modern parties.

Lastly, Dr. Hurstfield denies the validity of consent in Tudor England by another of those modern parallels which he says he dislikes using. Searching for "evidence that this was

Parliament and Representation in Medieval and Tudor England," *Jamestown Essays on Representation*, ed. A. E. Dick Howard (Charlottesville, Va., 1969), especially 29ff.

58. *The Tudor Constitution*, 284.   59. Hurstfield, 101.

a free society in which men reached their decisions by the reasonable processes of free discussion," he remembers "the emergence and misuse of a mass medium of communication of gigantic proportions" in our own lifetime. The consent allegedly present in Tudor Parliaments was similarly controlled, he says, by active propaganda and the very active repression of all forms of dissent.[60] Thus government could pretend to rule by consent and make laws with the agreement of the realm, when in reality it did as it pleased and forced hostile voices into silence. Now, of course, censorship, control of press and pulpit, the exploitation of the majesty of the monarch—were all features of Tudor government. By the absolute standards apparently set here, sixteenth-century England was not "a free society": what society is? But neither was it a despotism; there are stages between those extremes. One need do no more than remember that in every reign these supposedly tractable Parliaments, composed of men whose opinions had been manipulated by the pressures of government propaganda and repression, raised serious opposition to the crown and often forced changes in action and policy. I agree that "this was minority rule, an uneasy and unstable distribution of power between the crown and a social *élite*," though the *élite* was larger and the power distribution more stable than Dr. Hurstfield recognizes.[61] Tudor rule was certainly determined, hostile to political and religious dissent, equipped with formidable emergency powers—though it was also astonishingly incapable of creating that general habit of obedience for which it longed. We are asked to ignore legalism and look at the realities of the situation. Yet, seeing that these included an often painful legalism, a passionate deference to entrenched rights, unending disagreement, frequent resistance, and far more violent disobedience than is found in the following century, how can this system be called a despotism, even by the loose standards applied by Dr. Hurstfield? In theory, monarchy was limited by law and consent; in practice, this strong crown depended for the execution of all its notable powers

60. *Ibid.*, 103–104.   61. *Ibid.*, 104–105.

on the willing cooperation of a large political nation (down to village constables) over whom it had very few physical means of control, and whom—its own readiness to obey the law apart —it could only hope to retain cooperative by observing the rules of the game. I cannot accept Dr. Hurstfield's arguments for a despotism because I am forced to think the terms in which he has discussed the problem essentially wrong—imposed upon the sixteenth century rather than appropriate to it.

Yet it may be held that in stressing the rule of law I have overlooked too much. Anyone wishing to list acts of doubtful legality committed in the sixteenth century will have little difficulty in finding some; and the tally will be larger in Elizabeth's reign than in her father's, a fact which may account for Dr. Hurstfield's growing conviction that Tudor rule was despotic. Some of the state trials, however legal in form, were certainly rigged; willful power at times asserted itself; the treatment of Mary Queen of Scots cannot be described as being according to the rule of law; Elizabeth showed an improper readiness to imprison people without trial by way of asserting her authority or working off her spleen. The fact that the judges in Darnell's Case (1626) were forced by the precedents to accept an order of king and council as a bar to granting *habeas corpus* does not make those precedents any more reassuring. Many people may well feel that the Tudors were both ruthless and despotic in that area of which they themselves are exceptionally aware—in politics and the business of state. It is therefore necessary to define what is and what is not at issue in this discussion. In emphasizing the rule of law I am not condoning acts of brutality or willfulness. But moral reprobation offers no clue to the inquirer who would understand the nature of the Tudor state, while understanding that nature must not be read as equal to discarding all moral judgment. The opinion is wrong which confuses a demonstration of the realities with simple approval of the abuses that occur in reality, as is that which supposes that breaches of the law or morally repulsive behavior can occur only in a despotic system. Tudor law, like Tudor

life, was often savage; and Tudor rulers, like all rulers, occasionally did things which were not lawful. In the sixteenth century,
the rule of law in fact permitted quite enough horrors to make
the politically conditioned rare evasions of that rule seem morally little worse than many of the actions taken in perfect observance of it. I insist only that it is possible to separate recognition
and condemnation of vile behavior from an enquiry into the
true structure of the sixteenth-century political system, and I
maintain that to describe that system from its occasional perver-
sion of its own fundamental principles is to distort. No system,
of course, has ever been absolutely perfect and consistent in
political operation, least so when a society has become convinced
(as that of Tudor England was with good reason convinced)
that its very existence was frequently in danger. It is that system,
not its moral virtues, that have here been discussed. The faults
and lapses of Tudor governments do not disprove the existence
of the rule of law under which they governed. Our question
has been whether the Tudors governed as despots or as limited,
law-controlled monarchs, not whether they would be acceptable
in the houses of the gently nurtured.

The rule of law is not identical with either the rule of
charity or the rule of good sense, though these two are perhaps
more likely to prevail when law rules than when will is all.
The revolution which we call the Reformation had its victims,
none less deserved than Thomas Cromwell, who on the scaffold
implied a pointed distinction between the law by which he came
to die and the justice he had sought at the king's hands. Throughout his stage of the revolution, Cromwell saw to it that the
rule of law applied, as I hope to show elsewhere at much greater
length. With the worst will in the world, and often their will
was good, Henry VIII, Elizabeth, and their servants neither
could nor would escape from the two great limitations upon
their executive power: their dependence on a netwook of self-
reliant men throughout the realm and throughout society, and
the rule of law.